Drinking Dilemmas

Drinking and drunkenness have become a focal point for political and media debates to contest notions of responsibility, discipline and risk; yet, at the same time, academic studies have highlighted the positive aspects of drinking in relation to sociability, belonging and identity. These issues are at the heart of this volume, which brings together the work of academics and researchers exploring social and cultural aspects of contemporary drinking practices. These drinking practices are enormously varied and are spatially and culturally defined. The contributions to the volume draw on research settings from across the UK and beyond to demonstrate both the complexity and diversity of drinking subjectivities and practices. Across these examples, tensions relating to gender, social class, age and the life course are particularly prominent. Rather than align to now long-established moral discourses about what constitutes 'good' and 'bad' drinking, sociological approaches to alcohol foreground, the vivid, lived, nature of alcohol consumption and the associated experiences of drunkenness and intoxication. In doing so, the volume illuminates the controversial yet important social and cultural roles played by drink for individuals and groups across a range of social contexts.

Thomas Thurnell-Read is a Senior Lecturer in Sociology in the School of Humanities at Coventry University. Through his research and teaching, he uses contemporary leisure and consumption practices, particularly those relating to drinking and drunkenness, to explore a range of sociological issues relating to sociality, identity and diversity. His research on British stag party tourism in Poland has been published in a range of international journals and focuses on the social construction of masculinity through transgressive drinking practices. He is the editor (with Dr Mark Casey, Newcastle University) of *Men, Masculinities, Travel and Tourism* (2014, Palgrave Macmillan). He is a founder member of the BSA Alcohol Study Group and has been Co-Convenor of the group since July 2012.

Sociological Futures
Series Editors: Eileen Green, John Horne, Caroline Oliver, Louise Ryan

Sociological Futures aims to be a flagship series for new and innovative theories, methods and approaches to sociological issues and debates and 'the social' in the 21st century. This series of monographs and edited collections was inspired by the vibrant wealth of British Sociological Association (BSA) symposia on a wide variety of sociological themes. Edited by a team of experienced sociological researchers, and supported by the BSA, the series covers a wide range of topics related to sociology and sociological research and features contemporary work that is theoretically and methodologically innovative and has local or global reach, as well as work that engages or reengages with classic debates in sociology, bringing new perspectives to important and relevant topics.

The BSA is the professional association for sociologists and sociological research in the United Kingdom. It has an extensive network of members, study groups and forums, and a dynamic programme of events. The Association engages with topics ranging from auto/biography to youth, climate change to violence against women, alcohol to sport, and Bourdieu to Weber. This book series represents the finest fruits of sociological enquiry, for a global audience, and offers a publication outlet for sociologists at all career and publishing stages, from well-established to emerging sociologists, BSA or non-BSA members, from all parts of the world.

An End to the Crisis in Empirical Sociology?
Edited by Linda McKie and Louise Ryan

Bourdieu: The Next Generation
The development of Bourdieu's intellectual heritage in contemporary UK sociology
Edited by Jenny Thatcher, Nicola Ingram, Ciaran Burke and Jessica Abrahams

Drinking Dilemmas
Space, culture and identity
Edited by Thomas Thurnell-Read

'*Drinking Dilemmas* is an important and timely collection of papers on the study of alcohol, drinking and drunkenness. Thurnell-Read has brought together a range of distinguished authors to explore how drinking practices and individual identities are both spatially and culturally defined. This book will prove to be a useful resource for both scholars and students at all levels who wish to understand the multiple ways in which individual identities, alcohol consumption, drinking practices and intoxicated behaviors are interwoven.'

Geoffrey Hunt, Professor, Centre for Alcohol and Drug Research, Aarhus University, Denmark

'This timely collection of recent research on the role of alcohol in cultural life makes an important contribution to contemporary debates about the "demon drink". Contributors challenge the overwhelmingly negative connotations of much public health and policy discourse, examining the diverse symbolic meanings of drinking in a range of social, political and economic contexts. The book has a distinctive focus on place and space, crossing academic disciplines from sociology and geography to criminology, and crossing the globe from the Bigg Market in Newcastle to Mar Mikhael in Beirut, via France, South Africa and the extreme metal music scene in Leeds, UK.'

Christine Griffin, Professor, University of Bath, UK

Drinking Dilemmas

Space, culture and identity

Edited by Thomas Thurnell-Read

LONDON AND NEW YORK

First published 2016
by Routledge
2 Park Square, Milton Park, Abingdon, Oxon OX14 4RN

and by Routledge
711 Third Avenue, New York, NY 10017

First issued in paperback 2018

Routledge is an imprint of the Taylor & Francis Group, an informa business

© 2016 Thomas Thurnell-Read

The right of the editor to be identified as the author of the editorial material, and of the authors for their individual chapters, has been asserted in accordance with sections 77 and 78 of the Copyright, Designs and Patents Act 1988.

All rights reserved. No part of this book may be reprinted or reproduced or utilised in any form or by any electronic, mechanical, or other means, now known or hereafter invented, including photocopying and recording, or in any information storage or retrieval system, without permission in writing from the publishers.

Trademark notice: Product or corporate names may be trademarks or registered trademarks, and are used only for identification and explanation without intent to infringe.

British Library Cataloguing in Publication Data
A catalogue record for this book is available from the British Library

Library of Congress Cataloging-in-Publication Data
Thurnell-Read, Thomas, 1982– editor.
  Drinking dilemmas : space, culture and identity / edited by Thomas Thurnell-Read.
  1. Drinking of alcoholic beverages—Great Britain. 2. Drinking of alcoholic beverages—Social aspects—Great Britain. 3. Alcoholic beverages—Social aspects—Great Britain. 4. Drinking customs—Great Britain. 5. Great Britain—Social life and customs.
  HV5446.D75 2015
  394.1/30941—dc23
  2015025836

ISBN 13: 978-1-138-59636-8 (pbk)
ISBN 13: 978-1-138-93114-5 (hbk)

Typeset in Times New Roman
by Apex CoVantage, LLC

Contents

List of figures and tables ix
Acknowledgements x
List of contributors xi

1 **An introduction to drinking dilemmas: space, culture and identity** 1
   THOMAS THURNELL-READ

2 **Revisiting urban nightscapes: an academic and personal journey through 20 years of nightlife research** 13
   ROBERT HOLLANDS

3 **The symbolic value of alcohol: the importance of alcohol consumption, drinking practices and drinking spaces in classed and gendered identity construction** 28
   KIMBERLEY ROSS-HOULE, AMANDA ATKINSON AND HARRY SUMNALL

4 **Beer and belonging: Real Ale consumption, place and identity** 45
   THOMAS THURNELL-READ

5 **Illegal drinking venues in a South African township: sites of struggle in the informal city** 62
   ANDREW CHARMAN

6 **'Eat, drink and be merry, for tomorrow we die': alcohol practices in Mar Mikhael, Beirut** 81
   MARIE BONTE

7 **'A force to be reckoned with': the role and influence of alcohol in Leeds' extreme metal scene** 99
   GABBY RICHES

8 'Never, ever go down the Bigg Market': classed and spatialised processes of othering on the 'girls' night out' 114
EMILY NICHOLLS

9 Young people's alcohol-related urban im/mobilities 132
SAMANTHA WILKINSON

10 Parenting style and gender effects on alcohol consumption among university students in France 150
LUDOVIC GAUSSOT, LOÏC LE MINOR AND NICOLAS PALIERNE

11 Growing up, going out: cultural and aesthetic attachment to the night-time economy 172
OLIVER SMITH

12 'There are limits on what you can do': biographical reconstruction by those bereaved by alcohol-related deaths 187
CHRISTINE VALENTINE, LORNA TEMPLETON AND RICHARD VELLEMAN

13 Drinking dilemmas: making a difference? 205
MARK JAYNE AND GILL VALENTINE

Index 219

Figures and tables

Figures

5.1	Entrance to the shebeen. The public space is highlighted.	68
5.2	Plan view perspective of a 'neighbourhood' shebeen, showing the division between public and private space.	72
5.3	Internal seating within the venue, showing the VIP lounge. The use of seating and signs is illustrated.	74
6.1	Drinking patterns in Beirut.	86
6.2	Crew Express, Armenian Street.	90
6.3	Drinking outside in Mar Mikhael, Armenian Street.	93
6.4	Young Syrian (left) having a drink in Mar Mikhael with a group of Lebanese students.	94
10.1	Structure of the educational parenting styles of the father and mother	153
10.2	Distribution of types of alcohol consumers (AUDIT) by sex (chi-square test***)	158
10.3	Distribution of the types of alcohol consumers (AUDIT) among female students, by the level of study (chi-square test***)	159

Tables

10.1	Distribution of educational parenting styles (EPS) of mothers and fathers	155
10.2	Distribution of alcohol consumption among female and male students by the educational parenting style (EPS) of the father and mother	161
12.1	Profile of a sub-sample of interviews (conducted between March and September 2013)	190

Acknowledgements

Without the energies and efforts of everyone involved in the British Sociological Association Sociology of Alcohol Study Group over the past four and a half years this volume would not have been possible. Significant thanks are therefore due to the founder and original force behind the group, Patsy Staddon, and to Karl Spracklen, Amanda Rohloff, Laura Doherty and Carol Emslie, who have worked with me as group convenors at different times. Amanda, who sadly and unexpectedly passed away in December 2012, is fondly remembered and dearly missed.

The contributions to this volume all stem from presentations made at the *Drinking Dilemmas* conference held at Cardiff Metropolitan University in December 2013. Caroline Ritchie and her colleagues, who expertly hosted the event, therefore played a big part in preparing the ground from which this project grew. I am also grateful to Elaine Forester and Liz Brown at the BSA for their support with all the group's events over the years and, more generally, everyone who attended our various conference and workshops and contributed by sharing their research findings, insights and general enthusiasm.

Thanks are due to those who reviewed chapters and commented on the manuscript, including Laura Fenton, Emeka Dumbili, Karl Spracklen, Henry Yeomans, Laura Doherty, Patsy Staddon and Sébastien Tutenges. The assistance of the *Sociological Futures* series editors, Eileen Green, John Horne, Caroline Oliver and Louise Ryan, has been invaluable as has that of Alyson Claffey at Routledge and Alison Danforth at the British Sociological Association.

Contributors

Amanda Atkinson is a Senior Researcher within the Centre for Public Health at Liverpool John Moores University. Her research interests relate to youth leisure and health, gender, substance use, intoxication and media representations of these issues.

Marie Bonte is a geographer and PhD candidate at the University Grenoble Alpes where she teaches at postgraduate level. She is also a member of the PACTE research team, and a former fellow from the Ecole Normale Supérieure de Lyon. She is working on nightlife in Beirut, Lebanon. She is interested in cultural and political geography, Arab cities, the spatiality of alcohol and drinking and norms and transgression. She has published several articles about alcohol in Morocco, the gay nightscape in Beirut, the transition from day to night and public lighting in Beirut.

Andrew Charman trained as a sociologist and development economist, obtaining a PhD from Cambridge. His current research focuses on understanding township informal markets, studying the dynamics of micro-enterprises/entrepreneurship and investigating the politics of informality. His research seeks to apply social and cultural analysis to better explore and theorise the nature of informality and state regulation of informal activities. Andrew has experimented with new research approaches and methods to enhance stakeholder participation, whilst seeking to visualise outcomes through the use of cartography, diagrams, imagery and infographics. He has researched and published on the impact of the liquor control paradigm with respect to its economic, social and political implications for illegal drinking venues.

Ludovic Gaussot is Lecturer in Sociology at Le GRESCO (Groupe de Recherche et d'Etudes Sociologique du Centre Ouest – Group Research and Sociological Studies Centre West), University of Poitiers, France. His research interests include gender and gender relations, deviance and the sociology of knowledge. He has published broadly on a range of topics and is author of two books on alcohol and drunkenness: *Modération et Sobriété: Etudes sur les Usages Sociaux de l'Alcool (Moderation and Sobriety: Studies on the Social Uses* of Alcohol) and *Alcool et alcoolisme: Pratiques et représentations (Alcohol and Alcoholism: Practices and Representations)* published in 2004 and 1998, respectively.

Robert Hollands is Professor of Sociology in the School of Geography, Politics and Sociology, Newcastle University where he was Chair of Department until 2012. His research addresses a broad range of themes, including the sociology of city life, specifically concerning reconfigurations of the night-time economy, cultural tourism, cultural politics and social movements. Working with Paul Chatterton, Robert undertook the Economic and Social Research Council–funded research titled 'Youth Culture, Nightlife and Urban Change', taking in case studies of Newcastle, Leeds and Bristol. The project resulted in two books which have become key texts in the study of the night-time economy (NTE): *Changing Our Toon: Youth, Nightlife and Urban Change in Newcastle* (2001) and *Urban Nightscapes: Youth Cultures, Pleasure Spaces and Corporate Power* (2003). For the past 15 years he has been a research consultant to the Prague Fringe festival and more recently is recipient of funding to study the Newcastle-based Amber Collective to explore the possibilities of transformative art.

Mark Jayne is Professor of Human Geography at Cardiff University, UK. He worked for 10 years (2005–2015) at the University of Manchester and prior to this this he held research positions at Staffordshire University, the University of Sheffield and the University of Leeds where he worked with Gill Valentine on a number of projects relating to alcohol, drinking and drunkenness. Mark is a leading theorist of urban geographies. His work explores the cultural, social, political, legal, policy and economic intersections which shape and reform modern cities and considers how urban regeneration is regulated, who it affects and who it often marginalises or excludes. Mark (along with Gill Valentine and other collaborators) has undertaken two major research projects funded by the Joseph Rowntree Foundation on 'Family Life and Alcohol Consumption' and 'Drinking Places: Social Geographies of Consumption'. The two books these projects gave rise to, *Childhood, Family, Alcohol* published by Ashgate in 2016 and *Alcohol, Drinking, Drunkenness: (Dis)Orderly Spaces* (2011), have contributed to understandings of the social, cultural and spatial aspects of alcohol use both in the urban spaces of the night-time economy and the more intimate and hard-to-access setting of the family home.

Loic Le Minor is a sociologist working at Le GRESCO (Groupe de Recherche et d'Etudes Sociologique du Centre Ouest – Group Research and Sociological Studies Centre West), the University of Poitiers, France. His research addresses young people's experiences of drinking alcohol and has a particular focus on the intergenerational transmission of drinking styles and practices.

Emily Nicholls is Lecturer in Sociology at the University of Portsmouth. Her teaching primarily focuses on gender, sexuality and risk. Prior to this, she was Research Associate in the Department of Sociological Studies at the University of Sheffield and completed her doctorate in Sociology at Newcastle University. Drawing on in-depth, qualitative, semi-structured interviews with 26 young women, her Economic and Social Research Council–funded PhD research examines the everyday, embodied ways in which young women negotiate the boundaries of femininity through dress and appearance, drinking and risk management on a 'girls' night out', and the ways in which this is shaped by aspects of identity, including class, age, region and sexuality. She has also worked on policies, consultation exercises and research projects around domestic abuse and youth homelessness within local government.

Nicolas Palierne is a doctoral candidate at EHESS (Ecole des Hautes Etudes en Sciences Sociales) – Paris, CADIS. His research interests include the history of science, public health and the history of medicine.

Gabby Riches is a PhD fellow in the Research Institute for Sport, Physical Activity and Leisure at Leeds Beckett University, UK. Her doctoral research explores the role and significance mosh pit practices play in the lives of female heavy metal fans within the Leeds extreme metal music scene. Her research interests include the socio-spatial constructions of underground music spaces, women's participation in local metal scenes, non-representational theory, marginal leisures and embodiment. Her research on women's participation in mosh pit practices has been published in the *Journal for Cultural Research* (2011) and *Inter-Disciplinary Net Press* (2013), and by the International Association for the Study of Popular Music (2014).

Kimberley Ross-Houle is a Public Health Researcher at the Centre for Public Health at Liverpool John Moores University. Her background is in urban and gender research and her research interests include gender and identity, urban sociology, the sociology of the night-time economy and visual research methods. Kimberley is also writing her PhD thesis at the University of Liverpool titled 'Women's lived experiences and perceptions of representations and identity in urban space: A case study of Liverpool, UK'.

Oliver Smith is Associate Professor (Reader) in Criminology and Criminal Justice Studies at Plymouth School of Law, Plymouth University. He completed his PhD in 2010 and worked as a Teaching Fellow at the University of York for two years before moving to Plymouth to take up his current position. His research interests are in the utilisation of urban drinking spaces and the cultural and aesthetic attachments that people form to night-time alcohol-based leisure practices. He is the author of *Contemporary Adulthood and the Night Time Leisure Economy*, which was published by Palgrave Macmillan in 2014.

Harry Sumnall is a Professor in Substance Use at the Centre for Public Health, Liverpool John Moores University. He is interested in all aspects of substance use, particularly young people's health issues.

Lorna Templeton is a Research Associate at the University of Bath, UK, and Independent Research Consultant, Bristol. She has worked for more than 15 years exploring how children and families are affected by the substance misuse of a relative, and how research, practice and policy needs to be improved to better meet the needs of this large, but often marginalised, group. Lorna is a Trustee of Adfam, a member of Alcohol Research UK's Research Panel and a founder member of a new international organisation called AFINet, Addiction and the Family International Network.

Thomas Thurnell-Read is Senior Lecturer in Sociology in the School of Humanities at Coventry University. Through his research and teaching, he uses contemporary leisure and consumption practices, particularly those relating to drinking and drunkenness, to explore a range of sociological issues relating to sociality, identity and diversity. His research on British stag party tourism in Poland has been published in a range of international journals and focusses on the social construction of masculinity through transgressive drinking practices. He is the editor (with Dr Mark Casey, Newcastle) of *Men, Masculinities, Travel and Tourism*, published by Palgrave Macmillan in 2014. He is a founder member of the BSA Alcohol Study group and Co-Convenor of the group since July 2012.

Christine Valentine is a Teaching Fellow and Research Associate at the University of Bath. She has researched and published on the social and cultural shaping of bereavement in both British and Japanese contexts, and examined funeral welfare systems for people on low income both nationally and internationally. She is currently involved in research with families and individuals bereaved following a drug- or alcohol-related death, which aims to raise awareness and improve policy and practice to meet the needs of this group. She is a member of the Research Centre for Death and Society (CDAS) and a founder member of the Association for the Study of Death and Society (ASDS).

Gill Valentine is Professor of Human Geography and Pro-vice Chancellor for Social Sciences at the University of Sheffield, UK. Gill has secured over £4m of research funding, published 15 books, nearly 200 journal articles and book chapters, 10 official reports and supervised more than 20 PhD students. Gill was Co-founder and Co-editor *of Social and Cultural Geography*, as well as Co-editor of *Gender, Place and Culture*.

Richard Velleman is Emeritus Professor of Mental Health Research at the University of Bath, UK, and a Senior Research Consultant at Sangath Community, an NGO based in Goa, India. He is a clinical and academic psychologist and is a leading authority on substance misuse, with special interest in the impact of this misuse on other family members, including children. He is a founder of the Alcohol, Drugs and the Family UK research network and of AFINet (Addiction and the Family International Network: http://www.afinetwork.info/); and a member of the 15-person Scientific Committee of the EMCDDA (European Monitoring Centre on Drugs and Drug Addiction). His work in Goa involves developing and researching the use of community lay health workers to deliver psychological interventions to people with serious alcohol problems. His research and practice interests cover a wide spectrum within mental health, particularly the impact of substance misuse and mental health issues on family members, especially children.

Samantha Wilkinson is a Research Associate in the School of Sociology and Social Policy at The University of Nottingham and currently works on a project which aims to broaden understandings of good home care for people with dementia. Prior to this, she was a Human Geography PhD student at The University of Manchester, having previously completed a BA in Geography and a MSc in Environmental Governance at the same institution. She has presented findings from her thesis on 'young people, alcohol and urban life' at a number of conferences and she has written a chapter for the forthcoming reference works to be published by Springer in 2016, titled *Geographies of Children and Young People* (edited by John Horton and Bethan Evans), around the themes of alcohol, drinking and drunkenness and play/recreation.

Chapter 1

An introduction to drinking dilemmas
Space, culture and identity

Thomas Thurnell-Read

This book explores the social and cultural significance of alcohol, its consumption and its various effects and impacts at a time when alcohol is said to cost the British National Health Service £2.7 billion a year (The NHS Information Centre 2011) and to annually account for 3.3 million deaths globally (WHO, 2014). Yet, the chapters that comprise this volume do not position alcohol as exclusively negative. Throughout the volume, we see drinking as a means of forging personal identity, solidifying friendships and finding release from the pressures and anxieties of modern life.

The volume, therefore, follows in the footsteps of the influential Mary Douglas (1987) in refusing to view drink solely as a 'problem' through the lens of pathology and anomie. Instead, we note at the outset that 'drunkenness also expresses culture in so far as it always takes the form of a highly patterned, learned comportment which varies from one culture to another' (Douglas, 1987, p. 4). Much alcohol is consumed as part of what Douglas termed 'constructive drinking', where drinking is a constructive force far too embedded in the very fabric of social life – in its rituals, celebrations and binding social ties – to be reduced purely to its many real, but by no means automatic, negative outcomes. We therefore acknowledge, and indeed are drawn to, the beneficial cultural and social aspects of drinking and note how they invariably reflect an adherence to rule-bound and historically embedded social interaction.

In recent years, drinking and drunkenness has become a common focal point for political and media debates to contest notions of responsibility, discipline and risk. These debates have rapidly coalesced around the 'binge drinking' narrative which emerged little over a decade ago yet has so far proved to be a resilient rhetorical anchor around which debates have gathered (Plant & Plant, 2006; Nicholls, 2009). Alcohol has proved to be a handy scapegoat and one which has been used to explain away far more complex social and cultural changes in modern British society and beyond. Work in the social sciences has therefore necessarily sought to challenge the 'blame it on the booze' narrative which reduces context and causation to a simplistic model of alcohol as 'demon drink'. Important contributions to the field have shown that these concerns and the legislative responses to them, while at the forefront of our minds, are not new and, indeed, have a long historical lineage (Nicholls, 2009; Yeomans, 2014).

To these debates, social science perspectives have brought necessary insights. Indeed, we might suggest that the most clear and pressing issues relating to alcohol, drinking and drunkenness have at their core the tension between 'personal troubles' and 'public issues' that is deeply sociological in nature (Mills, 1959). For many years, alcohol and its various roles in specific social contexts have been present but rarely addressed directly within the sociological literature. Thus, we see the pub and drunkenness feature in Clarke and Critcher's (1985) neo-Marxist analysis of the tumultuous emergence of modern leisure in Britain. In Paul Willis' (1977) classic *Learning to Labour*, there are young working-class men for whom it was the pub more than the school in which the required standards of masculinity were learnt in readiness for a life of labour. And yet it is only recently that sociology and other closely related disciplines, human geography in particular, have built a sustained and still growing body of literature addressing alcohol and the associated issues of drunkenness and intoxication.

The expansion of what became known as the night-time economy during the 1990s is perhaps the single greatest catalyst for the emergence of valuable work across sociology, criminology and geography. Chatterton and Hollands' (2003) study, which Hollands reflects on in Chapter 2, particularly captured the concerns of an increasing number of academic researchers seeking to situate the individual amongst a fraught post-industrial restructuring of many British cities as commercial- and leisure-driven spaces. This changing urban environment – with its themed pubs, drinking circuits and the looming prospect of late/all-night openings – provided the backdrop for increasingly detailed studies of the classed and gendered divisions at work in Britain's night-time economy (Hollands, 1995). So too did risk, control and regulation emerge as key themes of the literature. Several studies of 'bouncers' (Monaghan, 2002; Hobbs, Hadfield, Lister & Winlow, 2003) explored the use of embodied capital and violence in controlling the night-time economy, and a more general mapping of the governance and regulation of drinking and drinking spaces demonstrated the competing forces at work in controlling night-time leisure on the British high street (Hobbs, Lister, Hadfield, Winlow & Hall, 2000).

In a study that would set the tone for others that followed, Tomsen (1997) explored the pleasures of 'the big night out'. What to one person is the fun and excitement of playful transgression is to another the very quintessence of chaos, mayhem and wanton abandon. As a field of study, alcohol studies in general and the sociology of alcohol in particular has needed to be aware of such relativity. The hysteria of media coverage and the hand-wringing of political and policy discussions were, clearly, missing the point; the apparent disorder and chaos were in fact highly desirable and represented for many drinkers a sense of cathartic fun and release. More recently, Fiona Measham has, across a range of studies and collaborations, defined and explored in great detail the 'new cultures of intoxication' where advanced drunkenness and this associated loss of control appear to be an integral and a desired feature of particularly younger drinker's engagement with alcohol (Measham & Brain, 2005). The tensions between the pleasures and dangers of the night-time economy, where both exuberant and destructive violence prove alluring and alarming (Winlow & Hall, 2006) mean that at the heart of many studies from this period is an important acknowledgment that the drinking cultures of the British night must be understood as contested and contingent. Without seeking to understand the many different actors involved in constructing and contesting the night we remain doomed to view the topic through a narrow lens of moral finger pointing.

Expanding on these insights, a number of key studies sought to understand how alcohol, drinking and drunkenness offer a source of identity, albeit a problematic one, in the face of changes in economic, social and political climate. The fun and camaraderie of drinking spaces was shown to provide, for many young men in particular, a sense of surety in a time of transition and uncertainty predicated by neo-liberal capitalism, globalisation and changing gender relations (Nayak, 2003; Blackshaw, 2003; Winlow & Hall, 2009; Smith, 2014). In these studies, specific drinkers and their drinking have been set within a broad and considered social milieu and have shown how understanding drink and its role in people's lives requires a link from the individual to the array of broad economic and social transitions and changes that have come to define the final decade of the 20th century and the opening decades of the present century. That drunken excess might offer catharsis to the impositions made upon the individual in late modernity remains, if not taboo, than a plausible explanation that academics have had to handle with tact. This breadth of scale, helping locate the individual and subjectivities within a far wider appreciation of historical and global shifts, is another example of where sociology and social science perspectives on alcohol have made valuable contributions. In many of the chapters in this volume, we see drinking practices understood within a bigger contextual picture of urban renewal (Hollands, this volume), neoliberal era and post-industrial anxiety (Smith, this volume; Thurnell-Read, this volume) and even the legacies of institutional racism (Charman, this volume) and war and civil conflict (Bonte, this volume).

Perhaps the most prominent contribution of sociology to the study of alcohol has been to explore and explain how gender permeates nearly every facet of drinking and, most strikingly, how societies respond with great variance to the drinking of men and of women. Elizabeth Ettorre's (1997) ground-breaking work on women and drinking exposed this deep gendering of drinking and did much to highlight how the 'problem' of drink is levied far more heavily upon women who drink than men. Indeed, where alcohol could serve to stigmatise the female drinker, for men it has been shown to be a significant resource in reproducing dominant codes of masculinity and, as an influential paper by the New Zealand sociologist Hugh Campbell (2000) detailed, the drinking of alcohol is performed and sustained in public drinking spaces which are shaped by formal and informal gender segregation. Gender continues to be central to much sociological research (for example, see Staddon, 2015) and is a direct or indirect theme of many of the chapters in this volume.

Why drinking dilemmas?

Despite recent advances, academic studies of alcohol still frequently struggle to reconcile the individual, social and cultural pleasures and benefits of drinking and drunkenness with concerns for health and well-being, public order and social policy. These 'drinking dilemmas' provide a fruitful site for academics to contribute to policy, media and health lobby discourses on the (un)acceptable functions of alcohol in modern society. One dilemma stems from challenging the common-sense notion of negative impacts of alcohol (Hollands, this volume), and then, against the weight of public perception and policy rhetoric, continuing to research and identify the many positive outcomes of drinking. Many studies in the area have sought to understand, if not necessarily sympathise with, individuals whose drinking practices are widely condemned and stigmatised. The media-led moral panic against binge drinkers, and before them 'lager louts', should not blind us from seeking to understand why so many might find either excitement or solace in drinking heavily.

There is not one drinking dilemma but many, and they are interconnected. These dilemmas involve tensions relating to gender, social class, age and the life course, and mean that the contested role of alcohol and drunkenness in contemporary debates about place, identity and sociality are at the heart of the volume. Why, in the face of evidence and advice (Yeomans, 2013) are many people still motivated to drink, often to excess? The boundary between acceptable and unacceptable drinking clearly bends and shifts in accordance with the social class, gender and age of the drinker. Thus, we see plans for those receiving social welfare benefits to be paid on preloaded store cards blocked from being used to purchase alcohol (Chorley, 2014) at the same time as research has revealed a link between heavy drinking and working in professions with cultures marked by high pressure and long hours (Badham, 2015). What use is talk of 'sensible drinking' when such disparities exist in how gender, social class, age and ethnicity refract how drinking and drunkenness are understood and perceived by others and by wider society?

Drinking practices are diverse and are spatially and culturally defined. It is this plurality from which many dilemmas stem. News stories about drunken excesses and violence, at least when they relate to drinkers of a particular social class, have become an easy currency for tabloid newspapers, and on social media a new era of self-publicity has made any clear distinction between public and private drinking hard to sustain. Thus, there are also huge variations in the visibility of certain drinkers and styles of drinking, meaning the night-time economy has received sustained media, policy and academic attention whereas drinking within the home (with a few notable exceptions, Holloway, Jayne & Valentine, 2008; Jayne, Valentine & Holloway, 2011) remains conspicuously absent.

Dilemmas also exist for the discipline of 'alcohol studies' and for the role of sociology and other social and cultural perspectives within it. Many of the contributions to this volume are not from sociologists. Indeed, geography is particularly well represented and demonstrates the notable valued, though relatively recent, contribution of geographical approaches to the study of alcohol, drinking and drunkenness. As Jayne and Valentine (this volume) rightly point out in closing this volume, a wealth of at times brilliant academic work has remained too insular and compartmentalised within disciplinary boundaries. Such work has also largely failed to reach out for dialogue with policy and health science disciplines that, of course, are also guilty of the same.

It is intended that this volume shows how sociological perspectives on drinking are a platform, or forum, which many disciplines with related concerns can relate to and foster dialogue within. Beyond sociology and geography, the collection ought to be of interest to a broad range of disciplines, including the health sciences, urban planning, leisure and tourism, youth work, gender studies and cultural studies. The scale and scope of these insights is important; both sociology and geography have made important contributions to the field in their ability to consider alcohol within the personal, group and community level as well as more broadly across national and global media, and policy and commercial contexts. Sociology has proved strong in highlighting how deep social divisions relating to gender, social class and sexuality shape and are in turn shaped by our understanding of alcohol and when, where and how it is consumed. From the minutiae of daily life and personal subjectivities through communities and to national, historical and global forces, sociological approaches to alcohol have, perhaps more than other disciplines, offered the potential to be an interface, an interdisciplinary forum through which dialogue can take place.

The subthemes of the collection – space, culture and identity – indicate the key concerns of the sociology of alcohol but these are concerns shared across disciplinary boundaries. We therefore tip our hats to our geography colleagues for highlighting the importance of space and place in understanding alcohol, drinking and drunkenness. This volume sees drinking explored across a diversity of spaces: from both online and offline spaces (Ross, Atkinson and Sumnall, this volume); the extreme metal club mosh pit (Riches, this volume); the township shebeen (Charman, this volume); and the Beirut neighbourhood street (Bonte, this volume); to the parks and bedrooms of suburban Manchester (Wilkinson, this volume). Across all contributions we see the legacy of Mary Douglas (1987) in understandings of the inescapably cultural nature of alcohol and drinking. Drink is also a canny modifier of identity and social relations with its promise of extended youth (Smith, this volume) or a reassuring return or continuation of locality and community (Thurnell-Read, this volume). It opens up our bodies and allows us to assert our identity and belonging in new ways (Riches, this volume) and it can also leave its traces in pain, grief and stigma (Valentine, Templeton and Velleman, this volume).

The structure of the book

Following this introduction, in Chapter 2 Robert Hollands revisits and reflects on his involvement in research into alcohol and the night-time economy spanning

20 years. We see how, as previously noted, the field of alcohol studies has changed significantly and, in no small part due to the work of the likes of Hollands, a new legitimacy has been gained. In the chapter, and Hollands' work more generally (particularly that conducted in collaboration with Paul Chatterton), we see how the diverse and often competing agendas of corporate rationalisation, regeneration and resistance are set against a backdrop of wider social, cultural and demographic changes in post-industrial cities typified by homogeneity and gentrification.

In Chapter 3, Kimberley Ross-Houle, Amanda Atkinson and Harry Sumnall make identity the focus of their analysis and explore how alcohol consumption practices play a role with the construction, performance and negotiation of identity. Alcohol is a cultural and social resource which individuals, particular young adults, look to in order to express sociality and belonging in the expression of selfhood. Here, as with later chapters, gender and class are particularly present in the use of alcohol branding and, as a recent and important development, social media is used to claim distinction and validation through alcohol consumption. As with Hollands, we see that the motivations and practices of individual consumers must necessarily be considered with reference to the actions and efforts of the elements of the drinks industry that go to great length and expense to position their brand as desirable.

Expanding on the theme of identity in my own substantive contribution, Chapter 4 explores how alcohol consumption, in this case that of 'traditional' Real Ale, taps into and supports a range of identity constructions linked to local and national identity. The chapter explores how consumers of Real Ale locate their drinking in terms of identity formation and loyalty to place. Expanding on this observation, the chapter considers the profusion of nostalgic imagery in Real Ale branding and suggests that invoking the symbols of industry, empire and heritage offers some consumers a sense of belonging and identity. This is, of course, gender specific, and the chapter closes with a discussion of how such masculine imagery acts to exclude and contain female drinkers.

Chapters 5, 6 and 7 move discussion into a diverse range of drinking spaces by looking at the South African township 'shebeen', the night-time neighbourhood in Mar Mikhail, Beirut, and the 'mosh pits' of the Leeds extreme metal 'scene', respectively. Common to all, despite their diverse social and geographical contexts, is the interconnection and co-dependency of space and alcohol consumption practices and experiences. Andrew Charman, in Chapter 5, explores the spatial micropolitics of shebeens and details how their proprietors carve out a livelihood and an identity within the landscape of post-apartheid South Africa. In Chapter 6, Marie Bonte describes the shifting spatial dynamics of drinking in Beirut where complex religious, ethnic and cultural fault lines underlay emerging spaces which the city's young people are using to find solidarity, sociality and, for many, an escape from pressures and legacies of civil conflict and social and political instability. Gabby Riches' analysis of the embodied and sensory pleasures of extreme metal music fans in Chapter 7 foregrounds the transformative role of alcohol for female participants, in particular, for whom drinking alcohol unleashes the potentiality of alternative bodily practices and gender subjectivities. In all three chapters we see how alcohol is an inseparable constituent of the spatial and social setting which, it can be added, evidently necessitates such rich qualitative inquiry to access and understand in all its nuanced detail.

In Chapter 8, Emily Nicholls explores the links between place, identity and drunkenness in the narratives of young female drinkers in Newcastle. We see how drinkers position themselves and each other in relation to constructions of respectability and control which draw heavily on perceptions of community, social class, gender and sexuality. Tellingly, certain drinking spaces and particular drinkers are subjected to discursive distancing and 'othering'. Young drinkers are also the focus of Chapter 9, in which Samantha Wilkinson explores the drinking practices of teenagers and young adults from two suburban areas in the north-west of England. Using innovative methods that seek to capture the fluidity and mobility of participants' experiences as they move through the streets, parks and bedrooms that make up the often overlooked settings of suburban drinking, the chapter demonstrates the centrality of friendship, sociability and autonomy to understanding young people's drinking practices.

The next three chapters demonstrate how debates about alcohol, drinking and drunkenness morph and shift across the life course. In Chapter 10, Ludovic Gaussot, Loic Le Minor and Nicolas Palierne explore the influence of parenting style on the drinking habits of French students. Using quantitative and qualitative data, the analysis unpacks issues of parenting style and how children are socialised and, as a consequence, how they engage in risky or sensible drinking. Again, as elsewhere in the volume, significant differences in gender exist with the persistence of gender stereotypes, meaning the drinking of female students is subject to far harsher monitoring and judgment than that of young males. Chapter 11 sees Oliver Smith question the continued involvement of adults in the night-time economy. Rather than 'growing up' and settling down, the participants of his study cling on to a social and aesthetic attachment to the spaces and experiences of the night-time high street in an extended and, for some, abortive transition to adulthood. In the corporate theming of drinking venues, particularly those designed to appeal to nostalgia, the allure of continued involvement in heavy drinking and hedonistic consumption practices is juxtaposed against the anxieties and tensions that go with growing old in the night-time economy. Finally, in Chapter 12, Christine Valentine, Richard Velleman and Lorna Templeton offer a unique and poignant insight into the experiences of the families and relatives of those killed by their addiction to alcohol. We see how the stigma of alcoholism occupies and shapes the grieving process of 'those left behind'.

The final chapter aims to offer a reflection that 'bookends' those offered in the Introduction and in Robert Hollands' reflections on the field in Chapter 2. Chapter 13 therefore sees Mark Jayne and Gill Valentine provide a stock taking of contributions made by different disciplines to social and cultural understandings of alcohol, drinking and drunkenness. The frequent citation of Jayne and Valentine in the chapters in this volume attests to their influence across disciplines and, in particular, in opening up new lines of inquiry both within and beyond the commercialised spaces of urban drinking (e.g., Jayne, Valentine and Holloway, 2011 stands out as a unique contribution to understanding the place of alcohol in that rarely accessed setting, the family home). Thus, the chapter gives an overview both of the progress and shortcomings of the varied social and cultural approaches to the study of alcohol and its impacts. It also makes a convincing and spirited call for a greater dialogue between social, health and medical scientists and a pragmatic approach to the recording of the impact of our work.

The future of the sociology of alcohol: progress and potential

The contributions to this volume originate from papers presented at the *Drinking Dilemmas: Space, Culture and Identity* conference held by the British Sociological Association's Sociology of Alcohol Study Group at Cardiff Metropolitan University in December 2013. Founded in July 2011, the study group has successfully brought together academics working on alcohol, drinking and drunkenness from a range of disciplinary fields and cultural contexts. Interdisciplinarity has been a feature of the group and this is reflected in the contributions to this volume. In Cardiff – and at the group's other events held in London (in March 2012, December 2012 and February 2015) and Leeds (July 2012) – contributions came not only from sociologists but also geographers, criminologists, health professionals and even, in one illuminating presentation on pub interiors, the field of art and design history. While some have made alcohol the explicit and direct focus of their scholarly activities, many have come to the group with alcohol as a supplementary or emergent theme of their research.

As Hollands observes (this volume), both the scale and the perceived validity of alcohol research looking beyond strict pathology at pleasures and motivations has come a long way. Yet, by way of concluding this introduction, it is important to note the numerous areas where work still needs to be done. This involves, in various senses, 'following the stream' and seeing where alcohol flows but is as yet unstudied. While this volume addresses a range of geographical and social contexts and a diversity of subjects, there remains a skew towards the study of younger drinkers (see Emslie, Hunt & Lyons, 2012 for a recent exception to this). Non-white drinkers are also conspicuously absent from the literature. This is worryingly pronounced in the British context meaning, barring a few notable exceptions (Valentine, Holloway & Jayne, 2010), we are left to look across the Atlantic at work on Caribbean drinkers in Canada (Joseph, 2012) and young Asian Americans in California (Hunt, Moloney & Kristen 2010) for insights into how race and ethnic belonging influence and shape experiences of alcohol and drunkenness (also see Charman and Bonte, this volume). There is a feeling that extreme youth drinking cultures have, as Hollands suggests (this volume), 'gone global'. Recent years have seen a notable, yet somewhat familiar, emergence of debates about youth drinking in countries such as China and France (Willsher, 2014). Drinking studies will undoubtedly grow in other countries; welcome recent work by sociologists has shed light on gendered drinking practices in Nigeria (Dumbili, 2015) and Japan (Ho, 2015).

Reflecting on social class, while media coverage and policy agendas have exhibited an undeniable bias towards working-class drinking habits, often with a notable preference for demonisation and pathologisation, the habits of middle-class drinkers are only recently receiving similar levels of academic attention (Järvinen, Ellergaard & Larsen, 2014). Further still, given the rise in exclusive 'VIP' bars and the continuation of exclusive private-member clubs, I would suggest that there is scope and, indeed, a pressing need to 'study up' by exploring the drinking habits of the upper classes and elites, particularly when they are linked to the maintenance and extension of privilege and professional closure. Looking at the attention given to British Prime Minister David Cameron's membership of the notorious 'Bullingdon Club', when a student at the University of Oxford, where 'dinning' appears a handy if distasteful euphemism for anarchic drunkenness (BBC News, 2007), we can see how the excesses of elites can prove to be a lightning rod for resentment that could yet be used to explore complex and long-established configurations of privilege and social inequalities.

Research has also been perhaps too keen to focus on the most obvious and spectacular examples of drinking and drunkenness, with the night-time economy tending to dominate both the public imagination and research activities of academics and researchers. Studies of non-drinkers in situations and social contexts where heavy drinking has become normative (e.g., Romo, 2012; Conroy & de Visser, 2013) indicate that there is space to explore a range of intensities of engagement with alcohol, including total abstinence. As previously noted, drinking in the home is another area in clear need of greater research and more nuanced theorising (see Brierley-Jones et al., 2014).

Beyond these considerations, the research field has a somewhat 'hollowed out' look. With attention focusing on economic restructuring and media and policy discourse at the structural level and, characteristically, the varied motivations, subjectivities, practices and experiences of drinkers at the individual level, vast swaths of middle ground have been left unquestioned. Studies offering real insight, from a critical standpoint, into the workings of the industry remain rare (Hastings, 2009). Indeed, looking back we see Chatterton and Hollands' (2003) discussion of producers of night-life spaces as a largely unanswered call for research to address the bar owners, pub companies, urban redevelopment agencies and various governmental and non-governmental bodies that all influence the shape and direction of alcohol policies and practices. The Campaign for Real Ale (CAMRA), subject of my own recent research, is joined by the Society of Independent Brewers, the British Beer and Pubs Association and the European Beer Consumers Union in being an influential body at the heart of shaping the current position and future direction of the drinks industry and of alcohol policies which, evidently, require research or, indeed, collaborative and cooperative links.

A final observation echoes that made by Jayne and Valentine in their closing chapter to this volume and concerns how alcohol studies ensures its relevance and its future through both an openness to collaborations across disciplinary and methodological boundaries and in a continued and concerted effort to disseminate findings in a manner that engages with public interests and concerns. While this volume highlights the diversity at the heart of contemporary academic research into alcohol, drinking and drunkenness, it is by no means meant as a comprehensive or definitive text. Rather, its strength should be judged on the range and scope of cases offered and the potential for these studies to prompt and inspire further research into such areas as this closing section has identified as being under-researched. Drinking dilemmas both old and new, it seems, will continue to fascinate.

References

Badham, V. 2015. Are you drinking because you're working long hours, or are you working long hours to justify drinking?, *The Guardian*, 20 January 2015. http://www.theguardian.com/commentisfree/2015/jan/20/are-you-drinking-because-youre-working-long-hours-or-are-you-working-long-hours-to-justify-drinking

BBC News. 2007. "Cameron student photo is banned". BBC News Online, 2 March 2007. http://news.bbc.co.uk/1/hi/uk_politics/6409757.stm

Blackshaw, T. 2003. *Leisure life: Myth, masculinity and modernity*. London: Routledge.

Brierley-Jones, L., Ling, J., McCabe, K. E., Wilson, G. B., Crosland, A., Kaner, E. F. and Haighton, C. A. 2014. Habitus of home and traditional drinking: A qualitative analysis of reported middle-class alcohol use. *Sociology of Health and Illness* 36(7): 1054–1076.

Campbell, H. 2000. The glass phallus: Pub(lic) masculinity and drinking in rural New Zealand. *Rural Sociology*, 65(4): 562–581.

Chatterton, P. and Hollands, R. 2003. *Urban nightscapes: Youth cultures, pleasure spaces and corporate power*. London: Routledge.

Chorley, M. 2014. "Benefits to be paid onto smart cards to stop claimants spending their money on alcohol or gambling." *The Daily Mail*, 29 September 2014. http://www.dailymail.co.uk/news/article-2773857/Benefits-paid-smart-cards-stop-claimants-spending-money-alcohol-gambling.html

Conroy, D. and de Visser, R. 2013. Being a non-drinking student: An interpretative phenomenological analysis. *Psychology and Health*, 29(5): 536–551.

Clarke, J. and Critcher, C. 1985. *The devil makes work: Leisure in capitalist Britain*. Basingstoke: Macmillan.

Douglas, M. 1987. *Constructive drinking: Perspectives on drinking from anthropology*. Cambridge: Cambridge University Press.

Dumbili, E. 2015. 'What a man can do, a woman can do better': Gendered alcohol consumption and (de)construction of social identity among young Nigerians. *BMC Public Health*, 15:167.

Emslie, C., Hunt, K. and Lyons, A. 2012. Older and wiser?: Men's and women's accounts of drinking in early mid-life. *Sociology of Health and Illness*, 34(4): 481–496.

Ettorre, E. 1997. *Women and alcohol: A private pleasure or a public problem?* London: The Women's Press.

Hastings, G. 2009. *"They'll drink bucket loads of the stuff": An analysis of internal alcohol industry advertising documents*. The Alcohol Education and Research Council.

Ho, S.-L. 2015. 'License to drink': White-collar female workers and Japan's urban night space. *Ethnography*, 16(1): 25–50.

Hobbs, D., Lister, S., Hadfield, P., Winlow, S. and Hall, S. 2000. Receiving shadows: Governance and liminality in the night-time economy. *British Journal of Sociology*, 51(4): 701–717.

Hobbs, R., Hadfield, P., Lister, S. and Winlow, S. 2003. *Bouncers: Violence and governance in the night time economy*. Oxford: Oxford University Press.

Hollands, R. 1995. *Friday night, Saturday night: Youth cultural identification in the post-industrial city*. Newcastle: Newcastle University.

Holloway, S. L., Jayne, M. and Valentine, G. 2008. 'Sainsbury's is my local': English alcohol policy, domestic drinking practices and the meaning of home. *Transactions of the Institute of British Geographers*, 33(4): 532–547.

Hunt, G., Moloney, M. and Kristen, E. 2010. *Youth, drugs, and nightlife*. New York: Routledge.

Järvinen, M., Ellergaard, C. and Larsen, A. 2014. Drinking successfully: Alcohol consumption, taste and social status. *Journal of Consumer Culture*, 14(3): 384–405.

Jayne, M., Valentine, G. and Holloway, S. L. 2011. *Alcohol, drinking, drunkenness: (Dis)orderly spaces*. Aldershot: Ashgate.

Joseph, J. 2012. Around the boundary: Alcohol and older Caribbean-Canadian men. *Leisure Studies*, 31(2): 147–163.

Leyshon, M. 2008. 'We're stuck in the corner': Young women, embodiment and drinking in the countryside. *Drugs: Education, Prevention and Policy*, 15(3): 276–289.

Measham, F. and Brain, K. 2005. 'Binge' drinking: British alcohol policy and the new culture of intoxication. *Crime, Media, Culture*, 1(3): 262–283.

Mills, C. W. 1959. *The sociological imagination*. London: Oxford University Press.

Monaghan, L. 2002. Regulating 'Unruly' Bodies: Work tasks, conflict and violence in Britain's night-time economy. *British Journal of Sociology*, 53(3): 403–429.

Nayak, A. 2003. Last of the real Geordies? White masculinities and the subcultural response to deindustrialisation. *Environment and Planning D*, 21(1): 7–26.

Nicholls, J. 2009. *The politics of alcohol: A history of the drink question in England*. Manchester: Manchester University Press.

Plant, M. and Plant, M. 2006. *Binge Britain: Alcohol and the national response*. Oxford: Oxford University Press.

Ritchie, C. 2011. Young adult interaction with wine in the UK. *International Journal of Contemporary Hospitality Management*, 23(1): 99–114.

Romo, L. K. 2012. 'Above the influence': How college students communicate about the healthy deviance of alcohol abstinence. *Health Communication*, 27(7): 672–681.

Smith, O. 2014. *Contemporary adulthood and the night-time economy*. Basingstoke: Palgrave Macmillan.

Staddon, P. 2015. *Women and alcohol: Social perspectives*. Bristol: Policy Press.

The NHS Information Centre. 2011. *Statistics on alcohol: England, 2011*. Leeds: NHS Information Centre. 26 May 2011.

Tomsen, S. 1997. A top night: Social protest, masculinity and the culture of drinking violence. *British Journal of Criminology*, 37(1): 90–102.

Valentine, G., Holloway, S. and Jayne, M. 2010. Contemporary cultures of abstinence and the nighttime economy: Muslim attitudes towards alcohol and the implications for social cohesion. *Environment and Planning A*, 42(1): 8–22.

WHO. 2014. *Global status report on alcohol and health*. Geneva: World Health Organisation.

Willis, P. 1977. *Learning to labour: How working class kids get working class jobs*. Aldershot: Ashgate.

Willsher, K. 2014. "France bill aims to call time on 'le binge drinking'". *The Guardian*, 15 October 2014.

Winlow, S. and Hall, S. 2006. *Violent night: Urban leisure and contemporary culture*. Oxford: Berg.

Winlow, S. and Hall, S. 2009. Living for the weekend: Youth identities in northeast England. *Ethnography*, 10 (1), 91–113.

Yeomans, H. 2013. Blurred visions: experts, evidence and the promotion of moderate drinking. *The Sociological Review*, 61(S2): 58–78.

Yeomans, H. 2014. *Alcohol and moral regulation: Public attitudes, spirited measures and Victorian hangovers*. Bristol: Policy Press.

Chapter 2

Revisiting urban nightscapes
An academic and personal journey through 20 years of nightlife research

Robert Hollands

No animal ever invented anything as bad as drunkenness – or so good as drink
(G. K. Chesterton)

Introduction

G.K. Chesterton's quotation, like the main title of this edited volume *Drinking Dilemmas*, aptly sums up our often ambivalent personal and social attitudes towards alcohol consumption. Most of us can probably recall both peak life moments as well as darker, more negative experiences while under the influence of alcohol. Socially, on the plus side, anthropologists like Mary Douglas (2003) remind us that in Western culture alcohol is a fundamental part of most celebration rituals – weddings, christenings and birthdays – helping to create community and sociability, or what the sociologist Emile Durkheim (1965) referred to in another context as 'collective effervescence'. Some have gone as far as to speculate about the link between drinking and creativity, though the evidence here is (forgive the pun) a little fuzzy (Moss, 2014). On the other hand, as a society, we are all aware of the social and economic downsides of alcohol abuse, including its cost to the National Health Services (NHS), and its link with violence and vandalism (Plant & Plant, 2006).

Yet, while we may be personally aware of such drinking dichotomies, as a society we are still somewhat less informed as to how alcohol use, and our perceptions about it, are influenced by wider economic, social, cultural and spatial factors and contexts (Jayne, Valentine & Holloway, 2011). Part of this may have to do with the fact that popular media representations have tended to focus primarily on issues of binge drinking, violence, vandalism and riotous stag parties (see Thurnell-Read 2011 for a discussion of the latter). But it may also have to do with the fact that some academic research on alcohol tends to reproduce some of these negative aspects, with dramatic titles such as *Binge Britain* (Plant & Plant, 2006). In contrast, 'nightlife studies', it might be argued, have always focussed on wider social context factors such as changing youth transition and shifting urban contexts, in an attempt to understand not only drinking behaviours but also drug use and wider cultural trends (Bhardwa, 2014; Hollands, 2015). For example, my own joint research has located the changing economy of the pub and club infrastructure (Hollands & Chatterton, 2003) within wider urban changes towards corporatisation, entrepreneurialism, branding and theming (Gottdiener, 2001; Harvey, 1989), as well as shifting youth transitions (Hollands, 1997). Similarly, the regulation of drinking concerns not just the role of policing and containment (Hadfield, 2006) but also promoting nightlife through urban regeneration strategies (Chatterton & Hollands, 2003; Hobbs, Winlow, Lister, Hadfield & Hall, 2000). Finally, meanings and representations of alcohol consumption are always connected to wider class, gender, sexuality, race and age (youth) identities and codes (Chatterton & Hollands, 2003; Hollands, 2002), and are never neutral in character.

The main aim of this chapter is to reflect on my own involvement in researching nightlife over a 20-odd year period and consider its contribution to our understanding of drinking contexts. In the first part of the chapter I trace the origins of one of the first academic projects to look at the social meaning of going out, my book *Friday Night, Saturday Night* (Hollands, 1995), to a changing interest in a more political economy of nightlife provision in the evolving city (Chatterton & Hollands, 2001). I then turn to an examination of a body of joint work on the concept of 'urban nightscapes' (Chatterton & Hollands, 2002; Chatterton & Hollands, 2003), first looking at our arguments, and then assessing some of the pertinent ones that relate to contemporary relevant issues in the field. The point of the exercise is, I hope, not some kind of self-indulgence, but rather an assessment of whether some of the main arguments about nightlife and drinking culture have held up, as well as signalling future promising areas of research.

Beginnings: from *Friday Night, Saturday Night* to *Changing Our Toon*

Discussing one's academic reflections on studying nightlife and drinking over a 20-odd year period is replete with issues and dilemmas of its own. First, I should state that I am not an alcohol historian; even I though recognise the important role drinking has had in many past civilisations. Despite alcohol having a long and fascinating history (see Brownlee, 2002 for a popular and readable treatment), my interest concerns the more immediate transition from traditional pubs of the industrial period to contemporary nightlife in the developing post-industrial city (Hollands, 1995). Second, I confess that I do not really consider myself an 'alcohol researcher'. Rather I came to this topic not so much through a concern with drinking per se, but through my research on youth transitions, and a developing interest in urban processes and changing cities. Third, it is always problematic reflecting on one's own work, even if you do so critically. The issue of vested interest can always be invoked, even if the purpose is to emphasise weaknesses as well as strengths, or to examine what can be learnt from someone else's research experiences. Finally, as my chapter title suggests, such a review is never just an academic exercise but also involves personal reflections in the sense that as sociologists we all choose to study certain things in particular ways – the decision is never, to invoke Weber (1949), a completely 'value free' one.

Rather, what we research and how we study it is, to cite another classical sociologist C. Wright Mills (1959), more a product of our own history, biography and social structure (sociological imagination) than we might first imagine. For example, alcohol use was pervasive in the 1970s rural Canada I grew up in, as both a rite of passage into adulthood as well as a connection to teenage drinking rituals and sporting cultures. Underage drinking, excessive consumption, and drinking and driving were extremely common and accepted practices then. Introduction to alcohol at a young age, usually by a relative, was a marker of adulthood, while teenage drinking games and consuming alcohol in relation to sporting events was part of everyday culture. University drinking culture was also infused with both sociability and fun aspects, as well as excesses (see Miller, Melnick, Farrell, Sabo & Barnes, 2006), with the added bonus of introducing me to 'English'-style pubs which had started to spring up in some Canadian cities at that time (leading to a lifelong fascination with them, I might add). Experiencing some of the positive social and communal functions of alcohol was perhaps reflected somewhat in the rather celebratory tone of my first book on nightlife, *Friday Night, Saturday Night* (Hollands, 1995), which I dedicated to the role two of my uncles had played in stimulating my interest in studying drinking. Yet these same experiences also made me question some of the negative behaviours associated with alcohol use, later arguing against excessive mono-drinking cultures in cities in favour of more alternative, creative and diverse provision (Chatterton & Hollands, 2001).

When I moved from rural Canada to the urban UK in the 1980s, to do a PhD at the Centre for Contemporary Cultural Studies (CCCS), University of Birmingham, my main research interest focussed on the issues of youth unemployment, training schemes and labour market transitions. While this may seem some way away from the study of nightlife, three aspects of this experience are relevant here. First, while my thesis focussed on transitions particularly, it also stimulated my interest in the experience of youth generally. Second, the CCCS's concerns with youth cultural analyses and subcultures (Hall & Jefferson, 1976; Willis, 1977), were particularly influential. In my published doctoral thesis (Hollands, 1990) I sought to bring together the study of transitions and cultures, with the book including a chapter on youth, leisure and public space. And third, my initial concern with youth transitions resurfaced in my later work looking at how they helped to structure consumption experiences in the night-time economy, including issues of class and social exclusion (Hollands, 2002).

The origins of my research into the field of nightlife were a product of both circumstance and place. First, I had moved from Birmingham to lecture at Newcastle upon Tyne, a city famous/infamous for its boisterous nightlife. Second, my lectureship required me to teach both a specialism (I chose youth studies), as well as cover a more general module on urban sociology. The expectation, from a red brick university, was that all staff should be seeking research funding, and I logically thought of bringing together my two teaching areas into a project. I was also influenced by some interesting work conducted by Les Gofton (who was also at Newcastle University then, but in agriculture), on the decline of traditional pubs (Gofton, 1983), and the rise of new drinking cultures in the city (Gofton, 1990). As a sociologist, living in Newcastle in the early '90s, I was intrigued by the constant stream of negative press coverage of nightlife in the city, particularly the area called the Bigg Market (also see Nicholls, this volume). The intended research project pulled together my interest in youth transitions and cultures by focussing in on urban nightlife. The project, titled 'Youth Cultures and the Use of Urban Space', was duly submitted to and awarded funding by the Economic and Social Research Council (ESRC) to begin in the summer of 1993. It was, I believe, the first funded research study of young people's actual experience of nightlife in the UK.

Ironically, in light of what was to transpire later as 'the drinking study', the main body of the research proposal only used terms related to alcohol use a handful of times, while the Bigg Market area of Newcastle was mentioned only once in passing. In essence, the research project was actually led by my interest in 'interrupted' youth transitions and its relationship with understanding contemporary youth cultural identities – nightlife just happened to be a convenient focus. Methodologically, the research proposed utilising semi-structured interviews with revellers, combined with participant-observation methods while accompanying particular groups of young adults on their nights out, and it was this latter aspect that created most of the 'public furore' that followed. When the university published the title of the award on a public circular, I soon received a phone call from a local journalist and agreed that, despite the fact the project had not yet started, I would discuss what type of research I planned to undertake (much of what follows here is chronicled in Hollands, 2000). Perhaps naively, I agreed to pose for a photograph in a local pub, glass in hand (mineral water no less!). The story – 'A Bigg Night Out' – was published in one of the local papers, the *Journal*, and despite a disproportionate focus on the Bigg Market and drinking, it was a reasonably accurate portrayal.

I was, I have to admit, completely unprepared for what was to follow. While researching nightlife or drinking habits is quite common today, then, it clearly created a bit of a media storm. The first story was quickly followed by another local story, which was not so favourable ('A Bigg Mistake'); the second story focussed on the idea that studying nightlife was a waste of public money. It was quickly followed by a rash of stories from most of the national press (many of them headline news), as well as international stories, including coverage on the front page of the *Egyptian Gazette*! Humorous headlines like 'Boozy Bob going on a £16,000 pub crawl' *(Daily Star)*, were inter-dispersed with negative reactions about nightlife being an unworthy topic to study. Particular emphasis was placed on the fact that we planned to use participant-observation methods, including accompanying people on nights out – apparently at taxpayer expense ('£16,000 Nights Are On Us!' *(Daily Mirror)*.[1] I conducted a number of local and international TV and radio interviews subsequently to defend the research objectives, even being asked to go on an at the time popular Channel 4 youth-orientated programme, *The Word*, which I declined. While the study of alcohol today is much more mainstream, researchers in this field may continue to find that their work is trivialised or not seen as legitimate by either the media or even by their colleagues. It also raises the important lessons of having a well-structured press release and exercising caution when speaking to journalists about your research.

I was determined to address many of the pre-emptive criticisms of the research by giving young adults themselves a primary voice in articulating their experience and concerns around nightlife, and the study was based on 60 in-depth interviews with a cohort who had collectively made approximately 22,000 visits to the city centre on nights out. Unfortunately, the press (and publishers), were far less interested in publicising the research when it was finished, including its numerous findings which called into question many of the so-called common-sense assumptions surrounding various aspects of nightlife. My main sociological argument was that nightlife patterns in the city were clearly affected by underlying economic and social change in the region, including changing class and shifts in gender roles and relations. Furthermore, blocked transitions to adulthood meant that going out had changed from an adolescent 'rite of passage' to a more 'permanent post-adolescent socialising ritual', and these consumption-based identities were becoming core local/community identities (Hollands, 1995; 1997; also see Smith, this volume).

Publishing the research myself through Newcastle University, *Friday Night, Saturday Night* (Hollands, 1995) went on to become a bit of a cult classic, being cited in 125 articles or books, according to Google Scholar.[2] Economic change in the region had meant that only 40% of our interviewees were in full-time work, and only 13% of this age cohort was married, as opposed to 42% 30 years previously. The average age of our sample was mid-20s, suggesting that nightlife was not just a teenage phase but was becoming a core part of local Geordie identity. As such, the social meaning of going out, according to this age group, was that they were twice as likely to go out to 'socialise with friends' than to 'get drunk', and more said they went out for 'music and dancing' than 'meeting the opposite sex'. Figures on the incidence of excessive drinking, sexual conquests and witnessing and experiencing physical violence where lower than anticipated, with sexual harassment, racism and classism more prevalent. The research also discovered that night-time revellers wanted greater flexibility of opening times and greater diversity of provision, prefiguring the issue of changed licensing hours and the more current debate about the need for alternative types of venues (see Hollands, Berthet, Nada and Bjertnes, forthcoming).

However, there were some definite limits to the study, not least concerning available resources. Despite the media focus on the money side of the project, £16,000 only paid for a one-year study, with the bulk of the money spent to pay for a half-time research assistant. The research was also conducted in a single city, Newcastle, so one question raised was how typical was its nightlife? Finally, the predominate focus, despite a recognition of wider economic and social change, was on consumers, giving priority to the social meaning of nightlife consumption. Despite these shortcomings, I had no plans for either a follow-up or extension to the study, until I received a letter from Paul Chatterton, a recently graduated doctoral student from Bristol, who informed me he was moving to take a job at Newcastle, and that we should think about working together. We applied to the ESRC again, this time for a £123,000 three-city (Newcastle, Leeds and Bristol) study of nightlife production, regulation and consumption, which we were awarded in 2000.

The project signalled a shift in emphases in a number of fundamental ways, particularly in the direction of what might be called a political economy of nightlife. First, it had become increasingly clear that while consumption experiences were still crucially important, nightlife in terms of its production, organisation and regulation was changing, and changing fast. In other words, it had become evident that UK cities in particular, rather than following a European path, were becoming increasingly corporatised, themed and branded, like many American cities (Hannigan, 1998; Gottdiener, 2001), and this included changes in nightlife ownership patterns as well as shifts in urban regeneration strategies (Hobbs et al., 2000). At the same time, opposition began to spring up in response to some of these trends, and cities also began to see alternative urban resistances to issues around homogeneity, social exclusion and gentrification (similar debates emerge in Bonte, this volume).

In the Newcastle follow-up study, published as *Changing Our Toon* (Chatterton & Hollands, 2001), while we continued to focus on young people's nightlife identities and experiences, we also sought to locate them within a rapidly changing economic and political landscape. Rather than being ashamed of its nightlife as it had been historically, Newcastle had begun to actively market itself through the 'party city' idea. Two examples drawn from this period mark this transition. In the Newcastle-Gateshead Buzzin' capital of culture campaign, we saw the city beginning to market itself through leisure and consumption: 'But now Newcastle Gateshead is buzzin' with a new cosmopolitan, café bar society . . . set to make it one of the most attractive leisure destinations in Europe'. Similarly, Northumbria University also began to see some mileage in utilising Newcastle's reputation for nightlife as a recruitment strategy with this advert: '. . . easy to get to, only 3 hours from London, renowned for its nightlife and low cost of living – ONE OF THE UK'S MOST EXCITING STUDENT CITIES' (Chatterton & Hollands, 2001). While Newcastle has more recently sought to shift its identity away from the mono-cultural notion of the party city towards arts and culture, it continues to trade on its nightlife to aid student recruitment. Additionally, it has continued to develop more gentrified and touristy types of themed and branded premises (Proctor, 2014). In the next section, I sketch out some of the more general arguments we put forth in our three-city study and assess the degree to which its arguments still hold some purchase.

Revisiting *Urban Nightscapes*

The book *Urban Nightscapes: Youth Cultures, Pleasure Spaces and Corporate Power* (Chatterton & Hollands, 2003) was the product of a £123,000 ESRC three-city, nightlife study, which occurred between 2000 and 2002. While following up the changing Newcastle case, we also strategically decided to study a wealthier although somewhat more alternative southern city, Bristol, along with a more prosperous northern city known for the development of its financial service economy, Leeds (known as the 'London of the North', see Chatterton & Hollands, 2004). We also conducted limited research in some other UK cities (Edinburgh, Manchester and Liverpool) and comparative research on nightlife in Barcelona and in a few North American (Canadian) cities.

In addition to studying nightlife in three contrasting cities, we decided to interview nightlife producers (owners and managers of premises), regulators (e.g., police, bouncers and relevant city council officials) and a wide range of different nightlife consumers, ranging from white-collar professionals, students, working-class youth and gay and lesbian revellers, as well as producers and consumers of alternative nightlife spaces. In addition, like the earlier work, interviews were supplemented with participant-observation methods accompanying different types of revellers on nights out. Ironically, there was no media reaction to the research this time, despite its significantly higher price tag! Part of this was due to the changing context of cities themselves, where there was a noticeable readiness to market themselves through culture and entertainment, including the importance of having a lively after-dark economy. Indeed, we were now being approached by a number of UK city authorities keen for us to study nightlife in their city! The success of cities such as Barcelona, following the holding of the 1992 Olympic games, Berlin and Amsterdam as places with alternative nightlife, and even developing post-socialist cities like Prague and Budapest, were all clearly benefiting from having a lively nightlife to boost their status as growing tourist destinations.

The general concern of *Urban Nightscapes* (2003, p. xi) is summed up as ' . . . an outlook which combines the study of political-economic forces, and in particular a concern about the increasing power of corporate and global capital in our daily lives, with critical ethnographies sensitive to the nuances of locality, agency and political resistance'. Urban nightlife, we argued, is increasingly becoming 'MacDonaldised', with big brands taking over our cities, leaving consumers with an increasingly standardised experience and a lack of alternative, creative provision. While some groups of young urban dwellers have actively begun to resist this, other sections have been more accommodating of these trends. In contradistinction to more agency-oriented notions of youth culture as a 'pick and mix' affair, we argued (paraphrasing Marx): 'Young people make their own nightlife, but not under conditions of their own choosing' (Chatterton & Hollands, 2003, 8).

We suggested that nightlife is best understood through three dimensions (i.e., production, regulation and consumption) which help to produce three different nightlife spaces (i.e., mainstream, residual and alternative). On the production side we were interested in changing patterns of pub and club ownership, particularly the tendency towards corporatisation, and the development of branding (Klein, 2000) and theming, in the creation of entertainment landscapes – what we referred to as *urban nightscapes*.[3] Similarly, with regard to regulation, we began to see a pattern of development in many cities of 'urban entrepreneurialism' (Harvey, 1989), with many places using nightlife as an urban regeneration strategy. Both of these factors have had a significant effect on nightlife consumption identities and inequalities, including class, gender and racial elements. Finally, we were interested in the formation of spatial divisions in the night-time city, with the decline of traditional (residual) pubs, the growth of the commercial mainstream and gentrified premises, as well as examples of alternative resistance in the city (see Riches, this volume, for analysis of such an alternative drinking space).

For example, our ownership survey of all city centre pubs in our three UK locations showed an overwhelming dominance of corporate providers, with approximately two thirds of all premises falling into this category. These internationally financed companies were crowding out both regional and independent owners through aggressive marketing, theming and branding (Hollands & Chatterton, 2003). This shift in ownership pattern has also had a clear influence on the style and types of premises available in cities. While traditional pubs may still have made up approximately one third of city centre provision in Leeds, for example, a growing number of themed, style and cafe bars made up 51%, while alternative pubs were only 4% of the total (Chatterton & Hollands, 2003, p. 43). While there were slight variations in our studies of the other two cities, all three studies suggested that nightlife in many UK city centres was becoming increasingly themed and homogenised, as well as gentrified and stylised, with corporate chains squeezing traditional and alternative provision to the margins of the city. This trend has been aided by city councils eager to accept and work with big chains, and to cater to the tourist trade and more upmarket consumers, rather than meet needs of the local population or pursue more 'social inclusionary' measures in terms of city centre use.

This dual process of homogeneity and gentrification in commercial mainstream nightlife highlights some further contradictions and issues. One contradictory effect here is the creation of a divided and segmented nightlife infrastructure, with the formation of an alcohol-fuelled, hedonistic and heavily regulated 'mass market' for ordinary revellers (often referred to as 'townies'), and more up-market provision for young gentrifiers (see Hollands, 2002 for a more detailed discussion; also see Nicholls, this volume). Yet, this gentrifying influence has also curiously resulted in pressure to extend up-market provision and social status to aspirational sections of the middle and working-class – what I would refer to as the 'Geordie Shore effect'.[4] What I mean here is the extension of 'celebrity culture', with all of its 'excesses', including what Marjana and Measham (2008) refer to as 'extreme drinking', to ordinary revellers' expectations of what makes a good night out. This contradictory process, however, overshadows the fact that all of these forms of nightlife consumption are based on fairly excessive drinking cultures, and it further signals that those left out of this newly glamorised landscape are further scapegoated as 'chavs' and 'scratters' (Nayak, 2006; Chatterton & Hollands, 2003, p. 191).

As *Urban Nightscapes* was researched some 15 years ago, two questions about revisiting the work arise. First, what nightlife patterns we researched are still persistent, and second, what has changed? With regard to the question of increased corporatisation, urban nightlife certainly appears no less concentrated than it did in 2003. For example, with regard to Newcastle, approximately five companies control the vast majority of popular clubs and pubs in the city (Bentley, 2012). Unfortunately, academic work on questions of nightlife ownership has been rather neglected, and I would suggest that more updated work on this research topic needs to conducted in both the UK and abroad. On the other hand, while the trend towards the further conglomeration of the beer industry has indeed happened with some concentration of ownership at the top, one of the phenomena that we did not predict was the growth of independent beer production, especially Real Ale and craft beer markets. The impact this market might have on producing new consumer drinking behaviours and identities is significant (see Thurnell-Read, 2014 and this volume).

Regarding gentrification, a plethora of general studies reveals that it has become a dominant trend in most cities around the world (see Atkinson and Bridge, 2004, for a variety of international examples). With regard to nightlife, there are two very different instances one could draw on to suggest that the phenomenon of going out has been a fundamental aspect of this process. First, returning to Newcastle, a recent article in the local paper is instructive here on two counts – one for suggesting that gentrification in nightlife has clearly occurred, and two, for revealing that this circumstance has been viewed as a purely positive development (Proctor, 2014). To quote from the article, a spokesperson from NE1 Ltd, the business improvement district company for Newcastle city centre, said: 'Now we have a clear movement towards mid to upmarket venues. It is absolutely fantastic for the city' (Proctor, 2014). The second example comes from a very different 'world city' – New York. Here, Laame Hae (2011) highlights some of the contradictions of gentrification as a 'nightlife fix', including issues of urban exclusion and social polarisation, and even conflict between gentrified residents and businesses. The rise of style, cocktail and even champagne bars is part of this trend, with many cities marketing themselves to tourists through reference to these types of upmarket venues.

Differences between cities, however, raises questions whether our *Urban Nightscapes* argument is overly UK-centric, and even more specifically, 'core' city-centric. Clearly there are varied national contexts, laws, nightlife ownership patterns and level of corporate involvement in different countries and cities. Yet, while ownership structures and patterns in other countries are varied, theming and branding clearly exists in the North American context (e.g., chains such as the *Hard Rock Cafe* and *Planet Hollywood*) and in Europe through the example of the club chain *Pacha* (see Chatterton & Hollands, 2003). Additionally, despite these variations, our framework has been discussed or used as a model for understanding provision in a wide range of contexts, ranging from smaller UK cities (see Haydock's 2009 study of Bournemouth), to different European cities such as Geneva (Berthet & Nada, 2010). Additionally, we recognise that drinking cultures may be specifically related more to particular countries and their alcohol policies (Measham & Brain, 2005), for example, the well-worn comparison of

Mediterranean versus UK patterns of drinking (see Plant & Plant, 2006). However, what might be once considered specific to Newcastle nightlife has clearly existed or has sprung up in many other parts of the UK, and been imported via stag parties to cities such as Prague, Tallinn and Krakow (Thurnell-Read, 2011), and international dance spots such as Malaga and Ibiza (Bhardwa, 2014). In other words, despite national differences, the extreme youth drinking culture has clearly gone global (Marjana & Measham, 2008).

The deeper shift first identified in *Friday Night, Saturday Night* (1995) towards the growing significance of post-adolescent consumption-based identities has continued apace and is clearly evident in some recent work on nightlife which demonstrates the ways in which prolonged involvement in nightlife activity and nightlife identity are affecting more traditional forms of identity created through work and adulthood (Winlow & Hall, 2009; Lloyd, 2012; Smith, 2014). For example, Lloyd's (2012) recent study of work and leisure identities of call-centre workers appears to show that such monotonous post-industrial work is seen by young people in terms of a 'comfortable inertia' or 'extended present' and that more of their everyday identity is now gained through consumption and going out. In addition, Oliver Smith's excellent work in his book *Contemporary Adulthood and the Night-Time Economy* (Smith, 2014; also this volume), concisely demonstrates the impact extended leisure lives and identities amongst post-adolescent young adults are having on their friendships, relationships and household and employment transitions.

Finally, the tendency for alternative nightlife spaces to be incorporated and squeezed out of city centres, as corporate mainstream and gentrified premises move in, has, we would argue, largely been borne out. While *Urban Nightscapes* looked primarily at the resistant potential of squatting and rave culture, as examples of alternative nightlife culture, both of these types have come under social pressure, not to mention legal attack. With regard to squatting, many countries and cities have enacted anti-squatting legislation, effectively making the practice illegal, or applied political and economic pressure on squats to shut down or become incorporated. Across Europe in the past decade, we have seen the closure of well-known and long-standing squats in cities such as Berlin (Art House Tacheles), Prague (Villa Malada), Barcelona (Kasa de la Muntanya), Geneva (Rhino) and Amsterdam (Vrankrijk). At the same time, we have also seen the criminalisation of rave and acid houses, particularly the 'free party' movement side, through the Criminal Justice Act in the UK, as well as rave's general incorporation into a fragmented, commercial mainstream dance culture, in most cities around the world (Chatterton & Hollands, 2003, pp. 217–222).

Critiques of our typology of alternative nightlife spaces were that it was either a bit of an ideal type and too rigid a concept, or that it was too fuzzy, defying any precise definition. While we recognise the contradiction here – determinism versus the idea that 'what is alternative today can become mainstream tomorrow', through 'cool hunting' (Klein, 2000) – we always saw the alternative as something to be struggled over. As such, despite the fact that alternative nightlife spaces in many cities has appeared to have declined or been incorporated into the mainstream, newer and different forms of resistance have continued to survive. For example, we have seen some vibrant urban cultural movements in the past few years springing up to resist corporate branding and gentrified development in cities such as Hamburg, through the Not in Our Name anti-creative city manifesto, while groups in Berlin have tried to maintain some of its organic alternative nightlife spaces by conducting a sustained campaign against the corporatisation of a cultural quarter project along the river called Media Spree (see Novy and Colomb, 2013 for a discussion of both cases). Finally, in conjunction with a number of young activist academics, I am currently researching the significance of a 2010 'nightlife strike' in Geneva, which was in partial protest against a current lack of alternative and affordable nightlife spaces, in a city that was once known as the squatting capital of Europe (Hollands et al., forthcoming). Further work on the resistant potential of alternative nightlife activities and spaces is an important contemporary urban issue, and should become more of a priority research area in this field of study.

Conclusion

Making a series of concluding comments is always dichotomous as they signal both the end of a discussion as well as new beginnings. In terms of looking back on one's research over a period of time, it is easy to think 'was it really that long ago?', and 'what has really changed?', while at the same time recognising that it is clear that the studies of nightlife and alcohol have developed apace in the past 20 years, as this edited volume itself testifies. Of course, there is always the tendency to explore what predictions were right and perhaps play down others that were not so accurate. Rather, I would like to finish by making three general points which emanate from my experience researching in the field, as core ideas that all nightlife researchers should at least keep in mind when conducting their own work.

My first point concerns the need for work on nightlife and alcohol use to continue to challenge common sense, simplistic and overtly negative ideas about this important social and cultural phenomenon. One of the main contributions of *Friday Night, Saturday Night* (Hollands, 1995) was to argue that that nightlife reflected wider economic, social and cultural issues and trends such as a changing post-industrial economy, prolonged youth transitions and the development of new consumption-based forms of local identity, and was not just about drinking, sex and violence. Such an approach also calls into question simplistic and mono-causal policy solutions to some of the very real problems urban areas dependent on mono-cultures of drinking might have. Restrictive and punitive alcohol policies are often simplistic and ill thought out, and fail to provide longer-term sustainable changes in behaviour, which often have deeper and more complex social origins.

Second, with the proliferation of nightlife and alcohol studies in the current period, it is important that researchers continue to develop and utilise broader theoretical frameworks for locating their often specific place-based empirical work, so they can continue to talk to one another and create a rich forum for debate. This was the point in *Urban Nightscapes* (Chatterton & Hollands, 2003) when we attempted to map out the field in terms of production, regulation and consumption, and develop a typology of mainstream, residual and alternative nightlife spaces. We also sought to think through the relationship between economic forces, political regulation and identities of consumption (also see Ross-Houle, Atkinson and Sumnall, this volume, and Thurnell-Read, this volume). This is by no means a call for theoretical orthodoxy in the field, though I would argue that a political economy of nightlife remains crucial for our understanding of it. Rather we need the development of a range of theoretical positions and debates that new and young researchers can locate their own research questions against. There can be a tendency within academic work today (particularly PhDs) to narrow down the field of enquiry so much theoretically and empirically, that the research seems unable to speak to a wider field. The point about providing an overarching, and somewhat ideal type theoretical framework, is not to 'be right about everything', but to help others to develop, extend and challenge the framework, thereby creating a vibrant and ever-changing subfield of study.

Third, and finally, I would like to make a plea that researchers of nightlife and alcohol, whatever specific topic they are studying, need to remain aware of the existence and importance of more creative and resistant night-time activities. Otherwise, we run the risk of reproducing some of the negative nightlife stereotypes and researching only 'social problem'-type issues. Our own work on alternative nightlife (Chatterton & Hollands, 2003, Chapter 9) demonstrated how it could create new and more egalitarian forms of creativity and sociability, while my recent work has shifted to show how disenchantment with a lack of diversity in cities could act as a political focus for urban cultural movements such as 'night strikes' (Hollands et al., forthcoming). In this sense, alcohol might finally take its rightful place in the background, as a positive social lubricant for stimulating community, sociability and creativity in the urban night-time economy, rather than just being a negative focus of societal attention.

Acknowledgements

First, a huge thanks to Thomas Thurnell-Read for his patience and editorial guidance/suggestions. Additionally, I would like to acknowledge the 'collective' nature of much of my thinking and research on nightlife by thanking Paul Chatterton especially (an inspiring colleague and co-writer), and numerous other research assistants and writing collaborators over the years. Also thanks to all the revellers we have interviewed over the years, without which there would be no such thing as nightlife studies.

Notes

1 I should mention here that our research budget for accompanying our participants on nights out was £150 to cover entry fee to clubs, representing less than 1% of the total grant.

2 The study can still be accessed free on the internet, minus some hand-drawn figures, as: http://research.ncl.ac.uk/youthnightlife/HOLLANDS.PDF)
3 Note that our concept of urban nightscapes has been included in a book of the 50 most important urban studies concepts (see Gottdiener and Budd, 2005).
4 'Geordie Shore' is a TV programme set in Newcastle that follows a group of supposedly typical Geordies on nights out in the city and abroad, which has resulted in (limited) celebrity status for some of those involved.

References

Atkinson, R. and Bridge, G. (Eds.) 2004. *Gentrification in a global context: The new urban colonialism*. Oxon: Routledge.
Bentley, E. 2012. "Who owns Newcastle: Mapping the owners of the toon's bars and clubs." *The Courier*, April 23. http://thecourieronline.co.uk/who-owns-newcastle/
Berthet, M. and Nada, E. 2010. *Voyage au bout de la nuit*. Ville de Genève: Department de la Culture.
Bhardwa, B. 2014. "The construction of dance consumer identities: An exploration of drug use, digital technologies and control in three dance settings." PhD diss., Lancaster University.
Brownlee, N. 2002. *This is alcohol*. London: Sanctuary Publishing Limited.
Chatterton, P. 2002. Governing nightlife: Profit, fun and (dis)order in the contemporary city. *Entertainment Law*, 1(2): 23–49.
Chatterton, P. and Hollands, R. 2001. *Changing our toon: Young adults and urban change in Newcastle*. Newcastle: Newcastle University.
Chatteron, P. and Hollands, R. 2002. Theorising urban playscapes: Producing, regulating and consuming youthful nightlife city spaces. *Urban Studies*, 39(1): 95–116.
Chatterton, P. and Hollands, R. 2003. *Urban nightscapes: Youth cultures, pleasure spaces and corporate power*. London: Routledge.
Chatterton, P. and Hollands, R. 2004. The London of the north? Youth cultures, urban change and nightlife. In R. Unsworth and J. Stillwell (Eds.), *Twenty-first century Leeds: Geographies of a regional city* (pp. 265–290). Leeds, UK: University of Leeds.
Douglas, M. 2003. *Constructive drinking*. Oxon: Routledge.
Durkheim, E. 1965. *The elementary forms of the religious life*. Translated and edited by J. Swain. New York: The Free Press.
Gofton, L. 1983. Real ale and real men. *New Society*, 17: 271–3.
Gofton, L. 1990. On the town: Drink and the 'new lawlessness'. *Youth and Policy*, 2: 33–39.
Gottdiener, M. 2001. *The theming of America: American dreams, media fantasies and themed environments*. 2nd ed. Boulder, CO: Westview Press.
Gottdiener, M., and Budd, L. 2005. *Key concepts in urban studies*. London: Sage.
Hadfield, P. 2006. *Bar wars: Contesting the night in contemporary British cities*. Oxford: Oxford University Press.
Hae, L. 2011. Dilemmas of the nightlife fix: Post-industrialisation and the gentrification of nightlife in New York City. *Urban Studies*, 48(16): 3449–3465.
Hall, S. and Jefferson, T. (Eds.) 1976. *Resistance through rituals: Youth subcultures in post war Britain*. London: Hutchinson.
Hannigan, J. 1998. *Fantasy city: Pleasure and profit in the postmodern city*. London: Routledge.

Harvey, D. 1989. From managerialism to entrepreneurialism: The transformation in urban governance in late capitalism. *Geografiska annale*, 71B(1): 3–17.
Haydock, W. 2009. "Gender, class and 'binge' drinking: An ethnography of drinkers in Bournemouth's might-time economy." PhD diss., Bournemouth University.
Hobbs, D., Winlow, S., Lister, S., Hadfield, P. and Hall, S. 2000. Receiving shadows: Governance liminality and the night time economy. *British Journal of Sociology*, 51(4): 701–717.
Hollands, R. 1990. *The long transition: Class, culture and youth training*. London: Macmillan.
Hollands, R. 1995. *Friday night, Saturday night: Youth cultural identification in the post-industrial city*. Newcastle: Newcastle University.
Hollands, R. 1997. From shipyards to nightclubs: Restructuring young adults' employment, household and consumption identities in the north-east of England. *Berkeley Journal of Sociology*, 41: 41–66.
Hollands, R. 2000. 'Lager louts, tarts, and hooligans': The criminalization of young adults in a study of Newcastle night-life. In V. Jupp, P. Davies and P. Francis (Eds.), *Doing criminological research* (pp. 193–214). London: Sage.
Hollands, R. 2002. Divisions in the dark?: Youth cultures, transitions and segmented consumption spaces in the night-time economy. *Journal of Youth Studies*, 5(2): 153–173.
Hollands, R. 2015. Waiting for the weekend?: Nightlife studies and the convergence of youth transition and youth cultural analyses. In D. Woodman and A. Bennett (Eds.), *Youth cultures, belonging, transitions* (pp. 69–83). Basingstoke: Palgrave.
Hollands R. and Chatterton, P. 2003. Producing nightlife in the new urban entertainment economy: Corporatisation, branding and market segmentation. *International Journal of Urban and Regional Research*, 27(2): 361–385.
Hollands, R., Berthet, M. A., Nada, E. and Bjertnes, V. Forthcoming. Urban social movements and the night: Struggling for the 'right to the creative (party) city' in Geneva. In J. Hannigan and G. Richards (Eds.), *SAGE handbook of new urban studies*. London: Sage.
Jayne, M., Valentine, G. and Holloway, S. L. 2011. *Alcohol, drinking, drunkenness: (Dis) orderly spaces*. Aldershot: Ashgate.
Klein, N. 2000. *No logo: Taking aim at the brand bullies*. London: Flamingo.
Lloyd, A. 2012. Working to live, not living to work: Work, leisure and youth identity amongst call centre workers in north east England. *Current Sociology*, 60(5): 619–635.
Marjana, M. and Measham, F. (Eds.) 2008. *Swimming with crocodiles: The culture of extreme drinking*. London: Routledge.
Measham, F. and Brain, K. 2005. 'Binge' drinking: British alcohol policy and the new culture of intoxication. *Crime Media Culture*, 1(3): 262–283.
Miller, K., Melnick, M., Farrell, M., Sabo, D. and Barnes, G. 2006. Jocks, gender, binge drinking and adolescent violence. *Journal of Interpersonal Violence*, 21: 105–120.
Mills, CW. 1959. *The sociological imagination*. New York: Oxford University Press.
Moss, C. 2014. "Does alcohol release the creative spirit?" *The Telegraph*, January 24. http://www.telegraph.co.uk/men/thinking-man/10587189/Does-alcohol-release-the-creative-spirit.html
Nayak, A. 2006. Displaced masculinities: Chavs, youth and class in the post-industrial city. *Sociology*, 40(5): 813–831.
Novy, J. and Colomb, C. 2013. Struggling for the right to the (creative) city in Berlin and Hamburg: New urban social movements, new 'spaces of hope'? *International Journal of Urban and Regional Research*, 37(5): 1816–1838.

Plant, M. and Plant, M. 2006. *Binge Britain: Alcohol and the national response.* Oxford: Oxford University Press.

Proctor, K. 2014. "From party city to trendy toon: How Newcastle went upmarket." *Chronicle Live*, December 13. http://www.chroniclelive.co.uk/news/north-east-news/party-city-trendy-toon---8280468

Smith, O. 2014. *Contemporary adulthood and the night-time economy.* Basingstoke: Palgrave.

Thurnell-Read, T. 2014. Craft, tangibility and affect at work in the microbrewery. *Emotion, Space and Society*, 13: 46–54.

Thurnell-Read, T. 2011. 'Off the leash and out of control': masculinities and embodiment in Eastern European stag tourism. *Sociology*, 45(6): 977–991.

Weber, M. 1949. *The methodology of the social sciences.* New York: Free Press.

Willis, P. 1977. *Learning to labour: How working class kids get working class jobs.* Westmead: Saxon House.

Winlow, S. and Hall, S. 2009. Living for the weekend: Youth identities in northeast England. *Ethnography*, 10(1): 91–113.

Chapter 3

The symbolic value of alcohol

The importance of alcohol consumption, drinking practices and drinking spaces in classed and gendered identity construction

Kimberley Ross-Houle, Amanda Atkinson and Harry Sumnall

Introduction

In late modernity the nature of identity formation has been extended from a process related to work, employment and occupation to one based on consumption practices and lifestyle (Giddens, 1991; Miles, 2000). The social practice of purchasing different consumer products forms part of an individual's self-presentation, whereby they act out and perform desired identities in different social settings through the symbolic meanings and lifestyles held by consumer items (Goffman, 1959; Bourdieu, 1984; Giddens, 1991; Miles, 2000; McCreanor, Greenway, Barnes, Borell & Gregory, 2005; Stead, McDermott, MacKintosh & Adamson, 2011; Atkinson, Kirton & Sumnall, 2012). For example, reasons for choosing and rejecting certain types of alcoholic beverages or brands and engaging or disassociating oneself with certain drinking practices can often be related to concerns over personal and social identity, image, social belonging, distinction and social status (Measham, 2002; De Visser & Smith, 2007; Atkinson, Elliott, Bellis & Sumnall, 2011; Atkinson et al., 2012; De Visser & McDonnell, 2012; Thurnell-Read, 2013). This chapter discusses the role of alcohol-related spaces and alcohol as a consumer item with symbolic meaning and importance beyond its functional value to highlight the importance of alcohol culture and related practice in the creation and performance of identities. It considers how the consumption of particular alcoholic beverages, and access to and behaviour and relations within particular drinking spaces, provide opportunities for classed and gendered identity creation. Spaces in which alcohol-related identities can be created and performed can include physical drinking spaces such as bars, nightclubs and the home (e.g., in the context of 'pre-loading'), mediated spaces (i.e., popular media) and in recent years online spaces such as Social Network Sites (SNS) where content relating to alcohol consumption can be shared between peers, as well as by alcohol companies. In discussing such issues, the chapter draws on findings of empirical studies exploring the role and place of alcohol and drinking practices in the identity formation of people aged 11 to 21 and the role of traditional and new media (specifically SNS) in informing, reinforcing and reproducing such alcohol-related identities (Atkinson et al., 2011; Atkinson et al., 2012; Atkinson, Ross, Begley & Sumnall, 2015). It further draws on recent research (Ross, forthcoming) exploring women's use of urban space in recently regenerated consumer spaces such as drinking environments.

Alcohol and spatial experiences relating to gender and social class

Spaces which are associated with leisure practices such as the consumption of alcohol are highly gendered and classed and thus provide opportunities to create and perform gendered and classed identities through the symbolic value held within alcohol and drinking practices (Griffin, Szmigin, Bengry-Howell, Hackley & Mistral, 2012; Waitt, Jessop & Gorman-Murray, 2011; Thurnell-Read, 2013). Drinking practices are therefore spatialised, and as a result individuals may alter and adapt their drinking practices depending on the space/setting in which they are participating (see Wilkinson, this volume). This section focusses on how identities associated with alcohol are created within night-life settings, with a particular focus on gender, social class and spatial drinking practices. It also considers perceptions of 'ideal types' in terms of stereotypes surrounding alcohol consumption and drinking practices, the role of the media in reinforcing such ideals and how these influence identity.

Within settings relating to alcohol consumption, an individual's drinking behaviour is influenced by different social concepts such as gender and class. Goffman (1976) discussed the notion of 'ideal types' in terms of the media's representation of the roles and identities with which different social groups are expected to conform. These ideal types are often gendered, with women being subjected to further restrictions in terms of their behaviour in the public sphere (Grosz, 1994; McRobbie, 2004a; McRobbie, 2004b; Griffin, 2004). Similarly, Young (1990) considers why women have very different 'everyday' experiences to men and explores the concept of the 'lived body', arguing that from a very early age, girls are encouraged to restrict their bodies in terms of their behaviour to a far greater extent than boys are. Young (1990) suggests the embodiment of what is considered habitual behaviour occurs when individuals modify their own behaviour in light of highly gendered and classed social expectations. This relates to Bourdieu's (2010) notion of the bodily hexis, the way individuals understand their own social value and how this relates to other social and peer groups. This social construction of behaviour means that individuals often feel constrained by what behaviour and lifestyle choices are deemed appropriate for their identity in particular social settings. Such constraints can influence choices relating to alcohol consumption and related drinking practices, as well as the ways through which individuals and social groups choose to engage with spaces associated with these practices. For example, the gendering of alcohol consumption can lead to individuals adapting and recreating gender-specific drinking practices and stereotypes associated with alcohol consumption (also see Nicholls, this volume). Gender is thus a concept that is reinforced through engagement with practices that relate specifically to masculine or feminine identities, and this is reinforced through media representations of alcohol consumption as well as lived drinking practices (Atkinson et al., 2012). Therefore, the act of engaging in these practices not only reinforces these gendered (and classed) stereotypes but also enables individuals and peer groups to use stereotypes in the construction of their own identity.

Atkinson et al. (2011, 2012, 2015) explored how drinking practices provide one way in which gendered identities can be created within specific spaces and the role of the media in reflecting and reproducing gendered drinking practices and potentially problematic stereotypes. This body of research highlights how narratives related to alcohol, drinking and intoxication within popular media such as magazines and television programmes often present intoxication within the public sphere as less acceptable for women than men and the night-life environment as a context in which women are vulnerable and at risk. Such narratives are also reflected in young people's own discussions around drinking, with intoxicated women being judged and young women adapting their own drinking behaviours in response to discourses of risk and safety within night-life settings. Moreover, drinking spaces such as pubs are framed and perceived as male-dominated spaces, whilst night-life drinking environments such as bars and clubs highlight sexualised settings. Similarly, Skeggs (1997) found that space and place were main themes in women's narratives in relation to leisure spaces such as those in which alcohol consumption takes place. Her work discussed how social and cultural capital are gendered as well as classed, and that the intersections of class and gender often lead to further dissention for women who may struggle to access and negotiate certain spaces as a result of both their class and gender. The concepts of social and cultural capital refer to the work of Pierre Bourdieu (1984), who argued that, in addition to 'capital' as economic value, forms of social and symbolic capital can be applied to objects and practices (Bourdieu, 1984). For example, alcohol, consumption and related practice can act as forms of cultural, symbolic and social capital that distinguish along lines of age, class and gender in differing ways in differing contexts (Järvinen & Gundelach, 2007; Lunnay et al., 2011; Atkinson et al., 2015). With this in mind, Skeggs argues:

> Class becomes internalized as an intimate form of subjectivity, experienced as knowledge of always not being 'right'. Restrictions on access to the 'right' knowledge, the 'right' cultural capital, which can be traded means that there are limits to their passing as middle class. Whilst many anxieties over bodies, homes, children and clothes may be experienced by middle-class women too, it is the particular manifestation that they take that gives them the classed character. The anxieties of working-class women are always made through reference to something to which they do not have access, be it money, knowledge or space. They know that nearly everything they do will be recognised as classed.
>
> (Skeggs, 1997, p. 90)

In terms of drinking spaces, Skeggs' research highlighted how women perceived to be middle class often find it easier to negotiate the male-dominated drinking spaces such as pubs, compared with women perceived to be working-class and how public intoxication is often perceived as behaviour of working-class women. Furthermore, within public drinking spaces such women also feel pressured to maintain a certain level of physical appearance compared with those considered to be middle class. Similarly, Ross (forthcoming) explored women's experiences in urban space in a relativity deprived but recently regenerated city. Women discussed how, in exclusive bars and nightclubs, they felt pressure to maintain appropriate identities in order to access these spaces. This included maintaining a certain physical appearance, whilst for men access was dependent on their financial status. Women discussed that through the regeneration and privatisation process these spaces had become 'celebritised' as a result of their image of exclusivity and glamour. Such pressure was also prominent in research recently conducted by Atkinson et al. (2011, 2012, 2015) in the same geographical location, in which the concept of a 'night out' provided young women with an ideal opportunity to refine, create and perform glamorised self-presentation within drinking contexts which reflect those presented by celebrity-based media.

Similarly, the work of Griffin et al. (2012) on youth drinking cultures highlights how femininity has become a more complex issue now that women have more freedoms in the public sphere. This has led to what Griffin et al. describe as 'hypersexual femininity' as the traditional roles of women become challenged (Griffin et al., 2012, p. 185). The research highlighted how young women feel they have greater freedoms in the night-life environment to engage in behaviours, such as heavy drinking or pole dancing, that for previous generations would have been associated with negative stereotypes. Despite such feelings of liberation, participants still modified these behaviours with regards to what is considered appropriate for women within public spaces (see also Waitt et al., 2011 and Lunnay et al., 2011). For example, the perceived appropriateness of women's behaviour in public spaces was constructed in relation to the visibility of male peers, with pole dancing being viewed as more acceptable in the company of male partners. This demonstrates how the night-time environment, and women's behaviour within such space, has become sexualised and is often subject to the approval and control of men through their presence in accompanying women. Moreover, heavy drinking was considered to be more acceptable when drinking in large groups because this practice was perceived to be safe, highlighting how women adapt their behaviour and create their identities in relation to perceptions of vulnerability and safety in drinking settings (also see Riches, this volume). Similarly, Atkinson et al. (2015) found that young females are conscious of being perceived as sexually permissive when drinking alcohol in the night-time environment and monitor their own drinking in relation to potential risks such as drink spiking. Such social self-control and monitoring of behaviour in relation to sexuality and risk is derived from and influenced by the media's portrayal of women in public spaces and what has been described as a 'fascination with the fragile female form and her vulnerability to violation' (Ross, 2010, p. 95; Atkinson et al., 2012).

McRobbie (2004a) points to how class differences within gender are alluded to within the media, with programmes using middle-class values to help refine the behaviours and appearance of working-class women (McRobbie, 2004a, p. 100). Media representations which often reflect and favour the views of the (often male-dominated) middle class promote 'ideal types' in relation to female identity. Such media-reproduced ideals may explain the high level of judgement and criticism placed upon working-class women who participate in such practices of drinking and self-presentation. Gendered and classed drinking stereotypes are also reinforced through media depictions of intoxicated (usually working-class) women as 'un-feminine' or as vulnerable as an outcome of intoxication generally being attributed to masculinity (Lyons & Willott, 2008; Atkinson et al., 2012; De Visser & McDonnell, 2012). The media help reinforce what is regarded as socially acceptable alcohol consumption and drinking practices, with working-class women being subjected to further restrictions and negative stereotypes because of their gender and social class (e.g., see The *Daily Mail's* coverage of 'Ladies Day' at various racing events, Styles, 2014). Such research demonstrates a contradiction in an individual's feminine identity in relation to alcohol consumption and drinking practices, in that women may have more freedoms in terms of what behaviour they choose to engage in, yet there are still gendered restrictions placed upon them. Thus, women's engagement in drinking practices and what is considered to be appropriate behaviour within drinking settings is influenced by wider societal perceptions of appropriate action in relation to femininity and class, as well as the circumstances surrounding drinking practices such as the presence of males. This suggests that women have to negotiate more complex interactions with regards to alcohol consumption and drinking practices than men, who still have classed and gendered associations placed on their identities but do not have the same restrictions imposed on them.

That said, men also engage in a complex process of negotiating stereotypes associated with masculine identities which relate to social class and peer group identity in particular social settings (Thurnell-Read, 2013). For example, decisions around abstaining and consuming lower levels of alcohol are closely related to societal and peer group perceptions of what it means to be a man. De Visser and Smith (2007) researched differences in the alcohol consumption of men aged 18–21 and found much pressure placed upon them to conform to what were considered to be masculine drinking practices and behaviours, in particular with respect to the amount of alcohol consumed in public drinking spaces and social settings. Similarly, the research by De Visser and McDonnell (2012) with students and young people found that, whilst there was little difference in the drinking patterns of men and women, public intoxication and other extreme alcohol-related behaviour was considered to be masculine (and as such not participating in such behaviour 'feminine') and a way for men to achieve and perform ideal masculine identities within the night-time environment (Skeggs, 1997; Waitt et al., 2011). Despite such pressures, the research found that men could maintain a masculine identity if the aim of cutting down or abstaining from drinking alcohol was to enhance performance in other masculine activities such as sport and fitness. However, there is evidence to suggest a contraction to this notion as participation in sports can also lead to increased alcohol consumption in relation to collective drinking rituals and group bonding and identity formation (Wichstrom & Wichstrom, 2009). As with women, factors such as profession and class often determine definitions of masculine behaviour (De Visser & McDonnell, 2012). Perceiving a man to be from a middle-class profession and financially successful influences what is considered to be appropriate drinking practice, with less pressure being placed upon them to maintain a masculine image through drinking to a lesser extent than those perceived to be from working-class professions. This demonstrates how perceptions of social class influence what is regarded as appropriate drinking practices as it intersects with perceptions of masculinity. Thus, alcohol consumption and engagement with certain drinking practices provide context within which individuals can associate with and reinforce gendered and classed identities. Furthermore, the ways through which these gendered and classed associations intersect with one another mean that women are often under more complex pressures than men to engage with societal expectations of drinking practices.

The symbolic value of alcoholic beverages and brands

Stereotypical associations between class, gender, alcohol consumption and drinking practices also influence the types and brands of alcoholic beverages an individual chooses to consume in public and within peer group contexts (Wearing & Wearing, 2000; Forsyth, Galloway & Shewan, 2007; Gilbert, 2007). In turn, alcoholic beverages as consumer items are important in symbolically creating and performing classed and gendered identities in particular social contexts and settings (Atkinson et al., 2012; also see Thurnell-Read, this volume). Research conducted by Atkinson et al. (2011, 2012, 2015) highlighted strong associations among gender, class and alcoholic beverage choice, which were reproduced and reinforced through media representations and as a result carefully selected for consumption or avoided in an attempt to craft particular identities and distinguish the self from others along lines of age, class and gender depending on the social setting. For example, young people held strong views on what drinks were appropriate for men and women, with certain drinks being openly discussed as more masculine (e.g., beer and cider brands) or feminine (e.g., wine and cocktails were labelled as 'pretty' drinks suited to female consumers) than others. Such drinks were also associated with particular gendered settings and contexts such as football and 'the pub' for men and 'exclusive' bars for women. Thus, there were spatial associations attached to certain alcoholic drinks, with spaces such as pubs often being associated with males, and the consumption of beer (Atkinson et al., 2012), resulting in these drinks having less social value for females (Atkinson et al., 2015). As with Ross's (forthcoming) research, 'celebritisation' of leisure (Cashmore, 2014) and space along lines of gender and exclusivity, which is reproduced within popular forms of media (e.g., magazines), also created a desire among women to consume products and space (e.g., expensive drinks such as cocktails, exclusive bars) believed to be associated with certain prosperous lifestyles (Atkinson et al., 2011, 2012, 2015).

We can see here then how alcoholic beverages are categorised along lines of both gender and social class, with specific types of alcoholic drinks and brands being seen as symbolic of economic and cultural capital and associated with certain social groups. Furthermore, Atkinson et al. (2011, 2015) found that cheap alcoholic drinks (e.g., Frosty Jacks cider and supermarkets' own brand beverages) are often associated with stereotypes such as homelessness and drug use, and described using derogative language. Similarly, among young men and women, brands such as WKD and Lambrini were associated with the working-class and discussed using derogative labels such as 'chavs'. Although such drinks were cheap, affordable and enjoyed by young people in terms of taste, they avoided being seen drinking certain brands of alcohol, particularly in public, on the basis of class and gender associations and the stereotypes and identities such drinks symbolised. Among young women in particular, drinks such as wine, Champagne and cocktails were perceived as 'posh' and as symbolising high cultural and economic capital through connotations of expense, exclusivity and sophistication. Whilst consuming alcoholic drinks associated with the opposite sex and certain social classes was regarded as inappropriate in public settings, young people were less judgemental of such practice if drunk in private away from the peer gaze (Atkinson et al., 2015). Similarly, Thurnell-Read (2013) explored the relationship between contradicting identities and beverage choice and found that for men to adopt appropriate masculine identities they had to negotiate their choice of drink and behaviour. Factors such as age and social class were important in determining the creation of appropriate masculine identities through appropriate beverage choice. Beer and lager were beverages perceived as socially acceptable in the performance and acceptance of masculine identities. However, distinctions were made between different social economic classes, with middle-class men having more scope to consume drinks such as wine that have feminine connotations. This body of research demonstrates how alcoholic beverages are chosen for their symbolic meanings and associations in that they were seen as representing certain social groups and identities. Not only is the labelling of alcoholic drinks and brands along lines of class and gender reflected and reproduced in media representations (Atkinson et al., 2011, 2012) but also it is such classed and gendered identities and lifestyles that alcohol marketers aim to reflect in their branding and advertising (Brooks, 2010; Nicholls, 2012; McCreanor, Lyons, Griffin, Goodwin, Barnes & Hutton, 2012; Atkinson et al., 2015). Similarly, those who consume brands and certain drinks do so in a way that complement their own individual or peer group identities in ways that reflect what is regarded as appropriate beverage choice and drinking practices along lines of gender and class (Atkinson et al., 2012; Griffin et al., 2012; McCreanor et al., 2012).

Alcohol consumption, brands and related practices provide a means of creating and performing classed and gendered identities in real-life drinking settings. The use of alcohol within night life as a commoditised setting provides an opportunity for the creation and display of symbolic value which in turn forms gender and classed identities (also see Smith, this volume). There are clear distinctions between what alcoholic beverages are associated with particular social groups and this is reflected and reproduced through media representations, alcohol marketing and the everyday experiences of alcohol consumers. In recent years, the process through which alcohol as a cultural consumer resource that individuals use and re-appropriate in the representation of gendered and classed identities has extended to online spaces such as SNS.

Online space and the creation and display of alcohol-identities

We have shown that the spaces in which alcohol-related practices and identities are carefully crafted and performed are both physical and mediated, with such practice recently entering online digital environments (Brooks, 2010; Atkinson et al., 2011; Hastings, 2009; Nicholls, 2012; McCreanor et al., 2012; Moreno, Briner, Williams, Walker & Christakis, 2009; Institute of Policy Research, 2013). Within online spaces such as SNS, individuals participate in various activities in the construction of alcohol-related identities along the lines of gender, class and age. This includes engagement with alcohol marketing (Brooks, 2010; Freeman, Chapman & Rimmer, 2008; Mosher, 2012; Nicholls, 2012) and the creation of, and participation in, peer-created alcohol content (Griffin, Bengry-Howell, Hackley, Mistral & Szmigin, 2009; Atkinson et al., 2012; De Visser & McDonnell, 2012; Griffin et al., 2012). This section discusses examples of how these online spaces provide an extension of real-life drinking spaces and in turn reflect, reinforce and reproduce gendered and classed identities.

There are strong associations between an individual's exposure to alcohol advertising, attitudes towards alcohol and drinking practices, particularly among young people (Anderson, de Bruijin, Angus, Gordon & Hastings, 2009; Smith & Foxcroft, 2009; Babor et al., 2010; Gordon, Hastings & Moodie, 2010). The alcohol industry has traditionally used a variety of multi-platform channels and modes such as radio, television, sponsorship and billboards to advertise their products. In recent years, marketing strategies have entered online and digital space such as websites, mobile app devices and SNS (Mosher, 2012). Not only do SNS such as Twitter and Facebook reflect existing social processes in terms of how people relate to one another and share information, but also they have created new forms of social interaction because of their popularity and vast number of members, meaning that users (including marketers) can connect and share information with people on a global scale (Pempek, Yermolayeva & Calvert, 2009; Murthy, 2008). Freeman et al. (2008) suggest that in response to alcohol marketing now being subject to stricter regulations with regards to advertising on media such as television and radio, alcohol companies have turned to social media to promote their products (Brooks, 2010; Hastings, 2009; Nicholls, 2012). As well as providing a space for alcohol brands to have a page of their own, SNS afford opportunities for brands to buy advertising space to promote their products. Companies within the alcohol industry are increasingly engaging with SNS; for example, Diageo (the company owning the Smirnoff Vodka brand) has spent 21% of its advertising budget on digital forms such as SNS since 2010 (Mosher, 2012). Thus, new technologies such as SNS provide a new and innovative opportunity for alcohol marketing, with added features such as virtual relationships and interactivity, offering new ways of engaging potential customers (Nicholls, 2012). With this in mind, the rapid use of SNS by the alcohol industry raises concern from a public health perspective (McCreanor et al., 2012) because these spaces are harder to regulate, and the global scale in which they operate means that users are exposed to a variety of drinking cultures and practices, including those who may be under the age of 18 years.

SNS are also one means through which individuals can display a reciprocal relationship with alcohol marketing (Ridout, Campbell & Ellis, 2012; McCreanor et al., 2012; Moreno, Christakis, Egan, Brockman & Becker, 2012; Institute of Policy Research, 2013; Moreno, D'Angelo, Kacvinsky, Kerr, Zhang & Ellis, 2014). Users of SNS can interact directly with the marketing pages of the alcohol brands through 'liking' the page (Facebook) or 'following' the brand (Twitter), re-tweeting marketing messages, or joining a group dedicated to a brand. They provide an opportunity to associate the self with particular brands and lifestyles, in turn constructing, negotiating and signalling identity in relation to alcohol to within digital spaces in classed and gendered manners (Boyd & Ellison, 2007; Livingstone, 2008; Moreno et al., 2009, 2012, 2014; Ridout et al., 2012; McCreanor et al., 2012). Research by Atkinson et al. (2015) incorporating an analysis of online marketing for five alcohol brands popular in the UK highlighted the ways in which alcohol brands draw on, reflect and as such reproduce the classed-, gender- and age-related lifestyles and identities in their marketing. Various marketing strategies were used to make clear distinctions between the social groups and lifestyles their products cater for. Similar to Nicholls (2012), lager brands used highly gendered lifestyle associations such as football and male humour (sometimes described as 'banter') and vodka brands made references to cocktail recipes young participants interpreted as feminine (Atkinson et al., 2015). SNS users were regularly interacting with and co-creating brand content. This interaction differentiates new media marketing from traditional marketing, as users unintentionally help market alcohol brands as cultural and symbolic items of pleasure and enjoyment to the online audience (Atkinson et al., 2015; Nicholls, 2012). In particular, the research highlighted alcohol brands as a key component of young people's drinking cultures as symbolic resources that young people actively used and re-appropriate in the representation of self online (Holt, 2002; Miles, 2000; Stead et al., 2011). As in 'real life', young people displayed certain drinks online within a peer context and avoided revealing the consumption of particular brands (e.g., men avoided displaying wine and women avoided displaying drinks they associated with the 'chav' stereotype) as a result of gendered and classed connotations. Moreover, the marketing of events (where alcohol was served) in local night-life spaces, which is often highly gendered (BBC News, 2012; Hopwood, 2013), was highly valued by young people as informative sources used when organising drinking occasions. Thus, SNS marketing may contribute to the normalisation of drinking behaviours and related identities through the creation of 'intoxigenic digital spaces' in which young people learn about alcohol (Griffiths & Casswell, 2010, p. 525; see also Nicholls, 2012; McCreanor et al., 2012; Institute of Policy Research, 2013). The creative interactive marketing techniques on SNS may further produce a stronger influence on identity than traditional advertising (Montgomery & Chester, 2009).

Despite the pervasive role of alcohol marketing on SNS, it was peer-related SNS content that appeared to hold much value and significance in the creation of alcohol-related identity construction. SNS provide a means for individuals, particularly young people, to display their relationship with alcohol and drinking practices within a peer context (Moreno et al., 2012, 2014; McCreanor et al., 2012; Ridout et al., 2012; Pempek et al., 2009). Users of SNS can post their own alcohol-related content in the form of photographs and statuses, resulting in online space becoming an extension of the lived experiences that users have in relation to their 'real life' alcohol consumption and engagement with drinking practices (Moreno et al., 2009, 2012; Griffiths & Casswell, 2010; Morgan, Snelson & Elison-Bowers, 2010; Ridout et al., 2012; McCreanor et al., 2012; Tonks, 2012; Institute of Policy Research, 2013). Young people regard this practice as fun and pleasurable, and important for gaining social capital (Griffin et al., 2009; Hebden, 2011; McCreanor et al., 2012; Institute of Policy Research, 2013; Atkinson et al., 2015). In line with previous research (Mendelson & Papacharsi, 2010; Institute of Policy Research, 2013), Atkinson et al. (2015) found this practice to be gendered, with more women participating in such behaviour and males perceiving the sharing of alcohol-related content online as a feminine activity. Moreover, the practice was highly managed, with both men and women carefully selecting what was appropriate content to share. Men did participate in such online display, but usually in the company or under the instruction of women. Both carefully controlled what beverages are displayed on SNS because of gendered and classed connotations. However, like in real life, further control of behaviour display was performed by women, reflecting the gendered and classed restrictions placed on them in real life (Skeggs, 1997; Young, 1990). Through analysis of young people's Facebook profiles and interviews, women appeared to express more concern about how such online alcohol-related content was received by their peers and found such monitoring anxiety provoking. They often restricted content in which they appeared intoxicated because of unsatisfactory appearance and content that may be perceived as sexually revealing to prevent being labelled as sexually permissive. Despite such negative experiences, discussions around ideal 'flattering' photos highlighted the key role of drinking occasions as an opportunity for young women to perform a glamorous form of feminine identity which could be captured on camera and displayed to a peer audience on SNS. Furthermore, the majority of the photographs displayed were taken during home-based 'pre-loading' contexts, with female participants highly valuing this context as a time in which they bonded with friends and carefully crafted self-appearance which could be photographed and displayed online. Thus, SNS act as an extension of the space through which individuals performed and created specific types of gendered identities (Skeggs, 1997; Young, 1990; Waitt et al., 2011) through drinking and drinking occasions. We can see here how many of the gendered and classed experiences that relate to physical drinking spaces are also reflected through the display of alcohol consumption and drinking practices on SNS.

The research further demonstrates how online spaces both reflect and extend the physical spaces of the night-time economy as spaces within which identity can be crafted in terms of physical appearance and 'celebritisation' (McRobbie 2004b; Griffin et al., 2012; Atkinson et al., 2015). This relates to how McCreanor et al., (2012) emphasise the importance of a 'globalised culture of celebrity' (McCreanor et al., 2012, p. 112) in such self-expression, whereby young people are increasingly engaging in a process of 'celebritising the self' through consumption (McCreanor et al., 2012, p. 112; Cashmore, 2014). Therefore, in this neo-liberal context, the marketing of alcohol alongside the consumption of alcohol and alcohol-related behaviours both on- and off-line provide opportunity for individuals to carefully construct identities (also see Smith, this volume). The consumption of cultural items and practices, including alcohol and drinking, plays an important role in this creation and expression in that they are not valued merely for their function, but for their aesthetic and symbolic value (Bourdieu, 1984; Miles, 2000; McCreanor et al., 2012; Stead et al., 2011; Atkinson et al., 2012). Thus, alcohol can be seen as a socio-cultural product with meaning and importance beyond its functional value (i.e., intoxication or even refreshment). Through their choice of alcoholic beverages, drinking practices and engagement with drinking spaces, individuals are able to signal and symbolise specific tastes and identities, often in a highly gendered and classed manner (Skeggs, 1997; De Visser & Smith, 2007; Lyons & Willott, 2008; De Visser, Smith & McDonnell, 2009; Atkinson et al., 2011; Waitt et al., 2011; Atkinson et al., 2012; Thurnell-Read, 2012, 2013). The process through which symbolic value is acquired from alcohol consumption, marketing and branding in the formation of identities has become ever more complex as it has extended to online space such as SNS (Järvinen & Gundelach, 2007; Lunnay et al., 2011).

Conclusion

Alcohol is an inherently social practice with wider cultural and symbolic relevance. As discussed, the value associated with alcohol goes beyond its functional properties in that it holds much symbolic and aesthetic value. The chapter has highlighted how the use and display of consumer products such as alcohol and alcohol-related practice forms part of an individual's self-presentation and offers one way through which identities can be created and performed in different social settings through the symbolic meanings and lifestyles embedded in alcohol and drinking (Goffman, 1959; Bourdieu, 1984; Giddens, 1991; Miles, 2000; McCreanor et al., 2005; Stead et al., 2011; Atkinson et al., 2012). It purports that this social practice is highly gendered and classed in nature, with more restrictions and pressure being placed on women and those perceived to be working-class. It further highlights the role of media and marketing discourse in influencing, reinforcing and reproducing such gendered and classed alcohol-related identities. In addition to physical drinking spaces, the chapter has highlighted how online spaces have become an extended space where alcohol and associated drinking practices can be displayed and constructed.

The research presented has implications for the study of drinking cultures and policy related to young people's drinking specifically. Research has suggested that whilst the number of young people consuming alcohol has reduced slightly over the past few years, a high level of young people still partake in alcohol consumption, with those in the UK consuming higher amounts than the European average (Fuller, 2009; Hibell et al., 2009; Smith & Foxcroft, 2009; Hibell et al., 2012; Atkinson et al., 2012; NWPHO, 2013; Fuller & Hawkins, 2013). To fully understand such trends, it is important to consider the changing nature of alcohol consumption and drinking practices with regards to SNS marketing and the role that SNS have in drinking culture, and the wider role that alcohol has in the creation of gendered and classed identities. Alcohol representation (through brand marketing and sharing of user alcohol content) on SNS may not influence drinking practices directly, but may be a mediator through which alcohol is experienced, and it is the subsequent representation of these behaviours online that establishes norms and reinforces alcohol-related behaviour. This process is gendered and related to notions of class and associated with a wider set of culturally embedded understandings of what it is to be a man or a woman and how masculinity and femininity should be 'performed' and accomplished (West & Zimmerman, 1987; Butler, 1999; Atkinson et al., 2012). Although a small body of research has considered how the use of SNS can influence both identity formation and alcohol consumption, more research is needed to explore the significance of SNS within drinking cultures.

Research suggests that young people often have very little understanding about the long-term risks associated with alcohol consumption (De Visser & McDonnell, 2012). One possible way of informing young people of the potential negative effects could be through SNS-based health campaigns to use SNS. Within multi-component approaches, SNS health promotion can potentially offer a useful opportunity to engage young people with public health messages. In doing so, campaigns must appropriate online cultures and appeal to diverse groups in relation to age, class and gender. However, this may prove difficult in online spaces that are infiltrated with pro-alcohol content via marketing and peers (Atkinson et al., 2015; Atkinson et al., 2011; McCreanor et al., 2012; Nicholls, 2012).

Examining the spatialized significance of alcohol to gender (i.e., masculine/feminine) and classed identities both on and off-line is worthy of consideration due to the poor health outcomes often associated with behaviours that constitute particular identities, since drinking behaviour is often influenced by 'demographic, social and attitudinal variables' (De Visser & Smith, 2007, p. 596). In responding to policy concerns surrounding potentially problematic drinking practices and related behaviours, an understanding of the relationship between alcohol consumption and identity is essential given the influence this social process can have on individual and group drinking practices.

References

Anderson, P., de Bruijin, A., Angus, K., Gordon, R. and Hastings, G. 2009. Impact of alcohol advertising and media exposure on adolescent alcohol use: A systematic review of longitudinal studies. *Alcohol and Alcoholism*, 44(3): 229–243.

Atkinson, A. M., Elliott, G., Bellis, M. A. and Sumnall, H. R. 2011. *Young people, alcohol and the media*. York: Joseph Rowntree Foundation.

Atkinson, A. M., Kirton, A. W. and Sumnall, H. R. 2012. The gendering of alcohol in consumer magazines: An analysis of male and female targeted publications. *Journal of Gender Studies*, 21: 365–386.

Atkinson, A. M., Ross, K. M., Begley, E. and Sumnall, H. 2015. *Constructing alcohol identities: The role of Social Network Sites (SNS) in young peoples' drinking cultures*. Alcohol Research UK.

Babor, T. F., Caetano, R., Casswell, S., Edwards, G., Giesbrecht, N., Graham, K. . . . Rossow, I. 2010. *Alcohol: No ordinary commodity research and public policy*. 2nd Ed. Oxford: Oxford University Press.

BBC News 2012. "Carnage UK pub crawl criticised by student unions." BBC News Online. 11 October 2012. http://www.bbc.co.uk/news/uk-england-hampshire-19909216

Bourdieu, P. 1984. *Distinction: A social critique of the judgment of taste*. Harvard: Harvard University Press.

Bourdieu, P. 2010. *Outline of a theory of practise*. Cambridge: Cambridge University Press.

Boyd, D. M. and Ellison, N. B. 2007. Social network sites: Definition, history, and scholarship. *Journal of Computer-Mediated Communication*, 13: 210–230. doi: 10.1111/j.1083–6101.2007.00393

Brooks, O. 2010. *'Routes to magic': The alcoholic beverage industry's use of new media in alcohol marketing*. Institute for Social Marketing, University of Stirling and the Open University.

Brown, R. and Gregg, M. 2012. The pedagogy of regret: Facebook, binge drinking and young women. *Continuum: Journal of Media and Cultural Studies*, 26(3): 357–369.

Butler, J. 1999. *Gender trouble: Feminism and the subversion of identity*. London: Routledge.

Cashmore, E. 2014. *Celebrity culture*. 2nd Ed. London: Routledge.

De Visser, R. O. and McDonnell, E. J. 2012. 'That's OK. He's a guy': A mixed-methods study of gender double-standards for alcohol use. *Psychology and Health*, 27(5): 618–639.

De Visser, R. O. and Smith, J. A. 2007. Alcohol consumption and masculine identity among young men. *Psychology and Health*, 22(5): 595–614.

De Visser, R. O., Smith, J. A. and McDonnell, E. J. 2009. 'That's not masculine': Masculine capital and health-related behaviour. *Journal of Health Psychology*, 14(7): 1047–1058.

Forsyth, A., Galloway, J. and Shewan, D. 2007. "Young people's street drinking behaviour: Investigating the influence of marketing and subculture." *Alcohol Insight 44*. London: Alcohol Education and Research Council.

Freeman, B., Chapman, S. and Rimmer, M. 2008. The case for the plain packaging of tobacco products. *Addiction*, 103(4): 580–590.

Fuller, E. 2009. *Smoking, drinking and drug use among young people in England in 2008*. London: NHS Information Centre for Health and Social Care.

Fuller, E. and Hawkins, V. 2013. *Smoking, drinking and drug use among young people in England in 2013*. London: NHS Information Centre for Health and Social Care.

Giddens, A. 1991. *Modernity and self-identity: Self and society in the late modern age*. Cambridge: Polity Press.

Gilbert, E. 2007. Performing femininity: Young women's gendered practice of cigarette smoking. *Journal of Gender Studies*, 16(2): 121–137.

Goffman, E. 1959. *The presentation of self in everyday life*. New York: Anchor Books.

Goffman, E. 1976. Gender advertisements. *Studies in the Anthropology of Visual Culture*, 3(2): 69–154.

Gordon, R., Hastings, G. and Moodie, C. 2010. Alcohol marketing and young people's drinking: What the evidence base suggests for policy. *Journal of Public Affairs*, 10: 88–101.

Griffin, C. 2004. "Good girls, bad girls: Anglocentrism and diversity in the construction of contemporary girlhood." In A. Harris (Ed.), *All about the girl: Culture, power and identity* (pp. 29–44). London: Routledge.

Griffin, C., Bengry-Howell, A., Hackley, C., Mistral, W. and Szmigin, I. 2009. 'Everytime I do it I absolutely annihilate myself': Loss of (self-) consciousness and loss of memory in young people's drinking narratives. *Sociology*, 43(3): 457–476.

Griffin, C., Szmigin, I., Bengry-Howell, A., Hackley, C. and Mistral, W. 2012. Inhabiting the contradictions: Hypersexual femininity and the culture of intoxications among young women in the UK. *Feminism and Psychology*, 23(2): 184–206.

Griffiths, R. and Casswell, S. 2010. Intoxigenic digital space? Youth, social networking sites and alcohol marketing. *Drug and Alcohol Review*, 29: 525–530.

Grosz, E. 1994. *Volatile bodies: Toward a corporeal feminism*. Indiana: Indiana University Press.

Hastings, G. 2009. *'They'll drink bucket loads of the stuff': An analysis of internal alcohol industry advertising documents*. The Alcohol Education and Research Council.

Hebden, R. 2011. Tertiary student drinking culture, Facebook and alcohol advertising: Collapsing boundaries between social life and commercialised consumption. Master of Arts in Psychology.

Hibell, B. Guttormsson, U., Ahlström, S., Balakireva, O., Bjarnason, T., Kokkevi, A., & Kraus, L. 2012. *The 2011 ESPAD report: Substance use among students in 36 European countries*. Stockholm: The Swedish Council for Information on Alcohol and Other Drugs.

Hibell, B., Guttormsson, U., Ahlström, S., Balakireva, O., Bjarnason, T., Kokkevi, A., & Kraus, L. 2009. *The 2007 ESPAD report: Substance use among students in 35 European countries*. Stockholm: Swedish Council for Information on Alcohol and Other Drugs (CAN)/Pompidou Group at the Council of Europe.

Holt D.B. 2002. Why do brands cause trouble? A dialectical theory of consumer culture and branding. *Journal of Consumer Research*, 29(1): 70–90.

Hopwood, D. 2013. "Warwick student backlash against 'sexist, racist and violent' bar décor." *The Independent*. 15 March 2013. http://www.independent.co.uk/student/news/warwick-student-backlash-against-sexist-racist-and-violent-bar-decor-8534217.html

Institute of Policy Research. 2013. *Would you like a drink? Youth drinking cultures, social media and alcohol marketing online*, Policy Brief. University of Bath.

Järvinen, M. and Gundelach, P. 2007. Teenage drinking, symbolic capital and distinction. *Journal of Youth Studies*, 10(1): 55–71.

Livingstone, S. 2008. Taking risky opportunities in youthful content creation: Teenagers' use of SNSs for intimacy, privacy and self-expression. *New Media and Society*, 10: 393–411.

Lunnay, B., Ward, P. and Borlagdan, J. 2011. The practise and practice of Bourdieu: The application of social theory to youth alcohol research. *International Journal of Drug Policy*, 22: 428–436.

Lyons, A. C. and Willott, S. A. 2008. Alcohol consumption, gender identities and women's changing social positions. *Sex Roles*, 59: 694–712.

McCreanor, T., Greenway, A., Barnes, H. M., Borell, S. and Gregory, A. 2005. Youth identity and contemporary alcohol marketing. *Critical Public Health*, 15(3): 251–262.

McCreanor, T., Lyons, A., Griffin, C., Goodwin, I., Barnes, H. M., Hutton, F. 2012. Youth drinking cultures, social networking and alcohol marketing: implications for public health." *Critical Public Health*, 23(1): 110–120. http://dx.doi.org/10.1080/09581596.2012.748883

McRobbie, A. 2004a. "Notes on 'what not to wear' and the post-feminist symbolic violence." In L. Adkins and B. Skeggs (Eds.), *Feminism after Bourdieu* (pp. 99–109). London: Blackwell Publishing.

McRobbie, A. 2004b. "Notes on postfeminisim and popular culture: Bridget Jones and the new gender regime." In A. Harris (Ed.), *All about the girl: Culture, power and identity* (pp. 3–14). London: Routledge.

Measham, F. 2002. 'Doing gender' – 'doing drugs': Conceptualizing the gendering of drug cultures. *Contemporary Drug Problems*, 29: 335–373.

Mendelson, A. L. and Papacharsi, Z. 2010. "Look at us: Collective narcissism in college student Facebook photo galleries." In Z. Papacharsi (Ed.), *The networked self: Identity, community and culture on social network sites*. London: Routledge.

Miles, S. 2000. *Youth lifestyles in a changing world*. Buckingham: Open University Press.

Montgomery, K. C. and Chester, J. 2009. Interactive food and beverage marketing: Targeting adolescents in the digital age. *Journal of Adolescent Health*, 45: 18–29.

Moreno, M. A., Briner, B. A., Williams, A., Walker, L. and Christakis, D. A. 2009. Real use or 'real cool': Adolescents speak out about displayed alcohol references on social networking websites. *Journal of Adolescent Health*, 45: 420–422.

Moreno, M. A., Christakis, D. A., Egan, K. G., Brockman, L. N. and Becker, T. 2012. Associations between displayed alcohol references on Facebook and problem drinking among college students. *Archives of Pediatric Adolescent Medicine*, 166: 157–163.

Moreno, M. A., D'Angelo, J., Kacvinsky, L. E., Kerr, B., Zhang, C. and Eickhoff, J. 2014. Emergence and predictors of alcohol reference displays on Facebook during the first year of college. *Computers in Human Behaviour*, 30: 87–94.

Morgan, E., Snelson, C. and Elison-Bowers, P., 2010. Image and video disclosure of substance use on social media websites. *Computers in Human Behavior*, 26: 1405–1411.

Mosher, J. 2012. Joe Camel in a bottle: Diageo, the Smirnoff brand, and the transformation of the youth alcohol market. *American Journal of Public Health*, 102(1): 56–63.

Murthy, D. 2008. Digital ethnography: An examination of the use of new technologies for social research. *Sociology*, 42(5): 837–855.

Nicholls, J. 2012. Everyday, everywhere: Alcohol marketing and social media, current trend. *Alcohol and Alcoholism*, 47: 486–493.

NWPHO 2013. *Local alcohol profiles for England. Q1 2013*. Online resource http://www.lape.org.uk/ (last accessed 3 June 2013).

Pempek, T. A., Yermolayeva, Y. A. and Calvert, S. L. 2009. College students' social networking experiences on Facebook. *Journal of Applied Developmental Psychology*, 30: 227–238.

Ridout, B., Campbell, A. and Ellis, I. 2012. 'Off your Face (book)': Alcohol in online social identity construction and its relation to problem drinking in university students. *Drug and Alcohol Review*, 31: 20–26.

Ross, K. 2010. *Gendered media: Women, men and identity politics*. Plymouth: Rowman and Littlefield.

Ross, K. Forthcoming. "Gender representations and experiences in urban space after regeneration: A case study of Liverpool, UK and Liverpool One". Unpublished PhD thesis: University of Liverpool.

Skeggs, B. 1997. *Formations of class and gender: Becoming respectable*. London: Sage.

Skinstad, M. 2008. *Facebook: A digital network of friends*. ed. 24th Conference of the Nordic Sociological Association, University of Aarhus, 14–17 August 2008.

Smith, L. A. and Foxcroft, D. R. 2009. *Drinking in the UK: An exploration of trends*. York: Joseph Rowntree Foundation.

Stead, M., McDermott, L., MacKintosh, A. M., Adamson, A. 2011. Why healthy eating is bad for young people's health: Identity, belonging and food. *Social Science and Medicine*, 72: 1131–1139.

Styles, R. 2014. "Forgot your coats, girls? Big hats and goose bumps take centre stage as scantily-clad racegoers arrive for Ladies Day in chilly York." *The Daily Mail* 21 August 2014 http://www.dailymail.co.uk/femail/article-2730843/Big-hats-goose-bumps-centre-stage-scantily-clad-racegoers-arrive-Ladies-Day-chilly-York.html#ixzz3Ir8NmnHJ (accessed 11 November 2014).

Subrahmanyam, K. and Greenfield, P. 2008. Virtual worlds in development: Implications of social networking sites. *Journal of Applied Developmental Psychology*, 29: 417–419.

Thurnell-Read, T. 2012. Tourism place and space: British stag tourism in Poland. *Annals of Tourism Research*, 39(2): 801–819.

Thurnell-Read, T. 2013. 'Yobs' and 'snobs': Embodying drink and the problematic male drinking body. *Sociological Research Online*, 18 (2).

Tonks, A., 2012. "Photos on Facebook: An exploratory study of their role in the social lives and drinking experiences of New Zealand university students". Unpublished master's thesis, Massey University.

Waitt, G., Jessop, L. and Gorman-Murray, A. 2011. 'The guys in there just expect to be laid': embodied and gendered socio-practices of a 'night out' in Wollongong, Australia. *Gender, Place and Culture: A Journal of Feminist Geography*, 18(2): 255–275.

Wearing, S. and Wearing, B. 2000. Smoking as a fashion accessory in the 90s: Conspicuous consumption, identity and adolescent women's leisure choices. *Leisure Studies*, 19(1): 45–58.

West, C. and Zimmerman, D. H. 1987. Doing gender. *Gender and Society*, 1(2): 125–151.

Wichstrom, T. and Wichstrom, L. 2009. Does sports participation during adolescence prevent later alcohol, tobacco and cannabis use? *Addiction* 104: 138–149.

Young, I. M. 1990. *Throwing like a girl and other essays in feminist philosophy and social theory*. Bloomington and Indianapolis: Indiana University Press.

Chapter 4

Beer and belonging
Real Ale consumption, place and identity

Thomas Thurnell-Read

Introduction

The role played by alcohol and its consumption in the creation of personal, group and national identity has received considerable academic attention. A central feature of this has been the recognition that, in addition to the many potential negative personal and social outcomes of heavy drinking, the consumption of alcoholic drinks invariably involves significant articulations of personal identity, collective belonging and, as Mary Douglas and her contributors (1987) have established, the construction and perpetuation of culture itself. We must acknowledge, therefore, that alcoholic drinks exhibit remarkable symbolic power. Indeed, some even take on totemic positions in relation to national culture, history and identity; Roland Barthes (1972, p. 67) famously asserted that the performance of drinking wine 'is a national technique which serves to qualify the Frenchman, to demonstrate at once the performance, his control and his sociability'. More recently, Marion Demossier (2010, p. 29) has used her extensive study of wine production and consumption in France to explore how 'through wine consumption, individuals compete and construct their identity and relate to concepts of what it means to be French, exploring the relationship between regions and the nation'.

In the British context it is beer, perhaps more than any other alcoholic drink, which has so readily been held as in some way symbolic of national identity. In classic studies such as *The Pub and its People* (Mass Observation, 1943), the omnipotence of beer drinking in working-class culture, and British urban life, was identified. More recently, however, a decline of 'traditional' pubs and a diversification of drinking practices (Chatterton & Hollands, 2003; Hollands, this volume) have meant that beer has played a troubled and ambiguous role in the 'binge drinking' discourses played out in policy and academic debates and across the media during the 1990s and 2000s (see Plant & Plant, 2006). Drinkers are seen to be foregoing the tradition of beer in favour of heavily branded spirits, myriad flavoured 'shooters' and alcopops designed to encourage rapid inebriation (Measham & Brain, 2005; Smith, 2014). Further still, the potential that British drinkers might abandon beer in favour of a more 'continental' and congenial wine-based 'café culture' of Mediterranean drinking has been used to speak of a preferred transition and has informed policy accordingly (Jayne, Valentine & Holloway, 2008; Haydock, 2014).

However, during this time we have also seen, in the UK and elsewhere, a growth in breweries and beers that distinguish themselves from mass-produced and nationally or globally marketed brands through their link to locality, place and the identity of specific towns, cities or regions. Drinking beer from small and local breweries is perceived, by some consumers, to be 'authentic' and a means by which identity can be communicated and performed through consumption (Spracklen, Laurencic & Kenyon, 2013). Meanwhile, work in the United States has shown that many of the smaller scale breweries to emerge in recent decades actively offer their patrons a chance to engage with place and locality through the consumption of geographically specific beers (Flack, 1997; Schnell & Reese, 2003; Daniels, Sterling & Ross, 2009). While I have explored the notions of craft and identity exhibited by those brewers involved in the production of such beers elsewhere (Thurnell-Read, 2014), this chapter makes an analysis of symbolic trends in Real Ale imagery and suggests that such should be considered to be part of the now sizable heritage industry which has emerged by the creation of events and cultural products that use 'history and heritage to inform a personal and collective sense of place and local identity' (Cohen, 2013, p. 581). Thus, the symbolic imagery of beer consumption now offers drinkers a vast array of often potent symbolic markers of identity and belonging.

As such, this chapter suggests that the consumption of beer involves the invocation of place and identity. The identity, place and heritage present in Real Ale naming, imagery and symbolism is, of course, selective in its construction and possibly rather narrow in its appeal. It is important to note how lines of inclusion and exclusion are first constructed and then animated through embodied consumption. Further still, the chapter identifies how this symbolism is strikingly gendered and, as such, appears to offer a specifically masculine conception of heritage and identity. The final section of the chapter therefore explores the evident exclusionary tendency within the symbolic imagery of Real Ale which can signify that while a particular image of 'traditional' masculinity is valorised, the feminine is either rejected or contained.

Consuming places and drinking identity

Noting the influence of Mary Douglas's (1987) work on 'constructive drinking' and that of Thomas Wilson (2005) on drinking cultures, whereby alcohol is a central constituent of culture and identity, this chapter seeks to locate an analysis of Real Ale drinking amongst a range of themes relating to how identity is constructed, performed and negotiated through consumption. The suggestion at the outset is therefore that beer is a particularly symbol-laden drink and its consumption can tell us important things about personal, local and national identity. Just as wine and French national identity (Barthes, 1972; Demossier, 2010), whisky and Scottish identity (Spracklen, 2011), beer and Czech identity (Hall, 2005) and vodka and Russian identity (Roberts, 2014) are semantically intertwined, so too might the pint of beer be seen as a sign or icon of British identity (Rojek, 2007, p. 197). Tellingly, a recent report by *VisitBritain* (2010, p. 12), the public body responsible for promoting Britain as a tourist destination, has reflected that 'in terms of "living culture", British pubs are a real strength – they are part of the image of Britain and a good experience to have during a visit'.

However, the role of alcohol as a symbolic marker of identity has been under-explored in the social sciences. Indeed, alcohol has largely been omitted from interesting recent work on the potential for food to inhabit the collective imagination and speak to ideas of national belonging, as well as to define 'other' nations through their 'foreign' tastes (Ashley, Hollows, Jones & Taylor, 2004). Just as Bell and Valentine (1997) have suggested in relation to food, drink can also be thought of as being 'scaled' across space and place; from individual tastes, pleasure and guilt of the body and self; through the familiar routines of home and community; and on through region and nation to the global. In several studies, for example, we see how particular beer brands have become woven into expressions of national identity and belonging in Ireland (Murphy, 2003), South Africa (Mager, 2005), the Czech Republic (Hall, 2005) and Scotland (Gutzke, 2012). Notably, as we return to later in the chapter, in all these studies the consumption of alcohol defines national identity but also overlaps with gender identity where beer and beer drinking are used to shape and define what it means to be an Irish, South African, Czech or Scottish man.

To further theorise this we can turn to various constructivist accounts which show how national identity emerges from and is sustained by acts of communicative action and symbolic meaning making which bind often disparate individuals around 'imagined communities' (Anderson, 1983) of common identity and a sense of belonging. Thus, in his work on *The Invention of Tradition*, Eric Hobsbawm (1983, p. 1) explored how national identity is asserted through customs and traditions which 'attempt to establish continuity with a suitable historic past'. While nationalism has all too often given rise to extremism and conflict (e.g., see Ignatieff, 2010), it can also be observed how the performance of belonging is also enacted in everyday, quotidian ways, with acts of consumption being a prime example. The symbolism of national identity and belonging works its way into daily life in numerous mundane and often unremarkable ways in what Michael Billig (1995) has termed 'banal nationalism'. As such, national identity is reproduced and 'flagged' in the daily lives of individuals and in a 'booming' heritage industry which draws on nostalgia and 'patriotic themes' (Billig, 1995, p. 113) and national and sub-national identities can be readily attached to relatively mundane consumption practices (Foster, 1999).

Consumption is therefore, as Bourdieu observed (1984, p. 100), 'a labour of identification and decoding'. Even banal everyday consumer items can and do support a complex and often deeply felt sense of belonging (see Smith, this volume). Particular products are instilled with meaning and, as enacted in their consumption, individuals actively pursue and create a meaningful connection. As

John Urry (1995, p. 28) has observed, 'the consumption of place and the consumption of goods and services are interdependent', meaning 'images of place are routinely used in the symbolic location of products and services'. This commoditisation of local culture entails 'the creation and valorization of resources that have a place identity and can be marketed directly or used in the marketing of the territory' (Ray, 1998, 6). Informed by this work, this chapter seeks to indicate how, rather than being a banal practice, the consumption of Real Ale involves the negotiation of identity and belonging.

Research methods

This chapter draws on a qualitative study of the British consumer pressure group the Campaign for Real Ale (CAMRA) and, more generally, the changing practices and meanings of beer consumption in Britain. Founded in 1971 with the aim of protecting Real Ale, defined as a traditional British style of beer involving secondary fermentation or 'cask conditioning', CAMRA now boasts more than 170,000 members spread across in excess of 200 local branches. During this time, and in the past decade in particular, a revival in the fortunes of Britain's small and independent breweries has seen a huge rise in their number, with CAMRA reporting in its annual *Good Beer Guide* that 1,285 breweries were operating in Britain in autumn 2014.

Research was conducted between August 2012 and May 2014 and comprised 53 semi-structured qualitative interviews with a range of relevant participants involved in CAMRA, including two of the four founders, several senior salaried staff and numerous local branch members. Most of these interviews took place in and around the English midlands, in or near London and, for a small number, in the rural county of Cornwall. Other key informants include beer writers, brewery staff and members of a university ale appreciation society. Participant-observation was carried out at CAMRA Annual General Meetings and branch meetings as well as a range of beer festivals, pub crawls and brewery tours. Additionally, archival and documentary analysis of CAMRA campaign materials (such as the monthly newsletter *What's Brewing?* and the annual *Good Beer Guide*) was conducted as was collection and qualitative analysis of brewery marketing materials, including beer branding, logos and imagery.

Place, identity and Real Ale

The notion of locality as being an implicit feature of Real Ale consumption has been evident since the founding of CAMRA which, as an organisation, sought to challenge the increasing homogenisation of beer production and associated loss of local variety. Thus, an editorial in the 1974 edition of CAMRA's flagship publication, the *Good Beer Guide*, expressed indignation that 'large brewing factories near the motorways are supplying beer for whole regions of the country, where once there were dozens of little breweries each producing ales of different strengths and flavours'. Similarly, a former CAMRA chairman made a clear connection between place and consumption when observing in an organisation publication marking the 21st anniversary of the campaign that:

> A pint of Jennings tastes best in a whitewashed hillside Cumbrian pub with panoramic views; Donnington Bitter is most welcome in a cool Cotswolds taproom with a stone flagged floor.
>
> (Hunt, 1992, p. 81)

Such sentiments express the important links made between Real Ale and locality. Consumption in general and, in particular, of products so closely associated with specific places as Real Ale often is, must be acknowledged as a means by which individuals and groups can perform and feel identity. Indeed, such can be seen to amount to 'the valorisation of place through an objectification of its cultural identity' (Coombe & Aylwin, 2011, p. 2028) and, further, an example of what Pike (2011) has referred to as 'geographical entanglement'.

These concerns remain at the core of CAMRA's work as a campaign group. Thus, David, a senior CAMRA staff member, observed during an interview that:

> It's increasingly important to people that they know what they're buying and where it comes from, these are signs of people just feeling a little bit lost in the global world where they don't feel they can bring influence on any of the big things that are happening around us, but they can when it comes to buying basic produce.

Consuming locality is therefore cast as a comfort in a changing world, and one which provides the consumer with 'ontological security' (Giddens, 1991). During interviews it became apparent that a clear appeal of involvement with CAMRA and commitment to drinking ales was rooted in a sense of loyalty to or of belonging to a specific locality. As such, Martin, a local CAMRA branch member, suggested that:

> Being from the area, you want to try any beer from the local breweries. The older ones you're familiar with and you have a degree of loyalty and the newer ones are something to try to show your support but, yeah, I'd say I do knowingly, I mean I'm drawn to the local beers.

Here, Martin's loyalty to the local area is seen as a positive and is deployed in his positioning of himself as a knowing, self-aware consumer. Similarly, during a student ale society visit to a CAMRA beer festival in Manchester, where ales by breweries from across the country were available, one member on arriving at the festival venue announced that it was time to 'do my duty' and seek out and consume ales from his home county, Yorkshire. Similar to Murphy's (2003, p. 53) observation that the Irish participants in her study were *more* likely to drink

Guinness while travelling or living abroad 'in order to feel closer to home or in order to say "I'm Irish" and use the product as a badge of identity', for this student, studying away from his home appeared to add significance and meaning to his consumption of his 'local' beers. Tellingly, a common means of social interaction amongst CAMRA members and Real Ale consumers is to 'place' each other in relation to beers and breweries. Thus, being from Cornwall, my own interaction with participants became 'placed' as they positioned me in relation to 'good' and 'bad' breweries relating to that region.

Gordon, another interviewee with an extensive career in the industry, having previously worked in brewing, as a publican and in an executive role for an organisation promoting independent breweries, reflected on the trend for local produce and was one of many interviewees to draw a link between consumer enthusiasm for local beer and that for local food. As such, he observed that:

> If you go to somewhere and you know there's a local brewery and you want to try it, if you go to Cornwall you want a proper Cornish pasty, if you go to Bury in Lancashire you want some black pudding and I'm interested enough in local food to want to do that and you want locally sourced meat and that is a definite customer trend.

Again, we see consumption of ale as one means of consumers relating to their locality and placing themselves within space and place meaning 'a sense of local patriotism expressible through a preference for buying locally-produced goods and services' (Ray, 1998, p. 17).

Another example relates to two members of the student ale society who were interviewed for the research and, as international students studying at a British university, both made clear reference to Real Ale being a means to 'get to know' the culture of their host country. Peter, who had held several key positions within the society committee, observed that:

> [International students] come along, one or two at first and they say let's come along for the English beer, for the culture, and for them it's not too easy to meet people if you come in just for one year so for them it's a way to meet people and learn about English culture.

Similarly, Brenden, an American student on an exchange year at the British university, spoke of joining the society as a means of meeting British students and learning about British culture:

> I liked it because I liked the ale, I enjoyed drinking the ales that is, but I enjoyed the British culture in general. My course has about 120 students and there are maybe 4 people actually from Britain in the course and none of them are on my actual module so I don't have any actual British friends from my course so it was nice being able to become friends with a bunch of Brits.

Elsewhere in the interview, Brenden spoke with pride of knowing the pubs of the local area, breweries from the region and, more generally, a familiarity with British drinking culture that marked him out from other international students more willing to remain within the 'bubble' of the international student community on campus rather than seek out involvement with local social life and culture.

Heroes, heritage and drinking nostalgia

The previous section identified how place and identity making are 'at work' in the consumption practices of Real Ale drinkers and that this is readily framed by participants in relation to a sense of personal belonging to specific places. However, adding to this sense of spatiality with its linking of personal identity and that of local and regional places, this section explores what might be described as a temporal theme within much Real Ale consumption. Specifically, the use of historical themes and 'tradition' is striking when reviewing the growth of Real Ale as a consumer practice. This orientation to the past is a central, if contested, facet of the Real Ale phenomenon.

Many of the widest-selling Real Ales, if not those most highly regarded by connoisseurs, draw on precisely such symbolism. Indeed, frequently, temporal and spatial specificity overlap. One prominent example is *Spitfire Kentish Ale* which was first brewed in 1990 and took its name from the iconic fighter plane flown during World War II in the Battle of Britain. That the original ale marked the 50-year commemoration of the Battle of Britain and that the Spitfire flew from and fought over the English county of Kent and the adjacent English Channel and North Sea thus exemplify how both the naming and imagery of Real Ale branding invoke specific conceptions of time and place. In a more general sense, military imagery is common, with notable examples being Woodforde's *Nelson's Revenge*, *Broadside* by Adnams, *Bengal Lancer* and *Seafarer* by London-based Fuller's Brewery and *Bombardier* by Wells and Young's. In a good example of Billig's (1995) banal nationalism, the latter even incorporates the red cross on white of the English St. George's flag.

Images of famous historical figures and famous events and industries are prominent. In particular, figures with links to locality are a common feature of ale branding and are frequently name checked both directly and indirectly. For example, *Wainwright* by the Lancastrian brewery Thwaits derives its name 'in honour of the famous fell walker, author and fellow Lancastrian Alfred Wainwright' (http://www.wainwrightgoldenale.co.uk), while *Darwin's Origin* by Shropshire-based brewery Salopian was first brewed in 2009 to mark the 200th anniversary of Charles Darwin's birth in the Shropshire town of Shrewsbury. Other ales make references to professions associated with the brewery locality. *Haymaker* by Hook Norton and *Boltmaker* by Timothy Taylor are examples of agricultural and industrial vocations being invoked by breweries based in rural Oxfordshire and urban Yorkshire, respectively. This appears to parallel Schnell and Reese's (2003, p. 59) observation of the preference for 'Blue-Collar' historical profession such as 'blacksmiths, or miners, or steamboat captains' amongst small American breweries.

The predominance of names and imagery which situate the beer in time and place is of interest to understanding how Real Ale appreciation is a leisure and consumer practice which serves to both construct and perform specific interpretations of identity. Richard, one of the brewers interviewed for the research, spoke of the importance of needing a 'theme' and chose to link his brewery and beers to local history by using names and images related to the route of the Roman road passing close to the brewery:

> We've got a very loose roman connection. All our beer names have got Latin in there somewhere . . . So yeah that's the brewery logo as such and then we've taken, we've got Gladiator, we've got Centurion.

While these brands, their names and their imagery, draw on quite disparate themes depending on the specificity of each brewery's locality, they all have in common a particular orientation to the past that can be seen to link to heritage and nostalgia. Worth noting, however, is that very few of these brands are in fact 'traditional' in that they are in the majority products devised and launched only in the past three decades. Indeed, there is considerable mileage in suggesting this to be a largely recent development, contemporary to rather than predating the great expansion of mass-produced commercial drinks and drinking spaces witnessed in Britain from the 1980s onwards (see also Hollands; Ross-Houle, Atkinson and Sumnall; and Smith, all this volume). For example, it is striking how Frank Baillie's (1973) compilation of Britain's breweries in his at the time influential book *The Beer Drinker's Companion* was characterised by a far more prosaic style of naming which saw most breweries producing beers named descriptively according to style and appearance. The now defunct Hoskins brewery of Leicester, for example, is typical of the period in producing beers simply named *Bitter*, *Mild*, *Best Mild* and *Nut Brown* (Baillie, 1973, p, 174). Thus, such Real Ale brands are notably contemporary yet attempt to draw on a sense of continuity with the past through the incorporation of the pre-existing symbolism of local history. As Hobsbawm (1983, p. 6) suggested, 'sometimes new traditions could be readily grafted on old ones, sometimes they could be devised by borrowing from well-supplied warehouses of official ritual, symbolism and moral exhortation'.

Returning to Urry (1995, p. 156), who identifies the preservation movements of post-industrial Britain as reacting to a 'profound sense of loss' through the ritualistic and highly symbolic construction of nostalgic images, we can see how certain consumer spaces come to 'stand for' particular places and communities by linking consumption to time and place. Drinking certain ales offers a way of connecting to locality through geographically and temporally specific symbolism. Further still, there is a sense of 'ontological security' (Giddens, 1991) being offered by the familiar array of symbolism that links the consumer, via the product, to an identifiable and desired past. As Vesey and Dimanche's study of heritage tourism in New Orleans (2003, p. 56) indicated, 'the idealised image is remembered by the public as a frame of reference to the past', meaning complexities and anachronisms are easily ignored as long as the central motif functions in a meaningful way for those who engage with it. Unpacking these observations further, it is important to explore what Laurajane Smith (2006) has described as 'the uses of heritage' where heritage is not a fixed thing that is preserved and protected but a social and cultural process that involves identity, memory and remembering, performance and place. Thus, she states that 'heritage is used to construct, reconstruct and negotiate a range of identities and social and cultural values and meanings in the present' (Smith 2006, p. 3). Both the construction and use of heritage, therefore, involve the selection and valorisation of some themes and symbols over others.

Many within the Real Ale 'scene' were aware of and demonstrated reflexivity in regards to the accusations that Real Ale thrived on 'safe' nostalgic and at times chauvinistic imagery. Roger Protz, perhaps the most prominent and certainly longest serving beer writer with links to CAMRA, wrote in an editorial to the 2002 edition of the *Good Beer Guide* that:

> Companies need to be bold. Nostalgia and tradition have their place but building brands for the future demands a more radical approach, which translates such values into a classic, continuing appeal. Most independent brewers have tended to reach for the comfort blanket of their heritage rather than looking to the future.

Some brewers interviewed had doubts as to the overuse of heritage themes by breweries founded only very recently. A local brewer, Steve, reflected that 'there is something disingenuous about that, trying to, you know, pretend you've got this glorious heritage'. However, also worth noting is that Steve's own beers alluded in their naming and imagery to the local area and its previous prominence in the automotive manufacturing industry. More critical, Robert, the proprietor of a specialist beer shop, also suggested a need to move away from the overuse of heritage themes by saying:

> There are some good beers out there but to be honest it's a matter of style *and* substance. It could be an amazing ale but if the bottle has a picture of a steam engine or a bloody wizard on it [laughs] I'm going to think twice about having it on our shelves.

In his sardonic reference to industrial imagery such as steam engines, and mythical or fantastical themes such as wizards, Robert appears to reject a nostalgic iconography which he positions as twee and dated. Likewise, although expressed with somewhat more ambivalence, a local CAMRA branch member Michael admitted that 'it's all very blokey and a bit geeky . . . but that's what we're here for isn't it'.

Notably, as will become central to the proceeding analysis which identified the implicit masculine basis of much Real Age imagery, beer is readily associated with the assertion of nostalgic forms of masculinity. The predominance of local history and industrial themes in ale marketing are therefore reminiscent of the 'male, conservative, hegemonic interpretation of heritage' identified by Edensor and Kothari (1994, p. 185) and the post-industrial 'golden age' nostalgia discussed by Strangleman (2002). The convergence of beer drinking, masculinity and nationalism is well noted (Mager, 2005, 2010; Gutzke, 2012). Hugh Campbell (2000) identifies how the practice of drinking beer and the setting, in the case of his study the rural pubs of New Zealand, are gender specific and much work is done to keep it so. As the previous discussion indicates, much of the symbolic landscape of Real Ale is implicitly masculine and, it should be argued, this feeds into actual physical spaces and practices. The widespread use of the phrase 'old man pubs' to informally describe local pubs that typically might serve Real Ale to an exclusively male clientele foreground this gendering of drinking spaces as masculine, perhaps in notable contrast with the emerging mixed-gender drinking spaces of style cafes and bars (see Latham, 2003).

More broadly, we might locate this within the wider perception of a loss of a reliable and reassuring traditional industrial male identity where the 'nostalgia for a bygone age' in the face of diverse socioeconomic upheavals means industrial heritage has a particular surety which appeals to discursive constructions of masculinity (Beynon, 2002, p. 127). Real Ale might therefore be seen as part of a wider ready market for the symbolic imagery of traditional masculinity. It is the passing away of a clearly identifiable industrial masculine identity that makes the symbolic allusions to it such a pertinent and, for many, welcome anchor for identity. As noted previously, Real Ale consumption appears to offer consumers, at least many of those interviewed for this research, a sense of certainty embedded in locality and tradition (see also Spracklen et al., 2013). As Hobsbawm (1983, p. 4) notes, 'we should expect [the invention of tradition] to occur more frequently when a rapid transformation of society weakens or destroys the social patterns for which 'old' traditions had been designed, producing new ones to which they were not applicable'.

We might therefore frame these debates within a compensatory thesis where 'men who have suffered pangs of emasculation in this new environment have sought to symbolically reaffirm their status as real men through compensatory consumption' (Holt & Thompson, 2004, p. 425). For instance, Gee and Jackson's analysis of the 'Southern Man' advertising campaign of New Zealand beer brand Speights suggests that the success of the campaign rests on a 'hegemonic representation of rural, white masculinity in southern New Zealand' which is 'notable for being unapologetic', yet, equally, the campaign might be read as 'a nostalgic valorisation of local hegemonic masculinity in a time of destabilised male identity politics' (Gee & Jackson, 2012, pp. 84–85).

'Top totty' and 'retro' women: The place of women in Real Ale

So far, this chapter has sought to illustrate how Real Ale drinking can be seen, like wine is in France, as 'a marker of national and regional identity and as a complex arena for asserting and negotiating questions of competition, power, identity and social ordering' (Demossier, 2010, p. 7). Evident in this has been the way in which the identification with place and time offered by Real Ale production and consumption is gender specific, with a distinctly masculine landscape of industrial, military and heritage themes and imagery apparent. As anthropologist Nelson Graburn (2001, p. 68) has observed, 'the concept of heritage requires a sense of ownership, and the consumption of heritage requires a sense of permission'. Many of the themes and imagery just mentioned are clearly coded as masculine and evidently involve a 'claiming' of territory where Real Ale, and beer consumption more generally, has been fenced off as a masculine space.

This final section furthers this discussion by exploring the ways in which, as a flipside of this assertion of masculinity through nostalgic heritage, women, and the female body in particular, are marginalised and excluded. As Tim Edwards (2000, p, 146) observes, practices of conspicuous consumption that provide some with 'the means to form an identity and to maintain or develop a particular status or standing in society' also 'operates to exclude others and to reinforce the underlying divisiveness of the overall situation'. As in Cara Aitchison's (2003) instructive work on leisure and gender, a picture can be drawn of how such exclusionary forces run through much leisure and consumption practices. It is clear that the bodies and embodiments of male and female drinkers are held to quite different standards and patterns of moral judgement (see Thurnell-Read, 2011, 2013; and Lyons, Emslie & Hunt, 2014, respectively). While the identity work of Real Ale consumption asserts a confident, if nostalgic, masculine identity, the symbolic position of women within this is highly problematic. A number of examples serve to illustrate this observation.

Perhaps the most striking case of this in recent years can be found in the ale called *Top Totty*, brewed by the Staffordshire-based brewer Slater's. Described by the brewery as 'a stunning blonde beer full bodied with a voluptuous hop aroma' the beer branding features the image of a blonde, bikini and bunny ear clad, female figure carrying a glass of beer on a serving platter. The beer gained notoriety when, in February 2012, Shadow Equalities Minister Kate Green expressed her concern during Prime Minister's Question Time that a product featuring such sexist imagery should be served in a bar in the Houses of Parliament. While the beer was promptly withdrawn – or, by other accounts, had simply 'run out' – Slater's brewery reported a huge increase in sales following media coverage of the controversy, and posters began to appear in pubs bragging, 'Banned from parliament but not from here'. While a predictable media-led 'backlash' ensued, framing the debate as 'political correctness gone mad', with Green being attacked specifically as 'humourless' and prone to 'knee-jerk puritanism' (Martin, 2012), the event illustrates how women are frequently overtly demeaned and marginalised in sexist Real Ale branding.

The response to the *Top Totty* incident exhibits similarities to the use of 'humour' and 'irony' as a defence within the sexist narratives of men's lifestyle magazines, serving to distance those outside of the group and, further still, act as a defence mechanism against allegations of political incorrectness, chauvinism and sexism (Whelehan, 2000; Benwell, 2003; Benwell, 2004). While not addressing chauvinism directly, Stan, one of the brewers interviewed about their work, said: 'At the end of the day it's a bit of fun isn't it? Some of the beer names are a bit childish, you know, puns and that'. Further, this (mis)use of female bodies in beer-related imagery draws some ready parallels with the 'Tennent's Lager Lovelies' described by Gutzke (2012). In this case, the Scottish brewery used female models on lager packaging during the 1960s and 1970s whereby the 'patriotic beer-drinking Scotsmen could claim lager as theirs in buying cans with pictures of nubile Scottish women in provocative poses' (Gutzke, 2012, p. 555). The implication running through this is that, as Aitchison (2003, p. 44) has observed in relation to leisure, women are positioned as a support function to the main event of masculine leisure and consumption.

Some well-intentioned attempts to 'open up' beer consumption to female drinkers have perhaps unintentionally further highlighted these symbolic gender boundaries. For example, *Animee*, a 'beer for women' launched in the UK by Canadian firm Molson Coors in 2011 with a £2m marketing drive, based its branding around smaller, curvier bottles, pale pastel colours, fruit flavours and the promise of a 'lightly sparkling' and therefore 'feminine' product (Atherton, 2011). That Molson Coors initially gave away free samples of the beer through the Toni and Guy chain of hair salons appeared to further reinforce a derivative, and to many commentators, patronising image of drinking femininity. Commenting on the launch of the brand, beer writer Melissa Cole astutely suggested that:

> There are several factors that stop women from buying beer: a lack of education, too much gassy rubbish and ugly glassware. Top of the list, however, is that they find the inherent sexism in beer advertising and marketing off-putting – and there's certainly little that says "it's not pink and fruity enough" and (the) UK beer industry have busily been disenfranchising women from the beer market for the past 40 years and are now clumsily trying to entice them back.

Critics of the evidently misguided campaign were quickly vindicated as the company announced the withdrawal of the product just over a year after its launch.

Two further examples of how attempts to address these issues have been counterproductive can be drawn from within CAMRA. In the March 1997 edition of *What's Brewing?*, the long-running CAMRA monthly campaign newspaper, a story titled 'Do you know this ale fan? . . . we'd like her number' ran alongside an image of a young woman holding a glass of ale between her legs, taken at the 1995 Great British Beer Festival. The story aimed to locate the woman in the photograph and recruit her to 'spearhead' the promotion of that year's festival. One campaign member, responding in the letters section of the following edition of the paper, said:

> If you want to shed the bearded blobby man image then show a picture of a clean cut, slimmer man. There are plenty in the organisation. Why want a picture of a woman when it is the man's poor image that needs altering?

More recently, in October 2014, CAMRA released to several university ale societies a promotional leaflet for distribution to students, with the aim of recruiting new members to the campaign. The leaflet, featuring a blonde female model wearing blue hot pants and a low-cut white top on the front page, and a pair of female models on the inside both appearing to be wearing 'pin-up' style bodices, provoked a spirited response, with many ale societies refusing to accept the leaflets and directly criticising CAMRA for the poorly conceived and executed initiative. It was reported on a Facebook page of young CAMRA members that a response from CAMRA 'HQ' had indicated that the campaign was authorised following a 'design brief' to several agencies to commission the leaflet. Accordingly, 'one of the popular themes submitted by an agency was the use of 1950s imagery using professional 'vintage' models to help echo beer advertising imagery of 60 years ago' and that a 'focus group of both young male and female focus groups (both equally represented) and certain committees liked this approach and felt it was something different for CAMRA'. They also apologised if it was interpreted as 'a discriminatory/sexist campaign' and stated that this was 'seriously not our intention'.

While to a great extent the unfolding of this particular example indicates some of the long-lying tensions within CAMRA as an organisation, here it is interesting to note how the attempt to include new members by targeting young women involves 'looking back' to a 'retro' image. The representation of femininity in such 'retro' images is telling. As Elizabeth Brunner (2013) suggests, the 'visual evocation of cultural nostalgia' in such 'patriarchal visual rhetoric' serves to contain women's presence in leisure and consumption.

One research participant in particular, Mary, a beer expert and writer involved in various elements of promotion and industry engagement with consumers, stated in an email correspondence that:

> Beer marketing campaigns need to be revolutionised. A lot of mass market beer marketing is either blokey, sometimes sexist, aimed at young men, laddish, often assuming that they are childish losers (a recent *Foster's* ad is a good example of that), and where women only feature as totty, or as harridans spoiling the party.

Mary's comment captures well how the boundaries enforced by the symbolism and imagery of ale branding work to signal beer drinking as a practice which is implicitly masculine and from which women are to be excluded. Furthermore, her reference to the depiction of men as 'childish losers' strikes a chord with Smith's work on the infantalisation of drinking culture (2014 and this volume).

Conclusion

This chapter has explored how Real Ale might be seen as a symbolic landscape infused with heritage and nostalgia. In particular, the chapter observes how industrial and pastoral symbolism emerges precisely at the time when such is passing away. Reminiscent of Roberts' (2014, p. 306) observation that chocolate and vodka packaging in post-Soviet Russia 'has increasingly been designed to reproduce, and promote, the myth of the Great Russian past', the use of nostalgic, yet bold, images of a proud British past can evidently not be disentangled from wider social changes. As AlSayyad (2001, p. 9) suggests, heritage involves not only preservation but also an 'attempt to resuscitate' motivated by both, on the pragmatic level, financial gain in attracting consumers but also 'to serve as 'banks' of national memory and pride to ward off the subversive effects of historical change'. Thus breweries and beers that draw on the nostalgic imagery and language of industrial heritage do so in a way which situates and 'places' both the brewery and its locality within a national narrative of Britain as a 'Great' industrial power.

This chapter has sought to show, following the likes of Billig (1995, p. 175), that by looking at the symbolism of heritage 'we are noticing the depths and mechanisms of our identity, embedded in routines of social life'. Like other forms of heritage, Real Ale can convey 'a sense of place and of the past' (McIntosh & Prentice, 1999, p. 590). As such, Real Ale consumption proves to be an interesting case which demonstrates the links between consumption and identity and how consuming alcohol can be a way of feeling one's identity and one's place in the world (Ross-Houle, Atkinson and Sumnall, this volume). As Cohen (2013) notes, it is important to consider how the 'validation' of heritage constructions and memory are enacted in both official and, importantly, unofficial ways. Taking the former, as noted earlier in this chapter, tourism authorities such as *VisitBritain* have repeatedly endorsed the 'iconic' British pint consumed in a 'traditional' British pub as an important, and saleable, expression of national culture, heritage and identity. Further still, an array of informal engagements with such cultural symbolism, many involving resistance and contestation, mean that the consumption of Real Ale demonstrates how alcohol and identity are linked.

Yet, parallel to Graburn's (2001, p. 81) observation that heritage and tradition invariably involve 'paradigms of belonging and ownership', this chapter has explored how the rich symbolism of Real Ale that frequently draws on images of long since passed industrial, imperial or pastoral Britain exhibits exclusion as well as inclusion. While the 'invented traditions' of nostalgia and heritage are valuable 'evidence' for historians as they throw 'considerable light on the human relation to the past' (Hobsbawm, 1983, p. 12), so too are they of analytical use to sociologists considering the present and potential 'uses' of heritage. This chapter has identified how belonging and identity are evidently constructed through the consumption of Real Ale, as well as how others are contained and excluded by the very same imagery.

References

Aitchison, C. 2003. *Gender and leisure: Social and cultural perspectives*. London: Routledge.

AlSayyad, N. (Ed.). 2001. *Consuming tradition, manufacturing heritage: Global norms and urban forms in the age of tourism*. London: Routledge.

Anderson, B. 1983. I*magined communities: Reflections on the origin and spread of nationalism*. London: Verso.
Ashley, B., Hollows, J., Jones, S. and Taylor, B. 2004. *Food and cultural studies*. Basingstoke: Routledge.
Atherton, S. 2011. Lager for ladies. Again. *The Guardian Online*. 19 July 2011. http://www.theguardian.com/lifeandstyle/wordofmouth/2011/jul/19/lager-for-ladies-again
Baillie, F. 1973. *The beer drinkers companion*. Trowbridge: Redwood Press.
Barthes, R. 1972. *Mythologies*. London: Macmillan.
Bell, D. and Valentine, G. 1997. *Consuming geographies: We are where we eat*. London: Routledge.
Benwell, B. 2003. *Masculinity and men's lifestyle magazines*. Oxford: Blackwell.
Benwell, B. 2004. Ironic discourse: Evasive masculinity in men's lifestyle magazines. *Men and Masculinities*, 7(1): 3–21.
Beynon, J. 2002. *Masculinities and culture*. Buckingham: Open University Press.
Billig, M. 1995. *Banal nationalism*. London: Sage.
Bourdieu, P. 1984. *Distinction: A social critique of the judgment of taste*. Cambridge, MA.: Harvard University Press.
Brunner, E.A. 2013. Impotence, nostalgia, and objectification: Patriarchal visual rhetoric to contain women. *Visual Culture and Gender*, 8: 31–45.
Campbell, H. 2000. The glass phallus: Pub (lic) masculinity and drinking in rural New Zealand. *Rural Sociology*, 65(4): 562–581.
Chatterton, P., and Hollands, R. 2003. *Urban nightscapes: Youth cultures, pleasure spaces and corporate power*. London: Routledge.
Cohen, S. 2013. Musical memory, heritage and local identity: Remembering the popular music past in a European capital of culture. *International Journal of Cultural Policy*, 19(5): 576–594.
Cole, M. 2011. 'Pretty' beers for women? A rather tasteless idea. *The Guardian Online*. 19 July 2011. http://www.theguardian.com/commentisfree/2011/jul/19/beer-women-brewers-marketing
Coombe, R. and Aylwin, N. 2011. Bordering diversity and desire: Using intellectual property to mark place-based products. *Special Issue of Environment and Planning A: Society and Space*, 43(9): 2027–2042.
Crewe, L. 2000. Geographies of retailing and consumption. *Progress in Human Geography*, 24(2): 275–290.
Daniels, E., Sterling, C. and Ross, E. 2009. Microbreweries and culture in the greater Madison area. *Geography*, 565: 12.
Demossier, M. 2010. *Wine drinking culture in France: A national myth or a modern passion?* Cardiff: University of Wales Press.
Douglas, M. 1987. *Constructive drinking: Perspectives on drinking from anthropology*. New York, Cambridge University Press.
Edensor, T. and Kothari, U. 1994. The masculinisation of Stirling's heritage. In V. Kinnaird and D. Hall (Eds.), *Tourism: A gender analysis*. Chichester: Wiley.
Edwards, T. 2000. *Contradictions of consumption: Concepts, practices, and politics in consumer society* (p. 131). Buckingham: Open University Press.
Emslie, C., Hunt, K. and Lyons, A. (2012). Older and wiser?: Men's and women's accounts of drinking in early mid-life. *Sociology of Health and Illness*, 34(4): 481–496.
Flack, W. 1997. American microbreweries and neolocalism: "Ale-ing" for a sense of place. *Journal of Cultural Geography*, 16(2): 37–53.

Foster, R. 1999. The commercial construction of 'new nations'. *Journal of Material Culture*, 4(3): 263–282.

Gee, S. and Jackson, S. 2012. Leisure corporations, beer brand culture, and the crisis of masculinity: The Speight's 'Southern Man' advertising campaign. *Leisure Studies*, 31(1): 83–102.

Giddens, A. 1991. *Modernity and self-identity: Self and society in the late modern age.* Redwood City, CA.: Stanford University Press.

Graburn, N. 2001. Learning to consume: What is heritage and when is it traditional? In N. AlSayyad (Ed.), *Consuming tradition, manufacturing heritage: Global norms and urban forms in the age of tourism.* London: Routledge.

Gutzke, D. W. 2012. Tennent's lager, national identity and football in Scotland, 1960s–90s. *Sport in History*, 32(4): 550–567.

Hall, T. 2005. *Pivo* at the heart of Europe: Beer-drinking and Czech identities. In T. Wilson (Ed.), *Drinking cultures.* Oxford: Berg.

Haydock, W. 2014. The 'civilising' effect of a 'balanced' night-time economy for 'better people': Class and the cosmopolitan limit in the consumption and regulation of alcohol in Bournemouth. *Journal of Policy Research in Tourism, Leisure and Events*, 6(2): 172–185.

Hobsbawm, E. 1983. *The invention of tradition.* Cambridge: Cambridge University Press.

Holbrook, M. B. and Schindler, R. M. 2003. Nostalgic bonding: Exploring the role of nostalgia in the consumption experience. *Journal of Consumer Behaviour*, 3(2): 107–127.

Holt, D. B. and Thompson, C. J. 2004. Man-of-action heroes: The pursuit of heroic masculinity in everyday consumption. *Journal of Consumer Research*, 31(2): 425–440.

Hunt, C. 1992. A sense of place. In R. Protz and T. Millns (Eds.), *Called to the bar: An account of the first 21 years of the Campaign for Real Ale.* St Albans: CAMRA Ltd.

Ignatieff, M. 2010. *Blood and belonging: Journeys into the new nationalism.* London: Random House.

Jayne M., Valentine, G. and Holloway, S. L. 2008. Fluid boundaries: British binge drinking and European civility: Alcohol and the production and consumption of public space. *Space and Polity*, 12(1): 81–100.

Latham, A. 2003. Urbanity, lifestyle and making sense of the new urban cultural economy: Notes from New Zealand. *Urban Studies*, 40(9): 1699–1724.

Lyons, A., Emslie, C. and Hunt, K. 2014. Staying 'in the zone' but not passing the 'point of no return': Embodiment, gender and drinking in mid-life. *Sociology of Health and Illness*, 36(2): 264–277.

Mager, A. 2005. One beer, one goal, one nation, one soul: South African breweries, heritage, masculinity and nationalism 1960–1999. *Past and Present*, 188(1): 163–194.

Mager, A. K. 2010. *Beer, sociability, and masculinity in South Africa.* Bloomington, IN.: Indiana University Press.

Martin, D. 2012. MPs' 'sexist' beer ban: Top Totty ale outlawed in the Commons bar. *Daily Mail*, 3 February 2012. http://www.dailymail.co.uk/news/article-2095482/MPs-sexist-beer-ban-Top-Totty-ale-outlawed-Commons-bar.html#ixzz3bRJjX7ke

Mass Observation. 1943. *The pub and the people: A worktown study.* London: Gollancz.

McIntosh, A. J. and Prentice, R. 1999. Affirming authenticity: Consuming cultural heritage. *Annals of Tourism Research*, 26(3): 589–612.

Measham, F. and Brain, K. 2005. 'Binge 'drinking, British alcohol policy and the new culture of intoxication. *Crime, Media, Culture*, 1(3): 262–283.

Murphy, B. 2003. Pure genius: Guinness consumption and Irish identity. *New Hibernia Review*, 7(4): 50–62.

Pike, A. 2011. Placing brands and branding: A socio-spatial biography of Newcastle Brown Ale. *Transactions of the Institute of British Geographers*, 36(2): 206–222.

Plant, M. and Plant, M. 2006. *Binge Britain: Alcohol and the national response*. Oxford: Oxford University Press.

Ray, C. 1998. Culture, intellectual property and territorial rural development. *Sociologia Ruralis*, 38(1): 3–20.

Roberts, G. H. 2014. Message on a bottle: Packaging the great Russian past. *Consumption Markets and Culture*, 17(3): 295–313.

Rojek, C. 2007. *Brit-myth: Who do the British think they are?* London: Reaktion.

Smith, L. 2006. *The uses of heritage*. London: Routledge.

Smith, O. 2014. *Contemporary adulthood and the night-time economy*. Basingstoke: Palgrave Macmillan.

Schnell, S. and Reese, J. 2003. Microbreweries as tools of local identity. *Journal of Cultural Geography*, 21(1): 45–69.

Spracklen, K. 2011. Dreaming of drams: Authenticity in Scottish whisky tourism as an expression of unresolved Habermasian rationalities. *Leisure Studies*, 30(1): 99–116.

Spracklen, K., Laurencic, J. and Kenyon, A. 2013. 'Mine's a pint of bitter': Performativity, gender, class and representations of authenticity in real-ale tourism. *Tourist Studies*, 13(3): 304–321.

Strangleman, T. 2002. Nostalgia for nationalisation: The politics of privatisation. *Sociological Research Online*, 7(1).

Thurnell-Read, T. 2011. Off the leash and out of control: Masculinities and embodiment in Eastern European stag tourism, *Sociology*, 45(6): 977–991.

Thurnell-Read, T. 2013. 'Yobs' and 'snobs': Embodying drink and the problematic male drinking body. *Sociological Research Online*, 18(2): 3.

Thurnell-Read, T. 2014. Craft, tangibility and affect at work in the microbrewery. *Emotion, Space and Society*, 13: 46–54.

Urry, J. 1995. *Consuming places*. London: Routledge.

Vesey, C. and Dimanche, F. 2003. From Storyville to Bourbon Street: Vice, nostalgia and tourism. *Journal of Tourism and Cultural Change*, 1(1): 54–70.

VisitBritain. 2010. 'Culture and heritage: Topic profile'. http://www.visitbritain.org/Images/Culture%20and%20Heritage%20Topic%20Profile%20Full_tcm29-14711.pdf

Whelehan, I. 2000. *Overloaded: Popular culture and the future of feminism*. London: Women's Press.

Wilson, T. 2005. *Drinking cultures*. Oxford: Berg.

Chapter 5

Illegal drinking venues in a South African township
Sites of struggle in the informal city

Andrew Charman

Introduction: Informality and the dilemma of control

The word *shebeen* is of Irish origin, though it has become adopted as a South African term of reference for an unlicenced and hence unregulated venue where alcohol is sold and drinking conducted. Shebeens are illegal, but constitute the great majority of alcohol retailing venues in South Africa's black urban townships. It is thought that there are approximately 250,000 such venues throughout the country (Petersen & Charman, 2010). These venues symbolise a historical legacy of exclusion, beginning under Apartheid and sustained into present times, through regulatory obstacles and policy concerns to maintain control over working-class communities. Whilst our concern is with informal drinking venues, shebeens' illegal status and illegitimate provision of social spaces pose questions that Africanist scholars are asking about the meaning of 'cityness'. The widespread exclusion, marginalisation and prosecution of informality across African cities in its diverse social-spatial manifestations and economic conditions have prompted Pieterse and Simone (2013, p. 12) to speak of 'rouge urbanism'. The idea refers to social expressions that are 'unruly, unpredictable, surprising, confounding yet pregnant with possibility'. Although these scholars were not thinking explicitly about alcohol serving venues, these businesses fit the description aptly (also see Bonte, this volume). Unlike other forms of informal businesses, shebeens are not simply businesses seeking to survive and entrench their position in the urban milieu, but social spaces and indeed spaces that sustain cultural forms and expressions.

This chapter makes two arguments. Firstly, we argue that shebeens have become 'emancipatory spaces' forged through the incremental struggles of shebeen owners as well as their patrons for a place within an exclusionary city. We employ the notion of 'emancipatory' in the sense of an achievement of resistance against state policies that aim to curtail working-class sociability around drinking; recognising nevertheless that the shebeen 'space' itself is socially complex and contradictory, liberating and simultaneously exclusionary towards non-participants. The shebeen owners, who are the main subject of this study, seek to advance their rights to the city through the everyday practices in which they construct and sustain their venues under the threat of state authority and local insecurity. Secondly, we argue that because the shebeen environment is one of great social complexity and contradictions, where emotions are sometimes embedded in drunken sociability, the shebeen owners are constantly seeking to manage the social dynamics through use of subtle (both inclusive and exclusive) strategies and the configuration of the spatial environment. We seek to show how, in some instances, this can reinforce the 'emancipatory space' of the shebeen and have positive outcomes on social cohesion and present a vision of inclusiveness.

The case of informal drinking venues provides a contrast between the hyper-regulated drinking spaces of the Global North and the emergent, informal and illegal forms of drinking spaces in the Global South that are, in our case, constituted as 'unruly and threatening'.

South African alcohol regulation

Alcohol control in the Global North has, in recent times, straddled a paradoxical agenda of deregulation and stringent regulation as the place of alcohol in the city shifts, with new cultures of drinking emerging. This is most notably embodied through the emergence of new urban nightscapes and the growth of a night-time leisure economy centred on revived inner cities (Chatterton & Holland, 2003). These changes, argue Jayne, Holloway and Valentine, (2006), have been driven through a politics of consumption, shaped by the various influences of market segmentation, gentrification and corporatisation (also see Hollands, this volume). The drinking dilemmas, in this context, are the opposing needs for deregulation as a strategy to stimulate economic growth whilst catering to the demand for inner-city drinkatainment (Bell, 2007 introduces this idea) and reregulation to maintain 'control' whilst extending responsibility from the state to private entities and the businesses themselves. The emergence of this night-time leisure economy has not gone uncontested. New forms of 'moral panic' around alcohol have reignited debates on the scope of regulation, focusing their target on drinking cultures, which include youth drinkers and alcohol consumption among 'sexualised' young women drinking new types of drink (Jayne, Valentine & Holloway, 2010, p. 7). Moral fear centres on notions of disorder that challenge middle-class sensibilities (also see Nicholls, this volume). As a consequence, more stringent tools of regulation have been introduced, including the intensive policing of the street (and public space), CCTV surveillance, prohibitions on begging and measures to discourage rough sleeping.

The experience and debates on alcohol regulation and deregulation in Northern cities are central to the conceptualisation of South African alcohol control policies. But whereas alcohol control in the Global North has been influenced by the democratisation of the nightscape and the inclusion of the working-class within a corporatized consumption city, subject to the exclusionary influence of alcohol, venues and drinking itself (see Valentine et al., 2010), alcohol policies in South

Africa have reinforced the spatial, racial and class divisions embedded in its colonial history.

The spatial separation between the working-class townships and the gentrified city as a consequence of Apartheid segregation largely ensures that the poor do not participate in spaces intended for middle-class use (Turok, 2001; Pieterse, 2009). Instead of fostering inclusion, alcohol control in the case of the city of Cape Town aims to erode working-class drinking practices and minimise spaces of drinking sociability within the township (i.e., urban periphery). Although the politics through which this outcome was achieved is insightful of the polarisation of alcohol control to reinforce dominant race and class interests that characterise South African alcohol control dilemmas, this topic is not central to the arguments of this chapter. Some of the details of the emergence of alcohol policy in the region are detailed in Herrick (2014), Smit (2014), Herrick and Parnell (2014), Charman, Herrick and Petersen (2014) and Charman, Petersen and Piper (2013).

There are two main mechanisms to enforce the prohibitionist regulation in working-class settlements. The first are restrictions of the times and days in which the few licenced alcohol outlets may conduct business, with sales prohibited on Sundays and off-sales trade restricted to 6.00 p.m., ensuring that venues are shut by the time that workers return home. The second are a set of regulations designed to prevent venues from operating in residential areas. Principal amongst these regulations is the requirement that the land on which alcohol serving and selling venues operate be zoned for commercial use (Province of Western Cape, 2008). This requirement is especially pernicious as under Apartheid all land within townships was zoned for residential use and no allowance was made for commercial use (Parnell & Pieterse, 2010). The land zoning tactic is reinforced by regulations that prohibit the sale of alcohol within 500 meters of a school or religious institution, whilst licences are in any case subject to the approval of ward councillors and consideration of public objections. There is a clearly articulated policy objective to eradicate unlicensed drinking venues (Winde, 2013). As a consequence, of the 8,000 liquor licences through the Western Cape Province in 2011, merely 14% had been awarded to black persons (Liquor Licence Board Data in author's possession). Whereas the central business district of Cape Town had 1,232 licenced liquor outlets and venues, serving a population of 206,805, there were a modest 117 alcohol-licenced businesses within the working-class townships with a population of 1,112,650, of which there were only 85 licensed alcohol-serving venues. In the informal settlements, such as the case we present, the informality of shebeens is a structural outcome of the exclusion of the poor from the regulated city.

The scholarship on the predicament of informal liquor traders in South Africa is contoured by an epistemological divide. Although the boundaries are intermeshed, the health science research occupies a position of endorsement towards the current regulatory position, whilst much social science research, in particular the writings of geographers, sociologists and historians, supports a more nuanced position recognising the political agenda that alcohol regulation underwrites. In health science literature, working-class drinking venues in general and shebeens in particular are seen as vectors of conflict in which 'harmful' drinking is normalised and violence seen as an anticipated outcome (Parry, 2005; Parry, 2010; Peltzer & Ramlagan, 2009). Shebeens are held responsible for liquor harms (including violence) within the venue as a result of their direct impact (e.g., through noise) and indirect impact (e.g., through facilitating hazardous drinking). The drinking culture of shebeens, it is argued, manifests in sexual harassment and violence, inter-personal violence among drinkers and violence as a consequence of opportunistic crime as drunk persons walk home (Morojele et al., 2006; Watt et al., 2012). Deeply set within this literature is the idea that working-class drinking cultures are inherently 'hazardous' and hence violent and the principal solution is strategic prohibition through reducing access to liquor (known as *supply reduction strategies*) (see Matzopoulos et al., 2008). The positioning of alcohol control in intellectual terms, through what Jayne, Valentine and Holloway (2011, p. 5) describe as 'surveillance medicine' which focuses not on alcohol harms per se but on the possible risks of illness and harm (also see Valentine, Velleman and Templeton, this volume), has meant that drinking itself has been conceptualised within this broad literature as a transgressive activity.

There is a small, though expanding, critical literature that challenges some of these ideas. At the heart of the counter-argument is the recognition that shebeens are an enduring feature of township life and their persistence is linked to the continued high levels of poverty (Charman, Petersen & Govender, 2014; Smit, 2014; Drivdal & Lawhon, 2014). These arguments are supported by historical writings that illustrate the role of shebeens in providing much needed social spaces and offering a form of resistance to the various attempts of the Apartheid state to control the urbanised population (see Rogerson & Hart, 1986; La Hausse, 1986; Mager, 2004; Crush & Ambler, 1992). At the same time there is recognition that urbanisation and the availability of industrially produced alcohol (including and especially bottled beer) began to fundamentally reshape drinking culture, supporting creation of a (new) malevolent drinking culture (Mager, 2010).

This chapter seeks to address the paradox that shebeens 'have been left unchallenged in most African areas' despite their problematic impact on alcohol consumption (Parnell & Pieterse, 2010, p. 158). We seek to provide a better understanding of why the culture of shebeen drinking has been so robust and resilient. At one level the chapter seeks to respond to the argument of Herrick and Parnell (2014, p. 5) that the current liquor control objectives have a 'legislative logic and public health imperative' even though control makes 'little ethical sense' given that 'alcohol provision, consumption and control in South Africa has conspired to actively produce shebeens'. At a deeper level we seek to situate shebeen drinking culture in a more nuanced theoretical framework, one that is determined not merely as an outcome of the unintended conspiracy of industrial self-interest and state control, but as the result of the everyday action of individual shebeeners to secure their place within the city and the social networks forged within their venues that bind them to community and reinforce their place and belonging (also see Bonte, this volume).

Research approach and methods

The research was undertaken in three waves. The first wave took place in 2011. The initial study focused on micro-enterprise activities, examining businesses using a mix of qualitative and quantitative tools. The research approach is reported in Charman, Petersen, Piper, Liedeman and Legg (2015). The names of the interviewees, their businesses and the geo-spatial localities at which their businesses operate were anonymised and assigned a number in keeping with ethical conventions. Each of the interviewees has been linked to a designated site and database number, with their gender (M = male and F = female) and time in business (e.g., 7 = 7 years) in parentheses for additional information (e.g., M,7).

In the second wave, undertaken in 2012, the researcher focused on two issues: first, the characteristics of the space and place of the shebeen environment, and second, the experience of the shebeens in coping with and responding to state control and their experiences of running the business. The first aspect entailed a detailed socio-spatial investigation of six 'types' of shebeen wherein the research sought to identify the spatial arrangement of each venue. The investigation drew on the theorisation advanced by Jayne et al. (2006) and Jayne, Valentine and Holloway (2008) of the influence of space and place on drinking, thus affording the social environment a strong role in determining outcomes of drunkenness. Spatial data were obtained from each venue to identify particular aspects of the type in terms of design, layout, use of objects, business practices and facilities, home-business dynamics (public vs private space), relationship with patrons, patron composition and distinguishing characteristics of venue use. These research findings have been reported in Charman et al. (2014).[1] The second aspect of the research process aimed to understand the perspective of the shebeen owners with regard to their daily struggles in running their business through a collective, participatory digital storytelling research process. The digital stories were developed through a workshop process over a four-day period wherein eight participants ultimately developed and produced 3-minute digital stories. The research objective was to enable the participants to script and tell their own story, drawing on actual experiences to express a social message they wished to share with their fellow participants and potentially a wider audience. This chapter draws on some of these stories.

In 2014, a third wave of research was undertaken. In this wave, the researchers sought to focus explicitly on understanding the 'micro-control' strategies that we identified in the first and second waves. The research objective was to comprehend, from the shebeener perspective, the strategies that they utilize and activate to minimise the potential risks of harm within the public space of the drinking venue. We had learnt through prior research, how, for example, shebeeners had used mechanisms such as opening hours, accessibility within their venues (i.e., door policy), music type and volume adjustment, the provision and non-provision of amenities and configuration of the space to influence the composition of their customer base and position their businesses within a niche segment. In some venues, the niche comprised old men and women who met to drink, sing hymns and engage in conversation; in other venues, the niche could be young men or women who preferred a venue with loud dance music. But we were unclear about how and why these measures were specifically mobilised to reduce risks and manage the complex and contradictory environment.

The research process in the third wave entailed two aspects and a participatory action learning component. We first conducted in-depth interviews with 23 shebeeners, half of whom were involved in wave two, whilst the remainder expressed an interest in participating in the research. The interview process sought to understand the use of micro-control strategies. Each of the interviewees had a unique database number, reflecting the third wave of the research (e.g., S/W3/1 = Sweet Home Farm interviewee/Wave 3/No 1). Through this process, we identified 40 micro-control measures: these included active interventions (such as surveillance, bouncers, body searching, music control, closing time, home escorts, restricting the range of alcohol available, door policies, etc.) and passive interventions (such as seating provision and layout, the use of lighting, bar rails, windows, security bars, etc.). In the second step, we brought the shebeeners into a workshop process to analyse collectively and in a participatory manner the mechanisms of spatial and social control utilised in each participant's venue as detailed in a preliminary poster analysis. The workshop research process enabled us to explore emergent themes (on drinking cultures) and learn of strategies (such as cooperation between particular businesses) that had not been identified in the individual interviews.

In the analysis that follows, we have drawn on evidence from all three waves. Specific individuals, whose experiences are discussed in more detail, partook in all three waves of research. We have sought to reflect different gendered views. Most of our case studies focus on female-run shebeens, which in turn reflects the numerical dominance of women in the sector and in Sweet Home Farm. In Southern African rural communities, beer brewing was traditionally the preserve of older (usually married) women (Crush & Ambler, 1992, p. 5), whilst in the emergent urban settlements of the 20th century, the brewing and commercial sale of beer became a critical livelihood for women excluded from the formal and male migrant–dominated labour market (La Hausse, 1988; Mager, 2010). Colonial critics reacted to the successes of (some) women, characterising these entrepreneurs as 'shebeen queens', a label which embodied notions of excessive profiteering and social influence (see Mager, 1999 and 2004). Whilst this label has been popularised, it detracts from the reality that most women shebeeners run small businesses and remain in the liquor sector as a result of a combination of home pressures (including their role in child rearing) and economic marginalisation which minimises their opportunities for formal employment.

Sweet Home Farm and shebeens

The research is set in the informal township (slum) of Sweet Home Farm. The settlement is 0.3 km² and has a population density equivalent to 30,138 persons per km². The 2011 national census identified 3,210 households and a population of 7,836 (StatsSA, 2012). Poverty is deep and near universal throughout the settlement, with 63% of households subsisting on less than R38,000 (£2,000) per annum. Using the census data, unemployment (the narrow definition) stands at 42%. There are no formal houses. People have constructed their houses using scrap materials, with the architecture of the shacks comprising iron sheets, cardboard, rough timber and recycled fixtures and fittings (Figure 5.1). Especially in the case of older residents, some have built a fence around their dwelling, allowing them to utilise the courtyard space for seating, storage of materials and hanging washing. In 2012 only a few households had legal access to electricity and instead the resourceful settlers tapped into the nearest accessible power grid, resulting in a gigantic web of wires which criss-crossed the settlement. Today most households are legally connected to the grid. But many challenges remain, including the absence of toilet facilities and water. The road infrastructure comprises a small grid of council-built roads, which serve merely a fraction of households, and a few rudimentary tracks. Most residents access their homes via a network of pathways that twist and turn through the dense settlement, with (some) shebeens providing entrance (front) and exit (back) points that connect different pathways and portions of the settlement. The difficult living conditions within the settlement are occasionally brought to public attention through grotesque events, such as moments of mob justice (Koyana, 2014), flooding (which occurs annually) and a brutal attack of stray dogs on a young child (De Wee, 2011).

The challenge of economic survival necessitates action. Many residents have established a shebeen to generate income, with such venues providing a relatively stable income from the sale of liquor and coin-operated juke boxes and pool

Figure 5.1 Entrance to a shebeen. The public space is highlighted. Image supplied by SLF. Used with the author's permission.

tables. But unlike other business options, they provide a public social space and therefore provide a social return that has benefits and costs. For the residents of Sweet Home Farm, leisure options are limited to shebeens, the public space of the street network, businesses such as hair salons (which demand expenditure) and religious institutions. There are ten churches and one mosque. Of the 401 businesses we identified in the first wave of research, 111 or 27.7% sold alcohol, either providing a social venue within which consumption was permitted and accommodated or as takeaway sales for off-site consumption. Across the settlement there are 14.2 businesses selling alcohol for each 1,000 persons, a figure equivalent to 3.46 outlets per 100 households. The majority (57%) of shebeen owners we surveyed were women. Most businesses had been in operation for more than three years, though 12 had been running for over a decade.

We were able to discern six broad types or categories of shebeens. This was an important finding, given the characterisation of the shebeen landscape in monolithic terms. Of those venues that most closely matched the public policy conceptualisation of venues where both genders drink heavily in a highly charged emotional environment in which loud music mutes conversation and the potential for conflict is greatest, we identified very few. These venues we labelled 'drinkattainment shebeens' because of the obvious similarities to the city night-time leisure economy in terms of youth, drinking, entertainment and exclusionary influences. We identified only two venues that met this characterisation. In general, most venues do not have formalised entertainment: merely 17% of venues had pool tables and 11% had jukeboxes, though most shebeens have music systems. The 'neighbourhood shebeen', which we discuss later in the case of Louise, shares some characteristics with drinkattainment venues but differs fundamentally in the diversity of patrons by age and gender and their relationships to one another. The shebeen owner knows most of the patrons individually and the patrons themselves are well acquainted.

In another type, we identified several 'conversational shebeens', such as the venue operated by Mamaduma, where music is either turned low or entirely absent, patrons are almost always seated and socialisation is via conversation. In these types the shebeen owner similarly knows his or her customers on an individual level. Mamaduma was one of the first persons to settle on the site in the late 1970s. She has traded alcohol since first settling in Sweet Home Farm. Her venue is a place for subdued interaction, allowing for conversation between patrons, who are mainly elderly men and women (Charman et al., 2014). When the researchers asked her how she maintains 'control' over her customers, she responded:

> They listen to my rules and I listen to theirs. These people are very important to me. Everyone comes here to relax [,] so if you cause trouble I send you away. I prefer to deal with the older crowd but I [also] select[ed] which young ones are allowed to drink here. . . . I am an older person, so no one can disrespect me. They either do as I say or leave (S/W3/2).

Mamaduma's experience of exclusion within the Apartheid city (and from the rights to live and conduct business) was enforced many times over through police raids and her occasional arrest. But she did not stop selling alcohol, nor will she cease trading. In her words: 'I have run from the police all my life . . . [and] I will never stop selling liquor, not until I die' (Field notes, September 2011). A further example of the dynamic between shebeen owner and customers in the conversational type emerged from our interviews with Rosline. She reported that her male customers (her venue was exclusive to older men) could only obtain alcohol on credit if the patron's wife gave her authorisation to do so (she would phone them) (Field notes, May 2014).

Along this trajectory of highly localised shebeens, we identified two variants of the 'traditional shebeen'. In one type, the venues sold home-brewed sorghum and traditional beer, whereas in the second type the venues sold both commercial and traditional beer, though sustaining traditional drinking customs. Typically, the spatial configuration of the traditional shebeen sought to reinforce traditional isiXhosa drinking customs, with the furniture, for example, positioned against the walls to create a circular effect with a fireplace in the middle of the floor; windows were usually absent and fixtures minimal (on traditional isiXhosa drinking, see McAllister, 2006). Absent were any signs, symbols or posters that herald the era of corporatized consumption. The final type we identified were venues where groups, usually of young unemployed men, meet to play pool and 'hang out'. In these venues, very little alcohol is either sold or consumed. The function of the venues is to provide a social space of solidarity; drinking is a secondary activity.

Regardless of their type, the shebeens of Sweet Home Farm have been subject to relentless law enforcement (Herrick & Charman, 2013). In the 2011 research we found that 65% (50 of 78) of the venues had been raided at least once in the past 12 months. Although legitimate police targets, the research found that much of the policing of shebeens is motivated by personal financial incentives. Faull (2013) has argued that the raiding of shebeens is partially motivated by the demands of the police hierarchy to bolster their statistics and thereby appease their political masters, who desire action against crime and drugs. We learnt from the surveyed businesses, however, that most shebeen owners were able to resist and subvert the authority of the police through strategies such as buying small quantities of liquor (thus reducing losses) (S8 [F,3]), maintaining constant surveillance so as to allow the shebeen owner sufficient time to close the venue and hide in the settlement (S26 [F,3]), paying bribes (S29 [M,2]) and (S56 [M,3]), hiding the alcohol stock off site (S55 [F,2]), situating the venue separately from their place of residence (S59 [M,1]), and locking the customers inside the venue at night (S64 [M, 20]). All of these research participants refused to close their businesses following raids by the police. As a woman who sold traditional beer exclaimed, 'I cannot stop [running the shebeen] because there is no other business that I know' (S77 [F,4]).

The meaning of the police raids on the lives of the shebeen owners, in terms of reinforcing their sense of exclusion within the city, was articulated most clearly through the digital stories. In Welcome's story, titled 'A tale of the oppressed', he recounts how he left Johannesburg as a consequence of the then political violence. In Cape Town, he settled in Sweet Home Farm and ran a shebeen, providing a venue whose main attraction was the game of pool. The business did well, initially, but then he was arrested for selling alcohol. At that moment, in his words,

'Everything changed. My life ended'. His story makes an explicit statement about his exclusion and marginalisation from the formal economy:

> I cannot get hired because of my age. [A pause]. This government of ours has issues with the voters of this nation [meaning the voters are apathetic]. All the laws oppress us, not the whites because we are the slaves of these laws. We live in shacks. Shebeens are not allowed. We are slaves to hunger. All our money is locked up in debt.

In Nobesuthu's story, titled 'Ncedani – A cry for help', the complexity of the daily risks which shebeen owners (especially single women) confront, from the state on one hand and abusive, sometimes violent, customers on the other hand, emerges. She recounts:

> I started my business in 2009 and things were going well. After some time . . . I started to not be fine. Mostly, it was because of people's drunken behaviour towards me. But I paid very little attention to that because I understood my reasons for selling alcohol . . . I have children who require money . . . [Then] something happened which broke my spirit . . . One day I wet myself out of fear. My anxiety felt as if it could jump right out of my mouth. The knock was so loud. I had never heard it before. It was the police! I had been taking a bath in my bedroom. I did not open [the door] because I was afraid. They kicked the door [open] and stormed in. I was naked. So I grabbed a towel and wrapped it around my waist. They headed for the fridge and started breaking my liquor. After this they started to beat me at gunpoint saying "what did we say about selling alcohol without a licence?" What was painful was that I left the house [i.e., was arrested] in my towel and nightie. I left my children; crying; hungry; with nobody to look after then. We see the police as animals . . ..

'Emancipatory spaces'

In such a context where 'all the laws oppress us', the resilience of shebeens serves to offer 'emancipatory spaces' wherein socialising and the consumption of alcohol itself marks an act of resistance and achievement of freedom from the slavery of legal and economic injustice. The chapter now explores this idea through the perspective of the 'everyday relationships and practices', following the work of Latham (2003), of one shebeener and her patrons.

Louise's place

Louise was another of the first people to settle in Sweet Home Farm. She was employed, at first, as a domestic worker. Her digital story tells of an incident that occurred whilst she was at work. A group of young children knocked at the door begging for food; within the group she saw her own child. She recognised that her future necessitated, first, that she earn more money and, second, that she work from home to care for her children. Louise thus set up a small grocery store. But this enterprise failed. She then established a shebeen (see Figure 5.1). The business proved successful, mainly because the value proposition lay not in the products themselves, but in her ability to draw members of her family into the business, to establish a network with other businesses and, most important, to establish a social space where neighbours, friends and acquaintances could coalesce in social solidarity. Louise runs a neighbourhood shebeen. She explained how her customer base 'grew by word of mouth', saying that:

> The youth come especially to play pool here. Friday and Saturday is popular for dancing whilst Sundays are chilled movie days and for [watching] sport. Customers come from far, even as far as Fish Hoek (a middle-class suburb) and lots of "Nigerians" also visit. Additionally, farm workers visit her shebeen early in the morning to fill their 'cooldrink' bottles with 'The Best' [a cheap wine]. She said that whilst most of the customers consume alcohol, many 'simply come for the entertainment of pool, dance and music' (S/W3/18).

The layout of Louise's property is shown in Figure 5.2. The public space of the shebeen comprises the main venue (A) and an external courtyard (B). The

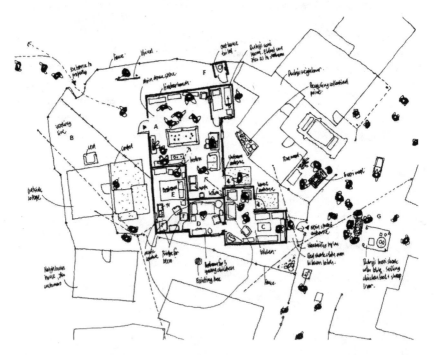

Figure 5.2 Plan view perspective of a 'neighbourhood' shebeen, showing the division between public and private space. Drawing by Thiresh Govender. Used with the author's permission.

private space comprises a lounge and kitchen (C), a bedroom (D) and the main bedroom (E). The patrons and members of the household share the toilet (F) and the urinal located (to the left) along the perimeter boundary. Outside the property, the neighbour operates a BBQ stand (G) selling meat to the shebeen customers. This is one example of the networked economy that link households together in inter-dependence. There are two entrances into the shebeen, one from the north-west (left corner of the diagram) and one (the main entrance) on the east, leading off the track. The shebeen itself thus provides a pathway that connects different places within the settlement. As people pass through the venue along the pathway the shebeen provides a point at which their journey pauses, allowing them a place to sit, engage in conversation or watch the goings-on of the pool table or patrons. Louise sells alcohol through a hatch that connects her lounge to the venue. Apart from providing a point from which she can maintain surveillance over the venue, the lounge and kitchen are culturally detached from the shebeen. The lounge furniture comprises a lounge suit, a coffee table, a television and hi-fi unit and a display unit housing crockery and glassware whilst exhibiting an assortment of ornaments, framed pictures and family photographs. The composition of furniture, fixtures and objects underlines a sense of orderliness and permanence, whilst providing a visual marking of the boundary between public and private space. The epicentre of the shebeen, notwithstanding the public-private space dynamic, is the main bedroom. In this space the bar fridge and the music system are situated. A small window has been built in the corner of the room to allow Louise to maintain surveillance over the venue and react to potentially problematic developments, through, for example, turning down the music volume or restricting beer sales. The significance of her bedroom underlines the social location of the shebeen within her domestic realm. Louise's customers are equivalent to an extended family and her shebeen, whilst public, is in her home. Her influence on the environment helps to provide a safe and relatively protected space for recreation.

In reflecting on the mechanisms she utilises to maintain 'control', Louise considered that 'interacting with customers is the key to safety . . . so that you know what's happening at all times. You cannot just sit in your room, you must observe.' In this respect, the layout of the venue fulfils the strategic objectives of surveillance and management, which includes separating the conversational drinkers from those playing pool or dancing. As she explains:

> There are no dark corners here so we can see everything that goes on, we even have someone who watches the pool table to make sure customers don't steal each other's coins. Then there are people in the community, youth, who keep an eye out for the police and also for unknown skollies (petty gangsters). They let me know when skollies or the police are approaching and I close the business . . . There is a section that some call the "VIP lounge" because it is usually used by people who want a bit more space to drink and leave their beers on the table and relax (S/W3/18).

Whereas the private space in her home is unequivocally restricted to family life and her matriarchal dominance, the space of the shebeen itself belongs in a public realm, beyond her absolute control and subject to subtle negation in which the authorship of the spatial arrangement is both hers and her patrons. The jukebox enables patrons to determine the choice of music. As in most shebeens in Sweet Home Farm, the patrons can influence the seating arrangement through positioning empty beer crates in order to create conversational nodes, both within and outside in the courtyard where on occasion people sit around an open fire. The architecture of the venue is constantly changing, evolving and permeable. Observing a 'responsive agility' within the shebeen architecture, Thiresh Govender (2013, p. 111) writes:

> . . . sophisticated control mechanisms of doorways, hatches and unwritten rules of user and proprietor behaviour guide the interplay between public and private. These thresholds comprise a careful combination of physical, ephemeral and symbolic devices that influence the use of compact space.

Louise (with the assistance of her then boyfriend) has continuously responded to her patrons' needs through restructuring the space; examples include the building of rails on which to place drinks, the creation of a VIP lounge (Figure 5.3), various hand-painted messages, the insertion of windows and the creation of separate

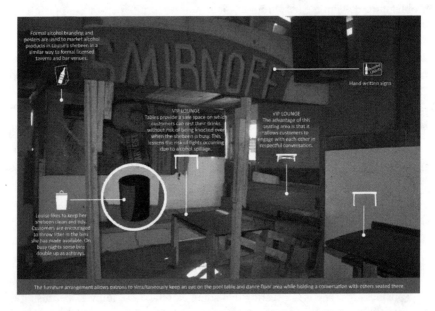

Figure 5.3 Internal seating within the venue, showing the VIP lounge. The use of seating and signs is illustrated. Image supplied by SLF. Used with the author's permission.

toilets for men and women. These responsive shifts have substantially altered the spatial configuration and social environment of the venue over the period between research in the second and third waves (2012–2014).

Creative outcomes

In his study of the leisure economy in Auckland, New Zealand, Latham shows how drinking can have a 'potentially productive element in the creation of social relationships and solidarities', focusing specifically on the coexistence of differences in culture, class, race and sexual orientation (2003, p. 1713). Shebeens are complex social spaces in which these identities are constituted, reproduced and challenged (also see Bonte on drinking spaces in Beirut, this volume). The socialisation that occurs around the shebeen experience is, in the case under consideration, nuanced and negotiated. The social environment varies according to the time of day and the composition of users and states of drunkenness amongst patrons. Shebeen owners, like Louise and Mamaduma, seek actively to influence the social space. One example is the construction of a VIP area in Louise's shebeen, enabling customers to sit away from the physical intensity of the dance floor and pool tables. Among her regular customers is 'Mr. Big', who always sits in the VIP area and dispenses patronage through purchasing drinks for other customers and his friends. Such gestures reduce venue segregation even though the VIP area provides a specific attraction to 'outsiders', including her Mozambican clients that travel from other settlements to 'chill out' at the shebeen on Sundays. The cohesiveness of the environment stands in contrast to scholarly arguments on the profound xenophobic nature of South African townships (see Crush, 2009). Another regular patron is a young transvestite, 'Rhianna', who hangs out with the regulars on Friday and Saturday evenings, entertaining the patrons with camp melodrama and then accompanying his friends to the 24-hour venues in the settlement once Louise shuts her doors. Such are the risks of crime that group drinking is as much about sociability and reciprocity as about ensuring the safety of individuals in moving between venues or going home. Louise told the author that she would never allow any of her regular customers to walk home alone, but would arrange an escort.

Among venues which attract youth, the need to maintain safety in periods of heighted drunkenness is a common objective. A male shebeener, Mr. M, described how he needs to closely monitor and respond to risks of conflict:

> Everyone has a mask on and they may only reveal their true self when it's too late so I do my own surveillance together with another person who is always here ... I confiscate all weapons when I see them until it is time to go home [at which point he returns their weapons]. I guard female patrons when they go out to the urinating passage for their safety. I have banned a trouble maker who broke a bottle on another guy's head; every time I see him I chase him away (S/W3/1).

These challenges are less pronounced in traditional and conversational types of shebeens. For example, Nobesuthu's venue caters specifically to 'older men' (over age 40) and she minimises her risks through closing early:

> I keep my opening times consistent because I am scared of skollies. The last bell rings at 8.30 p.m. . . . My patrons and I often get along. If another [person] comes around too drunk we ask them [to] leave because he will ruin everything for the others. We hardly have any music and when we do its traditional music. Young girls don't like it as much and as a result leave my place (S/W3/8).

Whilst the shebeen owner usually seeks to maintain cohesion within his or her venue, the customers similarly fulfil a role defending their local venue. In Welcome's shebeen, for example, his regular customers have taken it upon themselves to remove patrons who have threatened (physically and verbally) the safety and sociability of the venue and patrons (Field notes, March 2014). It is for this reason that Melissa Watt et al., (2012, p. 1276), in their study of violence against women in township drinking venues, found that 'smaller venues offered female patrons a greater sense of community, which women [patrons] perceived as a sense of protection'. Watt, et al. speculate on whether shebeen closure, as a result of regulatory impulses, will have 'the unintended consequences of forcing female patrons into the riskier environments of larger, unfamiliar venues'.

Conclusion

In this chapter we have sought to advance two claims. Firstly, we have argued that shebeens, whilst complex and contradictory, provide 'emancipatory spaces' in the context of an informal and marginalised settlement. The emancipatory proposition relates to two specific dynamics. First, it relates to the everyday struggles of shebeen owners to survive economically through undertaking a modest business whose success depends on their capacity to create a public space that reinforces cultural practices and social bonds. Second, it relates to the shebeen owners' simultaneous efforts to manage a public social environment that is 'pregnant' with possibilities, both positive and negative, and in its defiance of the alcohol control legislation presents a challenge of 'rogue urbanism' (Pieterse & Simone, 2013). This challenge seeks to thwart the authority of the state to define the terms on which working-class people are permitted to engage in public recreation around the consumption of alcohol. The space of the shebeen venue, in sum, is 'emancipatory' because it provides opportunities for social solidarity and building cohesion amongst people whom the city has excluded through institutional and economic means.

As a further contribution of the chapter, we have focused on subtle strategies through which shebeen owners have sought to mediate and minimise risks. One important strategy is the arrangement of the public space wherein the boundary between public and private is clearly established, whilst the architecture of the venue is constantly shifted and amended through changes to seating arrangements, images and iconography, music control and window positions, as some examples. We have also shown that some patrons, especially in the neighbourhood and conversational venues, are afforded a role in these responsive interactions. Furthermore, the creative outcomes which we discuss represent a challenge to the policy conceptualisations of illegal drinking venues as places and spaces that enhance danger and foster violence. Our argument is not that shebeeners are wholly effective in their endeavours, with the shebeen environment often becoming a 'vector of conflict', having direct and indirect impacts on individuals and the broader community. Some venues, such as those discussed, have potentially and probably been more effective than others in producing creative outcomes. We also recognise that drunken sociability has the potential to be both exclusionary and alienating. Instead, we have sought to illuminate how the struggle of shebeeners to survive and manage public space represents a struggle within a struggle where the overriding influences are those of marginalisation and exclusion. The possibilities for shebeens to become spaces that are 'conducive for health settlements' (Parnell & Pieterse, 2010, p. 158) rests, in part, on the inclusiveness of the poor within the city.

Acknowledgement

The author acknowledges the financial support of the Sustainable Livelihood Foundation. Neither the Foundation nor its funders had an influence on the decision to publish this article or its content. The author acknowledges the contribution of the following researchers: Thiresh Govender, Leif Petersen, Rory Liedeman, Thuli Ntshingila, Bronwyn Kotzen, Alex Cunningham and Khaya Mayile.

Note

1 A full report of these findings can be accessed via the emergentcity portal http://emergentcity.co.za/index2.html

References

Bell, D. 2007. The hospitable city: social relations in commercial spaces. *Progress in Human Geography*, 31: 7–22.
Charman, A. J. E., Herrick, C. and Petersen, L. 2014. Formalising urban informality: micro-enterprise and the regulation of liquor in Cape Town. *Journal of Modern African Studies*, 52(4): 623–646.
Charman, A. J. E., Petersen, L. M. and Govender, T. 2014. Shebeens as spaces and places of informality, enterprise, drinking and sociability. *South African Geographic Journal*, 96(1): 31–49.

Charman, A. J. E., Petersen, L. M. and Piper, L. 2013. Enforced informalisation: The case of liquor retailers in South Africa. *Development Southern Africa*, 1–16.

Charman, A. J. E., Petersen, L. M., Piper, L., Liedeman, R. and Legg, T. 2015. Small area census approach to measure the township informal economy in South Africa. *Journal of Mixed Methods Research*. (Published online before print.)

Chatterton, P. and Holland, R. 2003. *Urban nightscapes: Youth cultures, pleasure spaces and corporate power*. Routledge, London and New York.

Crush, J. 2009. *The perfect storm: The realities of xenophobia in contemporary South Africa*. Migration Policy Series, 50. Southern African Migration Programme.

Crush, J. and Ambler, C. 1992. Introduction. In J. Crush and C. Ambler (Eds.), *Liquor and labour in Southern Africa*. Ohio University Press, Athens.

De Wee, M. 2011. SPCA admits dog crisis in Philippi. *De Burger*. (July 13). http://www.news24.com/SouthAfrica/News/SPCA-admits-dog-crisis-in-Philippi-20110713.

Drivdal, L. and Lawhon, M. 2014. Plural regulation of shebeens (informal drinking places). *South African Geographical Journal*, 96: 97–112.

Faull, A. 2013. Policing taverns and shebeens: Observation, experience and discourse. *SA Crime Quarterly*, 46.

Govender, T. 2013. "Home sweet resilience: Lessons from Shebeens." *Slum Lab. Sustainable Living Urban Model*, 9.

Herrick, C. 2014. Stakeholder narratives on alcohol governance in the Western Cape: The socio-spatial 'nuisance' of drink. *South African Geographical Journal*, 96(1): 81–96.

Herrick, C. and Charman, A. 2013. Shebeens and crime: The multiple criminalities of South African liquor and its regulation. *SA Crime Quarterly*, 25–33.

Herrick, C. and Lawhon, M. 2013. Alcohol control in the news: The politics of media representations of alcohol policy in South Africa. *Journal of Health Politics, Policy and Law*, 38(5): 987–1021.

Herrick, C. and Parnell, S. 2014. Introduction: Alcohol, poverty and the South African city. *South African Geographical Journal*, 96(1): 1–14.

Jayne, M., Holloway, S.L. and Valentine, G. 2006. Drunk and disorderly: Alcohol, urban life and public space. *Progress in Human Geography*, 30(4): 451–468.

Jayne, M., Valentine, G. and Holloway, S.L., 2008. Geographies of alcohol, drinking and drunkenness: A review of progress. *Progress in Human Geography*, 32(2): 247–263.

Jayne, M., Valentine, G. and Holloway, S.L. 2010. Emotional, embodied and affective geographies of alcohol, drinking and drunkenness. *Transactions of the Institute of British Geographers*, 35: 540–554.

Jayne, M., Valentine, G. and Holloway, S.L. 2011. What use are units? Critical geographies of alcohol policy. *Antipode*, 44(3): 828–846.

Koyana, X. 2014. "Residents stone to death suspected rapists." IOL news. 4 March 2014.

La Hausse, P. 1988. *Brewers, beerhalls and boycott: A history of liquor in South Africa*. Johannesburg: Raven Press.

Latham, A. 2003. Urbanity, lifestyle and making sense of the new urban cultural economy. *Urban Studies*, 40(9): 1699–1724.

Mager, A. 1999. The first decade of 'European beer' in Apartheid South Africa: The state, the brewers and the drinking public, 1962–72. *Journal of African History*, 40(3): 367–388.

Mager, A. 2004. 'White liquor hits black livers': Meanings of excessive liquor consumption in South Africa in the second half of the twentieth century. *Social Science and Medicine*, 59(4): 735–751.

Mager, A. K. 2010. *Beer, sociability and masculinity in South Africa.* UCT Press, Cape Town.

Matzopoulos, R., Myers, J., Butchart, A., Corrigall, J., Peden, M. and Naledi, T. 2008. Reducing the burden of injury: An intersectoral preventive approach is needed. *South African Medical Journal*, 98(9): 703–704.

McAllister, P. 2006. *Xhosa beer drinking rituals: Power, practice and performance in the South African rural periphery.* Durham, N.C.: Carolina Academic Press.

Morojele, N. K., Kachieng'a, M. A., Mokoko, E., Nkoko, M. A., Parry, C. D. H., Nkowane, A. M., . . . and Saxena, S. 2006. Alcohol use and sexual behaviour among risky drinkers and bar and shebeen patrons in Gauteng province, South Africa. *Social Science and Medicine*, 62(1): 217–227.

Parnell, S. E. and Pieterse E. 2010. "The 'right to the city': Institutional imperatives of a development state. *International Journal of Urban and Regional Research*, 34(1): 146–162.

Parry, C. D. 2005. A review of policy-relevant strategies and interventions to address the burden of alcohol on individuals and society in South Africa: Original article. *South African Psychiatry Review*, 8(1): 1–20.

Parry, C. D. H. 2010. Alcohol policy in South Africa: A review of policy development processes between 1994 and 2009. *Addiction*, 105(8): 1340–1345.

Peltzer, K. and Ramlagan, S. 2009. Alcohol use trends in South Africa. *The Social Science Journal*, 18(1): 1–12.

Petersen, L. and Charman, A. 2010. Case study: Understanding the local economic impact of the closure of shebeens in the Western Cape as a consequence of the new Western Cape Liquor Act, 2008. *The Small Business Monitor*, 6(1): 102–109.

Pieterse, E. 2009. "Post-apartheid geographies in South Africa: Why are urban divides so persistent." Interdisciplinary Debates on Development and Cultures: Cities in Development – Spaces, Conflicts and Agency. Leuven University 15.

Pieterse, E. and Simone, A. 2013. Introduction. In E. Pieterse and A. Simone (Eds.), *Rogue urbanism: Emergent African cities.* Johannesburg: Jacana.

Province of Western Cape 2008. *Provincial Gazette Extraordinary*, 6582. Thursday, 27 November 2008.

Rogerson, C. M. and Hart D. M. 1986. The survival of the 'informal sector': The shebeens of black Johannesburg. *GeoJournal*, 12(2): 153–166.

Schneider, M., Norman, R., Parry, C., Bradshaw, D. and Pluddemann, A. 2007. Estimating the burden of disease attributable to alcohol use in South Africa in 2000. *South African Medical Journal*, 97(8): 664–672.

Smit, W. 2014. Discourses of alcohol: Reflections on key issues influencing the regulation of shebeens in Cape Town. *South African Geographical Journal*, 96(1): 60–80.

StatsSA. 2012. Census 2011. Sub-pace data available via: http://www.census2011.co.za/.

Turok, I. 2001. Persistent polarisation post-apartheid? Progress towards urban integration in Cape Town. *Urban Studies*, 38(13): 2349–2377.

Valentine, G., Holloway, S. L. and Jayne, M. 2010. Contemporary cultures of abstinence and the night-time economy: Muslim attitudes towards alcohol and the implications for social cohesion. *Environment and Planning A*, 42(1): 8–22.

Watt, M. H., Aunon, F. M., Skinner, D., Sikkema, K. J., MacFarlane, J. C., Pieterse, D. and Kalichman, S.C. 2012. Alcohol-serving venues in South Africa as sites of risk and potential protection for violence against women." *Substance Use and Misuse*, 47(12): 1271–1280.

Winde, A. 2013. 'Binge drinking is killing us and other (sober) truths. Liquor abuse is a national crisis which requires all of us to work together to change drinking behaviour, writes Alan Winde.' *Cape Argus*, 20 September 2013.

Wojcicki, J. M. 2008. 'She drank his money': Survival sex and the problem of violence in taverns in Gauteng Province, South Africa. *Medical Anthropology Quarterly*, 16(3): 267–293.

Chapter 6

'Eat, drink and be merry, for tomorrow we die'
Alcohol practices in Mar Mikhael, Beirut

Marie Bonte

Introduction

'The world is Beiruting again'

In 2011, an advertising panel surrounding the construction site of Zeituna Bay, the new waterfront bordering Beirut's downtown, proudly displayed the sentence 'The world is Beiruting again', taken from a French journal. This sentence echoes what many travel magazines and fashion weeklies have described as the rebirth of the city. Indeed, Beirut has been deeply impacted by the civil war that divided Lebanon between 1975 and 1990 (Kassir, 2003; Fregonese, 2009; Brones, 2010). Thanks to a relative political and economic stability over most of the 2000s decade, Beirut has recovered its strong and diversified nightlife (Kassir, 2003) not unlike the permissiveness that had blossomed during the '50s and the '60s. Now completed, the redevelopment of the waterfront embodies the idea that Beirut is a 'playground' (Khalaf, 2012) where rows of yachts, luxury restaurants and pubs add to the numerous bars and nightclubs of the city.

The 'playground' label, however, is double-edged. On the one hand, the permissiveness of the city and its dynamic night-time economy, as well as providing leisure provisions for Lebanese themselves, has attracted many tourists during the past decade, generating increased economic activity. On the other hand, the playground aspect of Beirut has a cathartic effect. Nightlife often provides an escape, as was the case during the civil war, and as it seems to be for a post-civil war generation that does not believe in a common future. Many troubles – such as the 33-day Israeli war on Hezbollah in 2006, the crisis of 2008 during which the armed opposition forces, in particular the Hezbollah militia, clashed with the government and seized control of a part of Beirut, and the wave of attacks that followed Lebanon's involvement in the Syrian war – have once again plunged the country into great instability. Despite the number of tourists decreasing every year since 2011 and growth in the wider economy slowing down, the night-time economy of Beirut has continued to prosper as people have sought refuge in bars to flee the chronic uncertainty of their country and carry out what Khalaf (2012) has called a 'culture of escapism'.

On studying alcohol in Beirut

To a certain extent, Beirut's nightlife has become more 'Lebanese' over the past years because of the decline in tourism. The city remains sleepless, appropriated at night by revellers who enjoy flows of alcohol and a variety of bars and clubs. Notably, Beirut nightlife is very nomadic. Partying is a fast-changing process that constantly reshapes the boundaries of the urban nightscape as certain bars, clubs and entire districts fall in and out of fashion. Thus, Beirut's bar scene transformed rapidly between 2011 and 2012, with the district of Mar Mikhael emerging as the new nightlife hotspot. In this new nightlife area, other ways of drinking and other patterns of occupying space by drinking emerged. Strikingly, the drinking in Mar Mikhael often takes place in the public space of the street adjoining the bars whereas, in contrast, in other areas of the city, alcohol consumption has generally taken place behind closed doors within drinking venues. This chapter is an attempt to describe and analyze these new ways of drinking as they are situated in the context of Beirut's nightlife and alcohol-related practices. It focuses on the issue of drinking on the street as a way to overcome some social barriers as well as an action that challenges the traditional meaning of Beirut's nightscape.

By studying space through the lens of alcohol, this chapter is part of an ongoing research project exploring night-time leisure in Beirut. It intends to be a contribution to the field of alcohol, drinking and drunkenness which has, in recent years, made considerable advances in relation to geographical understandings of drinking (Jayne, Valentine & Holloway, 2011). Themes such as emotions and affect (Jayne, Valentine & Holloway 2010), as well as the historical geography of alcohol production (Burnett, 1999), pub life and identity have been studied and allow us to understand how space and place shape drinking and drunkenness, and vice versa. Moreover, alcohol consumption has been identified as a main feature of sociality in the city at night (Chatterton & Hollands, 2003; Shaw, 2014). Nevertheless, these advances have invariably concerned drinking spaces in Western countries, where drinking is widely accepted and, despite many controversies, is generally seen as an accepted aspect of European and North American societies. In Lebanon, however, while standards are changing, alcohol consumption is far less central and certainly less widely tolerated. Beirut's case provides, then, a decentering insight into the study of alcohol. It addresses drinking practices in an area where alcohol often refers to a question of morality and respectability. In Beirut, drinking is both linked to leisure time, party and nightlife and refers to morality and visibility. Here, religion and social class are central issues. The location of drinking areas and drinking practices are then partly shaped by this socio-spatial context. The study of the circulation and consumption of alcohol in a district of Beirut reveals that the spatiality of alcohol can be better discussed when taking into account these new territories of empirical investigations.

Flows and encroachments

To question the meaning of new drinking practices emerging in Mar Mikhael, I explore Bayat's (2010) concepts of 'art of presence' and 'encroachments'.

Constructed in a Middle-Eastern context, they refer to the capacity to overcome constraints – here, social and economic constraints – by discovering new spaces within which one can be seen and heard (Bayat, 2010). This 'art of presence' becomes more crucial in times of uncertainty and political violence. More broadly, my analysis of a new drinking territory relies on Mary Lawhon's (2013) socio-material hybrid work on alcohol which positions alcohol as a social construct composed of both the natural resources needed to make it and, importantly, the social and cultural features that are ascribed to it. Thus, Lawhon reframes alcohol through the lens of urban political ecology and considers it as a flow that circulates. From this perspective, alcohol is not already in place but comes into and flows through space via interlinked social, economic and political interactions. By focusing on the process of getting alcohol into drinking places, she further enhances our understanding of alcohol and drinking. The case study of Mar Mikhael then considers alcohol as a socio-material flow in which circulation is shaped by norms and economic processes. Alcohol therefore circulates, continues with consumption and reappears with drunkenness. It creates sociability and transforms the meaning of place by re-configuring social norms in drinking areas.

I base my analysis of the emergence of a new drinking territory on extensive qualitative fieldwork which started in 2011 and focused on Mar Mikhael for a cumulative period of eight months in 2013 and 2014. The study first relies on site observations and second on semi-structured interviews. These interviews involved different kinds of actors: revellers, barmen and pub managers who were between the ages of 22 and 37 at the time of interview. Interviews were complemented by simplified questionnaires conducted in situ among people in the district of Mar Mikhael, with questions relating to drinking practices and attitudes. Further still, the analysis presented in this chapter also draws on a variety of secondary sources, including press articles and content from websites and social networking sites, especially Facebook. To understand how drinking practices and places are mutually constructed, I start the chapter by analyzing drinking patterns at work in Lebanon where alcohol is both welcome and despised, and often consumed in an ostentatious way. I then examine the emergence of the new drinking territory of Mar Mikhael, where drinking can be characterized as vertical and visible, contrasting with the alcohol consumption practices that have long dominated Lebanese drinking cultures. Expanding on this, the analysis concludes with a discussion of the temporary reconfiguration of prevailing norms and standards of behaviours at work and its relevance to wider understandings of the role of alcohol in the social life of Beirut.

Drinking patterns in Lebanon

Sober Lebanon?

The social approach to alcohol, drinking and drunkenness traditionally makes a distinction between countries where alcohol is present and welcome, and countries where alcohol is prohibited. In the latter, countries where alcohol is formally or informally prohibited, sociability shaped by alcohol is officially absent or hidden and finding alcohol is a real challenge. Offering a glass of alcohol is not a standard of hospitality (Gangloff, 2012), with coffee and tea being the drinks most commonly shared socially in public or private places. Problematically, in such countries, there is often no official discourse on moderation. Alcohol is not a public health concern for the state, because it would mean recognizing that alcohol is consumed. It does not mean that alcohol is totally absent but most of the population is abstinent. Indeed, alcohol is sometimes informally and traditionally produced and consumed. Lebanon in general, and Beirut especially, are interesting cases within the Middle-East and among predominantly Muslim countries. They are known for posing great challenges to alcohol producers who want to enter a market where most people do not drink. In some cases, alcohol is forbidden by law, as in Saudi Arabia or Kuwait. In other countries, such as the United Arab Emirates or Qatar, the sale is highly controlled, meaning only foreign residents can buy alcohol, doing so with a specific authorisation and at licensed shops. In countries such as Egypt or Syria, alcohol consumption is not strictly forbidden by law but subject to social prohibition and control, according to standards of morality and respectability. Although matters of alcohol may be addressed ambiguously in the Quran (Chebel, 2009; Amir-Moezzi, 2007) and are such subject of ongoing debate, drinking remains contrary to social rules.

In Lebanon, the sale and purchase of alcohol are legal. Because alcohol is only available in some parts of Lebanon, the country can be considered as *in-between* in that only a part of the population drinks. Two main factors explain this situation. First, as a multi-faith society, Lebanon includes Christian communities for whom alcohol is not prohibited. Indeed, there is a long history of alcohol production and consumption in the form of the traditional production of Arak, a beverage made with distilled grape juice and anise seed. Moreover, Lebanon is generally considered a more permissive country than its neighbours (Kassir, 2003), resulting in a greater availability and visibility of alcohol. These features contribute to the hybridity of people's drinking practices. A survey conducted in 2011 by the World Health Organisation shows that in terms of alcohol consumption, Lebanon is ranked 149th amongst 193 countries. However, this seemingly low ranking should be balanced by other statistics. For example, only 47% of adults consider themselves as abstinent from alcohol (Ghandour, Karam & Maalouf, 2009). This percentage is considerably less than the regional average that amounts to 87.8% of adults. Drinking alcohol is widespread among the student population: 40% of Muslim students who consider themselves as believers are used to drinking alcohol regularly. This rate rises to 89% for non-believers[1]. The population of drinkers in Lebanon is not strictly linked to religion: many people enjoy drinking regardless of their faith. As such, Lebanon produces wine and Arak, and brews its own beer. Hard liquors such as whisky and vodka are imported; the sustained demand is mostly driven by the night-time economy. This observation is not unique to Lebanon: alcohol plays a key role in shaping night-time activities (Chatterton & Hollands, 2003), and its promotion is central to the appeal of spaces at night (Shaw, 2014). Both the night-time and drinking activities are associated with moments of relaxation and friendship, and many people interviewed in Beirut spontaneously associate alcohol with the night-time. Indeed, during field work when the survey question 'What is nightlife for you?' was asked, 63% of people directly responded 'alcohol', 'drinking' or 'getting drunk'.

In Lebanon and in Beirut, alcohol is available in some places and not in other places. The city then can be described as a patchwork of 'wet' and 'dry' territories that reveal the complex geographies of alcohol in Beirut.

Geographies of alcohol and drinking in Beirut

To understand this circulation, I draw on Lawhon's (2013) reading of alcohol in urban environments. She bases her analysis on the understanding of cities coming from urban ecology, which considers cities as spaces of flows (Amin & Thrift, 2002; Castells, 2004). The concepts of circulation and metabolism are useful critical lenses through which to examine the urban environment and geography of alcohol. As a part of urban metabolism, the flow of alcohol in Beirut avoids certain areas and can be redirected to new urban nightscapes. In other words, the process of circulating is socially constructed (Smith, 2006), and the patterns are not always stable but frequently change and are reconfigured. Getting alcohol into a place depends on economic processes, cultural logics or historical legacies. If the circulation of alcohol is influenced by the spatial context, as a socio-material hybrid it is intended in turn to shape spaces and relations. In other words, the flow of alcohol is dynamic, meaning that, as Lawhon (2013, p. 686) suggests, 'the flow does not end with consumption; alcohol also reshapes other flows and relations'.

In Beirut's case, the spatiality of alcohol is linked both to the residential pattern and the urban nightscape. The circulation of alcohol is shaped by the religious-based separation of city. The city is approximately divided into two parts, a Christian section on the east side, and a Muslim one on the west side. Places where Christians and Muslims live together are rather few. This is a special legacy of the civil war during which the two sides were tightly divided through the 'green line' which has formally disappeared now but reappears in urban mobilities (Bonte & Le Douarin, 2014). This patchwork also shapes the flow of alcohol in Beirut, with alcohol more freely available in some areas and more fiercely prohibited in others. For instance, in Dahiya, the Shi'ite Beirut suburb controlled by Hezbollah, selling, buying and drinking alcohol is strictly forbidden, and social pressure is exerted to prevent drinking (Deeb & Harb, 2013). However, this does not mean that residents of such 'dry' districts do not drink as people may cross the immaterial borders to reach Christian areas to have a drink or two, away from the inquisitive gazes and the social control. As a matter of fact, many bartenders interviewed – taking all districts into account – report a significant decrease in consumption during the month of Ramadan.

The circulation of alcohol through the city is also determined by the location of bars, pubs and nightclubs. While this is not to say that alcohol is sold only in pubs and nightclubs, it also being available in supermarkets and grocery stores in Christian areas, it is these nocturnal leisure spaces that are specifically meant to be occupied by drinkers. The social act of drinking takes place in bars, where alcohol is bought, transformed – sometimes admirably by skilful bartenders – and consumed at the same place, shared and is supposed to bring people together. Consequently, the flow of alcohol and Beirut's nightscape are mutually constructed. The flow avoids residential and mainly Muslim areas. There are no pubs in these areas, and the restaurants do not provide alcohol. Alcohol reaches bars, nightclubs and pubs, which are mostly concentrated in a few nightlife areas. The map in Figure 6.1 highlights the nightlife districts in Beirut. The city's downtown includes numerous luxurious restaurants and pubs clustered around Uruguay Street where people sit on terraces, under the gaze of watchmen and valet parking attendants. On the west side of the city, Hamra vaguely reminds onlookers of the street's vibrant history: during the 1960s and until 1975, the district housed pubs and cafés that attracted students, journalists and intellectuals. Today, pubs have flourished once again and they welcome nostalgic young people who idealise the leftist political tradition associated with those places (Dot-Pouillard, 2013). The seafront offers a variety of restaurants where alcohol is available as well as beach clubs that welcome huge parties. On the eastern side of the city, alcohol is available almost everywhere but concentrated in nightlife districts such as Monot, Gemmayzeh and Mar Mikhael which contain a rich variety of drinking places. The circulation of alcohol then follows paths shaped by residential patterns and nightlife areas and ways of drinking are standardized and referred to as *ostentatious drinking*.

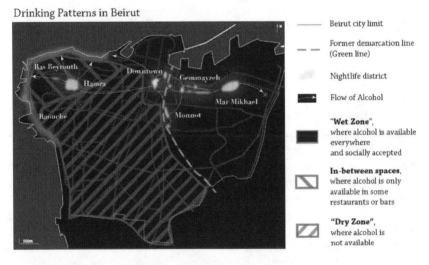

Figure 6.1 Drinking patterns in Beirut. Image supplied by L. Le Douarin and M. Bonte.

Ostentatious drinking

Only a few years after the end of the civil war, Beirut has recovered its strong and diversified nightlife (Kassir, 2003). The city now is on the one hand considered as the paradigm of a violent city that remains divided, and on the other hand as the archetype of the city which rises from its ashes and where partying allegedly has a unifying and cathartic role to play in post-conflict reconstruction and reconciliation. The current nightscape made up of bars and nightclubs is also composed of young and rich partygoers. Despite the greater permissiveness in the city, night-time leisure is less a moment of brotherhood and cohesion than a privilege reserved to a happy few. During the night, one can face a proliferation of real or symbolic barriers which are carefully maintained (Kegels, 2007). The first barrier is economic; the entrance to bars and nightclubs is often free but one must drink for a "minimum charge" that can reach 50 or 60 US dollars (USD) per person which is prohibitively expensive for many customers. Besides this economic consideration, people have to overcome a social or symbolic barrier, embodied by the bouncer or the unwritten nightclub etiquette which, most notably, uses a dress code to ensure only the 'right kind' of patron is granted access. For instance, at the Metis Club on Monot Street, revellers are expected to make reservations. The challenge is to get a table as close as possible to the DJ, in order to watch and show one's central place in the club's social arena. Typically, the women look very glamorous, with heavily made-up eyes, short sparkling dresses and fashioned hairstyles. The men, carefully dressed with designer shirts, arrive in luxury cars which are then left with valet parking. The impression is therefore one of a visible sense of performance, as if going onto a stage. Going out in Beirut, however, often means coming inside, with nocturnal venues if not fully hidden, then featuring a clear and well-maintained separation between inside and outside. Big doors are well guarded and windows are often lacking or obscured. This may be less true for bars and pubs in Hamra or Gemmayzeh where the separation is more tenuous, but it remains clear that having access to Beirut's nightlife is often a privilege.

The word 'ostentatious' used here refers to the way in which drinking is used as a form of social performance as well as a way to display one's wealth. It means that the visibility of what is drunk is more important than the act of drinking itself. It involves in many cases having a table, often itself subject to a 'minimum charge', to which customers order a bottle of wine, vodka, or champagne then brought to the table in a highly visible, and somewhat ritualistic, manner. Drinkers then commonly take group pictures with friends which clearly aim to draw attention to both the well-dressed appearance of the group and of the bottle or elegant and expensive-looking cocktail. Such pictures are evidently produced to be consumed publicly when published on social network sites, allowing others to view the assembled scene of drinks and drinkers. This, of course, does not come cheap. Bottles of wine and spirits may cost hundreds of dollars and the price of champagne at SkyBar, one of the most prominent luxury venues in Beirut, can reach 10,000 USD. On such occasions, the bottle may be delivered with fireworks or with a spotlight following the bartender to the table, both adding to the sense of occasion as clearly heightening the visibility of both the consumer and the act of consumption. Such ostentatious drinking can be considered as being part of what Veblen (1899 [1970]) has called 'conspicuous consumption'. Based on a theory of leisure class, conspicuous consumption refers to people who spend money on luxury products or in luxury venues. These lavish expenditures give an indication of their wealth and social status.

Importantly, ostentatious drinking is not necessarily related to drunkenness. While the kind of alcohol that circulates and the music that is played may be similar to other parties all over the world, behaviours involved by drinking radically change. Going out and drinking, especially in nightclubs, often involves remaining sober. Maintaining a proper behaviour is then essential, partly because the partygoers may know one another or be related in a certain way. Many revellers belong to the Lebanese upper or upper-middle class which is visible but not numerically important. They can be identified as Veblen's 'leisure class' even if they work, because they are, through their financial security, more sheltered from everyday problems than many other city residents experience (this includes unreliable electricity and water supplies, and the high costs of living and housing). Nightlife and particularly drinking are then a display of wealth, excess and waste that can be referred as to 'reckless expenditure' (Bataille, 1967). Ostentatious drinking is productive of social status and distinction (Bourdieu, 1979) both in reference to economic capital and in cultural capital by demonstrating taste in the selection of the venue or of the drinks and by symbolic abilities and embodied practices such as the emphasis on remaining sober and in control. After being a question of morality and visibility, and, by this, a question of place, alcohol is consumed in Beirut as a symbol of wealth and status for a limited group of partygoers.

Mar Mikhael: a new drinking place

From Gemmayzeh to Mar Mikhael

As nightlife in Beirut is a very nomadic process, the flow of alcohol is always about to be redirected to new drinking places. Since 2012, the status of the neighbourhood of Mar Mikhael as Beirut's growing party scene is unanimously acknowledged. This small district, actually made up of one main thoroughfare, the Armenia Street, and narrow surrounding streets, is a mixed residential area. Historically, most of the population living there has been Armenian (Krijnen & De Beukelaer, 2015). In recent years, Mar Mikhael has become home to pubs, restaurants and art places alongside other businesses such as mechanics and industrial shops opened during the day. The attractiveness of the district is partly due to its architecture and so-called 'authenticity'[2], both the cause and result from the process of gentrification[3] that the neighbourhood is facing. This gentrification is characterized as 'creative' even though there is no state politics to assist entrepreneurs or to facilitate the process. Creative industries here refer both to production and marketing of cultural or artistic goods and services (Zouain, Liatard & Fournier, 2011)[4]. The process of bar and pub openings then followed the two waves of installation of creative entrepreneurs. The first wave started in 2008 and comprised pioneers attracted by the low prices and charm of the neighbourhood. A small number of bars and restaurants opened there, for the same reasons, as in the example of Entourage. As a bartender from this venue explained:

> We wanted something bigger. We had a vision . . . At the beginning we just opened during the week-end because people were not used to come here. Now we have regular customers. They like being in the middle of nowhere.
> (R., bartender at Entourage, 18 March 2011)

Some of these pioneers were bartenders in Gemmayzeh, the former trendy place and neighbouring district. For instance, the owner of Torino Express, which is one of the first bars that opened in Gemmayzeh, went on to successfully launch Internazionale in Mar Mikhael. The same process happened with the manager of Charlie's, who opened Sector 75 in 2011, a name referring to 1975 and the outbreak of the civil war, a crucial turning point in Lebanon's history. Those initiatives have been followed by a second wave of openings starting in 2012. Attracted by the area's developing creative industries (Zouain, Liatard & Fournier, 2011), the number of bars and restaurants has increased exponentially in 2013 and 2014 with increased levels of involvement from investors. As such, by the end of March 2014, there were approximately 45 venues in Mar Mikhael; only two months later, five more bars had opened. One important aspect of the speed with which new venues open is the relative ease with which new venues are established as owners take advantage of the weaknesses of state and municipality, often not waiting for the final planning permission agreements before commencing renovation of premises and opening for business. According to the Ministry of Tourism, about three quarters of bars operate illegally (also see Charman, this volume). Often this means that the venue only possesses a license to operate as a restaurant rather than as a bar. While some such venues sell food, many only sell alcohol.

This 'revival' has caused a rapid increase of prices, with rental fees for ground-floor commercial venues nearly tripling since 2011[5]. At the same time, large-scale real estate projects developed (Krijnen & De Beukelaer, 2015) and live alongside other initiatives like the Radio Beirut, the first radio café in the Middle-East which is also a live music venue and a social hub for cultural activities, or 961 Beer, a micro-brewery making original and 'patriotic' beers.

Overflows of alcohol in Mar Mikhael

The 'revival of Mar Mikhael' through the implantation of creative industries redirected the flow of alcohol towards the area. Available in the dozens of bars and pubs settled in the main street or in the adjacent lanes, as well as in the grocery shops which open late, alcohol has changed the social space of the district and its visual aspect. As one interviewee explained:

> It's new now. Two years ago there was only one or two places, one called Entourage.... Entourage was very different; all Mar Mikhael was in Entourage. Just before it closed, two pubs opened, just besides ... For Lebanese people you take your site, your table, you have your drink, your shit ... on your table. Now you take your plastic cup which is definitely not Lebanese. Plastic ... when did they have plastic cups?
>
> (Interview with C.C., 16 July 2013)

In this new drinking territory, about half of the venues are small, cramped bars. They do not have more than three or four tables and a dozen seats. Consequently, during busy periods, customers are standing inside or outside, even crawling across the bar when, as it is most nights, the place is full. In contrast to the closed or at least heavily regulated frontages of the upmarket bars previously described, Mar Mikhael's bars are characterised by their openness: the limit between the street and the interior is very tenuous, if not non-existent. In Mar Mikhael, patrons enjoy wider sidewalks – a rare thing in Beirut – where they can stay without violating the 2012 anti-smoking law that some managers are committed to implementing. Some places do not even have a place to sit, instead offering drinks to 'take-away' in plastic cups. For instance, the Crew Express neighbouring Radio Beirut is a partial self-service venue where customers take beers from large fridges and pay for them at the counter which opens directly onto the street (Figure 6.2).

Figure 6.2 Crew Express, Armenian Street. Photograph by M. Bonte, June 2013.

The openness of such venues is characterised by the absence of doors or wide windows like at Internazionale. It is then quite easy to come and go from the street to the bar, and to walk from bar to bar. Paradoxically, it is also possible to stand at the same place for a whole night and see a very diverse range of people. The Calle pub – at the juncture between Gemmayzeh and Mar Mikhael – takes this principle of an open public drinking space even further. Indeed, the name of the venue, the Spanish translation of 'street', literally signals the spatial configuration as prioritising an openness which crosses over between the venue and the street outside. The street lights, the tags and graffiti on the walls, and the paved floor are elements meant to recreate an external atmosphere inside. Many people surveyed in the street said they appreciate Mar Mikhael for this spatial configuration that allows being outside, drinking, and meeting new people, with one commenting that 'I like it, this is casual', while another explained that 'this is a more friendly atmosphere than in classy pubs, and alcohol is cheap'.

Drinking has indeed become the main purpose for the revellers, and the main nocturnal activity of the area. This feature is claimed by both bartenders and revellers. The owner of one bar described how:

> A bar is made to talk. Here, we don't dance. You have to go to the night-clubs to dance. Here, we drink and laugh.
> (Interview with M., owner of Vyvyan's, 25 March 2013)

The cramped bars have a huge range of alcohol options, from cocktails hastily prepared to beers, or more potent shooters of fashionable branded liquors and spirits such as Jägermeister. Alcohol served in Mar Mikhael is cheaper than in other districts such as Gemmayzeh or Downtown. The prices also decrease during the 'Happy Hours', a period that can extend well beyond a literal hour and continue as late as 11 p.m., where the discount on drinks can amount to 70% of the normal price. People who come to Mar Mikhael then often drink heavily and do what can be called 'vertical drinking'. This way of drinking implies having cheap alcohol in large quantities, in places where there are few or no food options and few seats. This is emphasized by the settlement, that preceded the booming of Mar Mikhael, of three grocery stores that sell alcohol until 3 or 4 a.m. Many customers buy beers individually and drink them outside, on the ground or leaning against the parked cars. Significantly, on Armenia Street drinking is more obviously associated with drunkenness and disorder, meaning that during the busiest periods, a mixed crowd invades the pavements of the avenue, and can be observed singing and shouting and, on occasions, even climbing over cars unfortunately parked there.

The flow of alcohol plays a role in the reconfiguration of this emerging leisure space. As a Christian area that prior to the current nightlife boom boasted enticingly cheap rents and business rates, Mar Mikhael alcohol is consumed in large quantities and according to new standards. As alcohol flows into this space it reappears both in new behaviours such as 'vertical' street drinking and, in turn, plays a role in the creation of a new sense of place. Thus, the sociocultural context of Mar Mikhael both facilitates and is in turn reshaped by the flows of alcohol and the actions of drinkers.

Cheap and cheerful: temporary reconfiguration of social norms

Blurred lines: alcohol and social barriers

The drinking place of Mar Mikhael contrasts with other nightlife districts such as Downtown firstly because of people's appearance. Indeed, the way people are dressed, as well as the way they behave, is noticeably more casual than the more ostentatious presentation of self (Goffman, 1959/1990) previously described. When they come to Mar Mikhael, drinkers wear ripped jeans and have messy hair – sometimes with dreadlocks – and young women trade high heels for more comfortable shoes. Intricate make-up and brushings become scarce and eccentric or neglected outfits predominate. This 'come as you are' aspect of Mar Mikhael was often stressed by customers interviewed:

> Mar Mikhael is a gathering concept. Just wear shorts, and flip-flaps, and get a drink.
>
> (Interview with C.C., 16 July 2013)

These features may be a fashion phenomenon as well, yet they are related to different behaviours. Because of the permissive aspect of the area, and as a result of the real or potential drunkenness, allowed by that permissiveness, manners become more casual. The implicit but strict rules of behaviour observed in nightclubs (Kegels, 2007) seem to have vanished when people sit on the ground (Figure 6.3, A&B), drink a greater quantity of alcohol and sometimes even dare to smoke cannabis joints (a common practice usually strictly confined to private and domestic areas). A more informal atmosphere seems to dominate, where the interactions between fellow drinkers are more direct and uninhibited. Finally, unlike other drinking territories such as Alleway Street in Hamra or Uruguay Street, the music is played at a very acceptable noise level, thus encouraging encounters and conversations amongst friends and between new acquaintances. Thanks to the lower prices, people with more modest incomes can afford drinking there and enjoy the socializing aspect of alcohol. Importantly, while the religious context of Mar Mikhael, being as it is located in a Christian area, is important, some clients appear to prefer going there because of its apparently non-sectarian character[6] (Krijnen & De Beukelaer, 2015). The prominent display of political flags, slogans and posters, almost omnipresent elsewhere in the city, is far less obvious in Mar Mikhael. Moreover, the area is rather far from the predominantly Muslim residential areas where social control towards alcohol may be stricter and where alcohol is almost impossible to find.

Alcohol practices in Beirut 93

Figure 6.3 Drinking outside in Mar Mikhael, Armenian Street. Photographs by M. Bonte, June 2013 and May 2014.

The noisy and messy aspect of Mar Mikhael then provides anonymity that enables drinkers to go out and exhibit themselves without being too exposed. Through its informality, it works like a backspace (Goffman, 1959/1990) which is paradoxically visible. Tellingly, the space allows gay and lesbian people, who in other contexts have to hide their sexual orientation or identity to avoid insult, harassment, denunciation and even arrests, to enjoy a more open expression of their sexual identity. While Beirut's society remains rather homophobic and queer-friendly locations – outside the half dozen expensive bars and nightclubs clearly but not officially labelled as 'gay' – are rather few, in Mar Mikhael, it is not unusual to see men or women holding hands or kissing each other, without being evicted from the bar area. Young boys 'wearing T-shirts, tight jeans and sometimes circumspect make-up' (Merabet, 2004, p. 30), who are clearly recognizable as queer, can also enjoy partying and drinking outside. Through these 'playful deviances' (Redmon, 2003), the small district turns to be a more mixed area that gathers people who usually do not interact with one another, because of their different social or religious backgrounds. Mar Mikhael is therefore a space in which there is a coming together of a far more diverse array of participants than might be witnessed elsewhere in other night-time leisure spaces in Beirut. As a result, Mar Mikhael appears to successfully pull in those drawn by a relaxed, casual and more tolerant atmosphere more reminiscent of the streets of some European capitals. This last assertion refers particularly to Syrian residents or refugees who, by reaching Beirut, can diversify their leisure activities, especially at night. Figure 6.4 illustrates a group of young Syrians having drinks with a group of Lebanese, shouting and laughing. It appears that cheap alcohol and weak social control offer young migrants a window, even temporary, where they can afford, and sometimes be offered, a drink or two.

Figure 6.4 Young Syrian (left) having a drink in Mar Mikhael with a group of Lebanese students. Photograph by M. Bonte, June 2014.

Loud encroachments

The case study of Mar Mikhael finally raises the question of partying and drinking at times of uncertainty. These acts are related to pleasure and fun; at night, the prevailing standards of behaviour are more flexible and social barriers do not totally disappear but become fuzzier. The flow of alcohol changes the meaning of place. Drinking outside appears as an 'art of presence' that challenges the traditional definition of what is a public space and that allows a distinction (also see Wilkinson, this volume).

When they leave the bar for the street, people drink in a space formally considered as public and which is not supposed to accommodate this kind of practice. Indeed and as already mentioned, drinking and particularly drunkenness may be commonplace, yet they belong to private practices and behaviour. In Beirut's society, getting drunk, or for that matter being queer, are often relegated to private practices and behaviours. But in Mar Mikhael, drinkers are no longer protected by the bar that isolated them and ensured social homogeneity and privacy. In other words, they become public because they become visible. The shared drinking space combined with a common 'regime of visibility' (Lévy & Lussault 2003) invite us to reconsider the traditional and normative understanding of public space. Indeed, public space is invariably defined by its accessibility, as an open and shared space – a space accessible by *the public* – that could be a microcosm of society or a site of negotiation and, supposedly in Beirut's case, a site of resolution of differences and reconciliation (Kastrissianakis, 2013). However, some researchers now encourage another approach that considers public space as an urban practice, 'another way of making the city habitable' (Kastrissianakis, 2013). Mostly based on Isaac Joseph's approach of public spaces as places for action that encounter intrusion and are ever-changing (Joseph, 1992), this performative definition tends to multiply the number of spaces called public, as well as they turn to be more disseminated and unstable, never permanently settled and constantly negotiated.

In Mar Mikhael, during the course of the night, revellers transform the street from a place accessible by *the* public to a place made by *a* public. They *made it* public by drinking and by taking up space outside. In other words, they change the place by an 'art of presence' (Bayat, 2010). The concept of 'art of presence' explains how ordinary people change their society or express their discontent not only through active political use of public space like demonstrations, but also rather through ordinary practices of everyday life. Thus, for Bayat (2010) going to university as a woman, selling goods in the street to strive for a better life or, as explored here, drinking in the street are ways in which to imagine how:

> A society, through the practices of daily life, may regenerate itself by affirming the values that deject the authoritarian personality, get ahead of its elites, and become capable of enforcing its collective sensibilities on the state and its henchmen.
>
> (Bayat, 2010, p. 249)

These practices are called 'quiet encroachments' and can make 'oneself heard, seen, felt and realized' (Bayat, 2010, p. 26). In Mar Mikhael, the art of presence lies on drinking in the street and normalizing changing norms and values, and the discontent refers to conflicts in the region, political instability and underlying violence which, put together, create a sense of fear and uncertainty.

Consequently, revellers here by their 'art of presence' infringe upon a daily life which does not always suit them. They first distance themselves from ostentatious drinking, by asserting a cheap and cheerful way of drinking. This performance of drinking outside then becomes a way to stand out from chaos (Kegels, 2007) and a political life from which they feel dispossessed. Drinkers create a place where political neutrality is appealing. For example, one person suggested that 'Mar Mikhael is for people having fun and we don't care about politics. They don't represent us' and another that 'here you have people who fuck life'. The peaceful and merry although quite drunken atmosphere makes Mar Mikhael's drinkers 'the only reasonable people' in Beirut. In other words, this is a distinction (Bourdieu, 1979) which does not happen exclusively in the social space but rather at a political level. This practice is nevertheless visible, noisy and kind of disordered. In Mar Mikhael, noisy drinkers make *loud* encroachments and, by their practice *a priori* commonplace, question and challenge a state of affairs rather than the affairs of the state.

Conclusion

As a part of a wider study on Beirut's nightlife, this chapter was an attempt to consider drinking as a practice and an action which meaning changes in times of uncertainty and violence. The emergence of Mar Mikhael as the new hotspot of a nomadic nightlife, combined with the redirection of the flow of alcohol through the city, changed the drinking practices and the patterns of occupying space by drinking. Vertical and visible drinking contrasts with the dominant ways of consumption and reconfigures the prevailing norms and standards of behaviours. Further, in Mar Mikhael, through loud encroachments, people claim a right to have fun and a right to the party(-ing city). Adopting a geographical and de-centred standpoint, it showed how studying drinking beyond the West deepens our understanding of alcohol as a socio-spatial object. This reshaping may be spatially limited and temporary; however, it shows how ordinary people change or question a state of facts and remains an act, an 'art of presence'.

Notes

1 In Lebanon, the religious community is reported on the identity card before being a question of faith.
2 Indeed, many traditional homes from the '30s survived and sometimes welcome restaurants, such as the Villa Clara hotel or Toto.
3 Understood here in its broad definition, namely 'a socioeconomic and cultural transformation because of middle-class colonization or recolonization of working-class spaces', involving the displacement of 'people with less power and means' (Krijnen & De Beukelaer, 2015).

4 The NGO GAIA-Heritage suggested a typology of creative industries bringing together architecture, design, new technologies, advertising, communication, art galleries.
5 These figures refer to an interview with Karl Sarkis, managing director of Blox Real Estate Services.
6 The Armenian community remained neutral during the civil war, and today, the Armenian districts – which are also huge commercial areas – attract customers from all religions (Khayat in Ghorra-Gobin, 2001).

References

Amin, A. and Thrift, N. 2002. *Cities: Rethinking the urban*, Cambridge: Polity Press.
Amir-Moezzi, M. 2007. *Dictionnaire du Coran*, article « vin », Paris: Bouquins – Robert Laffont.
Bataille, G. 1967. *La part Maudite*, Paris, Ed. de Minuit.
Bayat, A. 2010. *Life as politic: How ordinary people change the Middle East*. Stanford, CA.: Stanford University Press.
Bonte, M. 2011. *Les territoires de la fête à Beyrouth: Innovations nocturnes dans le quartier de Gemmayzeh*. Master's thesis, ENS de Lyon – IFPO Beyrouth, 125 p.
Bonte, M. and Le Douarin, L. 2014. Dans les pas de la nuit: Les rythmes urbains de Beyrouth à la tombée du jour. *Revue des Mondes Musulmans et Méditerranéens*, 136.
Bourdieu, P. 1979. *La distinction: Critique sociale du jugement*, Paris: Ed. de Minuit.
Brones, S. 2010. Beyrouth et ses ruines (1990–2010): Une approche anthropologique. Thèse de doctorat, Université Paris Ouest Nanterre.
Burnett, J. 1999. *Liquid pleasures: A social history of drinks in modern Britain*. London, New York: Routledge.
Castells, M. 2004. Space of flows, space of places: Materials for a theory of urbanism in the information age. In S. Graham (Ed.), *The cybercities reader* (pp. 82–93). London: Routledge.
Chatterton, P. and Hollands, P. 2003. *Urban nightscapes: Youth cultures, pleasure spaces and corporate power*. London, New York: Routledge.
Chebel, M. 2009. *Dictionnaire encyclopédique du Coran*, article « vin », Paris: Broché.
Deeb, L. and Harb, M. 2013. *Leisurely Islam: Negotiating geography and morality in Shi'ite South Beirut*. Princeton, N.J.: Princeton University Press.
Dot-Pouillard, N. 2013. Boire à Hamra: Une jeunesse nostalgique à Beyrouth? In M. Catusse and L. Bonnefoy (Eds.), *Jeunesses arabes: Du maroc au Yémen, loisirs, cultures et pratiques*. Paris: La Découverte.
Fregonese, S. 2009. The urbicide of Beirut? Geopolitics and the built environment in the Lebanese Civil War. *Political Geography*, 28(5): 309–3018.
Gangloff, S. 2012. "Boire en Turquie: Pratiques et représentations de l'alcool dans la Turquie contemporaine, Intervention à l'IFEA, 1 Mars 2012.
Ghandour, L., Karam, E. and Maalouf, W. 2009. Lifetime alcohol use, abuse and dependence among university students in Lebanon: Exploring the role of religiosity in different religious faiths. *Addiction, Society for the Study of Addiction*, 104: 940–948.
Goffman, E. 1990 (1st ed. 1959). *The presentation of self in everyday life*. London: Penguin Books.
Jayne, M., Valentine, G. and Holloway, S. 2010. Emotional, embodied and affective geographies of alcohol, drinking and drunkenness. *Transactions of the Institute of British Geographers*, 35(4): 540–554.

Jayne, M., Valentine, G. and Holloway, S. 2011. *Alcohol, drinking, drunkenness: (Dis)orderly spaces.* Ashgate: Surrey.

Joseph, I. 1992. L'espace public comme lieu de l'action. *Annales de la Recherche Urbaine*, 57–58, pp. 210–217.

Kassir, W. J. 2003. The potential of Lebanon as a neutral place in international arbitration. *The American Review of International Arbitration*, 14: 545-571.

Kastrissianakis, K. 2013. Rethinking public space in Beirut: Competing territorialities and sphere-building since the Ta'if Agreement. Oral presentation, History and Theory of Architecture Research Seminar. University of Cambridge. Feb. 19, 2013.Kegels, N. 2001. In good times or bad? The discourse of national identity of the Lebanese upper class youth. In S. Khalaf and R. Khalaf (Eds.), *Arab youth: Social mobilization in times of risk.* London: Saqi Books.

Kegels, N. 2007. Nothing shines as bright as a Beirut night. *Etnofoor*, 20(2): 87–101.

Khalaf, S. 2012. *Lebanon adrift: From battleground to playground.* London: Saqi Books.

Khayat, T. 2001. Espace communautaire et espace public, comment dépasser la contradiction? In C. Ghorra-Gobin (Ed.), *Réinventer le sens de la ville: Les espaces publics à l'heure globale*, Paris, Montréal, Budapest: l'Harmattan.

Krijnen, M. and De Beukelaer C., 2015. Capital, state and conflict: The various drivers of diverse gentrification processes in Beirut, Lebanon. In L. Lees, H. Shin and E. Lopez (Eds.), *Gentrification, globalization and the postcolonial challenge.* Bristol: Policy Press.

Lawhon, M. 2013. Flows, friction and the sociomaterial metabolization of alcohol. *Antipode*, 45(3): 681–701.

Lee, H. 2009. Mar Mikhael: The new Gemmayzeh? *NOW Lebanon*, August 16.

Lussault, M. 2003. Régime de visibilité. In J. Levy and M. Lussault (Eds.), 2003, *Dictionnaire de la géographie et de l'espace des sociétés* (p. 997). Paris: Belin.

Merabet, S. 2004. Disavowed homosexualities in Beirut. *Middle East Report*, 230: 30–33.

Redmon, D. 2003. Playful deviance as an urban leisure activity: Secret selves, self-validation, and entertaining performances. *Deviant Behavior*, 24: 27–51.

Salem, R. 2010. Tradition in trouble. *The Executive*, September 2, pp. 1–4.

Shaw, R. 2014. Beyond night-time economy: Affective atmospheres of the urban night. *Geoforum*, 51: 87–95.

Smith, N. 2006. Foreword. In N. Heynen, M. Kaika and E. Swyngedouw (Eds.), *In the nature of cities: Urban political ecology and the politics of urban metabolism.* Oxford: Routledge.

Veblen, T. 1899 (1970). *Théorie de la classe de loisirs.* Paris: Gallimard.

Wilson, M. 2005. *Drinking cultures: Alcohol and identity.* New York, Oxford: Berg.

Zouain, G. S., Liatard, F. and Fournier, Z. 2011. Les industries créatives dans la ville: Le cas du quartier de Mar-Mikhayel à Beyrouth. *Travaux et Jours*, 85: 139–185.

Chapter 7

'A force to be reckoned with'
The role and influence of alcohol in Leeds' extreme metal scene

Gabby Riches

Introduction

Despite the amount of attention that has been paid to the ways in which drinking practices influence the construction of identities, expressions of identities and localised authenticities (Spracklen, Laurencic & Kenyon, 2013; Wilson, 2005), the gendered aspects of drinking practices within male-dominated subcultures remain underrepresented. This chapter aims to reveal how alcohol heightens feelings of affect within the Leeds' metal music scene and how it messily intersects with subcultural practices, embodiment, and spaces while also raising important methodological and ethical considerations regarding the consumption of alcohol within subcultural ethnographic fieldwork. The research predominantly focuses on the drinking practices of female metal fans and how it influences their mosh pit experiences. Within existing popular music and leisure studies debates, little attention has been paid to the pleasures women derive from alcohol and the ways in which drinking practices produce a sense of subcultural belonging between men and women (Holloway, Valentine & Jayne, 2009). To address these gaps in the literature I explore female metal fans' drinking experiences and how it affects their participation in male-dominated bodily practices. The chapter illustrates that drinking practices within male-dominated subcultures trouble conventional understandings of risk, marginalisation, transgression and gender when they are felt and performed through the female body.

Drinking beer, raising hell: extreme metal and its transgressive practices

Extreme metal music, which comprises subgenres such as thrash, death metal, black metal and grindcore, is a marginal, transgressive subgenre that remains at the edges of traditional heavy metal culture. Extreme metal scene members position themselves as 'different' and oppositional to mainstream culture through various transgressive practices. Extreme metal transcends conventional musical and discursive boundaries through guttural distorted vocals, down-tuned guitars and exceedingly complex and fast drumming, producing unsettling and unconventional lyrics, song titles and album artwork. However, the scene's transgressive discourses have implications for and are shaped by particular bodily practices. Although extreme metal has typically been associated with bodily excess such as heavy drinking, aggressive dancing and illicit drug use (Frandsen, 2011; Kahn-Harris, 2007), some subgenres and its fans embrace it more than others. Within the Leeds' extreme metal scene the valorisation and celebration of excessive drinking, as part of an embodied heavy metal identity, is evident through musicians having beer on stage during their performances, band lyrics, interactions with metal fans, and empty plastic pint cups strewn across the floor after a gig. Weinstein (2000) notes that the ingestion of large quantities of beer demarcates the corporeal politics of metal, a practice that increases the sense of excitement experienced at live metal concerts and one which closely aligns with the masculine norms, behaviours and discourses of the subculture.

Extreme metal scenes and its practices have been conceptualised as masculinist because they are sites of male domination which construct and reproduce hegemonic performances of masculinity. As men have more access to upward mobility, physical space at gigs, and are seen as 'authentic' subcultural members this reinforces essentialist understandings of gender in which female fans are considered marginal, passive, and inauthentic members (Hutcherson & Haenfler, 2010; Kahn-Harris, 2007; Weinstein, 2000). Similarly, 'excessive' drinking practices have also been aligned with performances of hegemonic masculinity and male bonding that are established through the absence of women (Campbell, 2000; Palmer, 2010). However, compared to mainstream pubs and drinking establishments, female and male metal fans consider metal venues in Leeds to be places to enjoy live music and engage in transgressive practices, and not as 'pick up joints' (Donze, 2010). In this way metal venues are constructed as 'safe spaces' where women can engage in excessive drinking practices and risky bodily comportments (moshing) without the threat of sexual harassment or being propositioned by male scene members. But because metal spaces are male dominated and shaped by masculine and heteronormative discourses, female fans that engage in drinking and mosh pit practices are simultaneously transgressing conventional gender norms of 'appropriate' female behaviour whilst garnering subcultural legitimacy by adhering to the masculine norms of the subculture through alcohol consumption and engaging in physically aggressive practices.

Moshing, another transgressive bodily practice, consists of people slamming into each other and getting swallowed up into the vortex of moving bodies. Drinking and moshing are both transgressive bodily practices and responses to the music and for many female metal fans that were involved in the research, they go hand in hand. Mosh pits are dynamic spaces that emerge and are shaped by the movements of audience members as they sporadically encounter and collide with one another at a live metal music performance. They are socially constructed spaces in front of the stage where head banging, crowd surfing, stage diving, body slamming and aggressive pushing are encouraged and contained. It consists of bodies being touched, pushed, shoved, lifted, carried, caught, picked up and thrown within a disordered, active moving space. Mosh pits are more than just expressions of an alternative identity and world view (Simon, 1997; Tsitsos, 1999); they are entanglements of emotions, physicality, performativities and complex sensations which alcohol consumption can either deflate or heighten. Colliding into bodies in an intimate metal venue, feeling the buzz from alcohol and connecting with the music is an emotional practice that is an important aspect of metal fans' lives, particularly female fans. In this way, emotions allow us to make sense of particular spaces, places and ourselves and these liquored emotions shape and are shaped by our interactions with people and spaces (Hubbard, 2005; Jayne, Valentine & Holloway, 2008b).

Intoxicated, corporeal geographies: the sensuous city of Leeds

Cities can be conceptualised as roiling vortexes of affect. Thrift (2007) points out that despite the pervasiveness of affect as a vital characteristic of cities there has been minimal academic research on the affective qualities of city life. Affect has become a part of how cities are experienced, felt and promoted. Leeds, a postindustrial city in the North of England, is characteristic of the changing 'postmodern' cities in the United Kingdom that have been redeveloped and re-imaged following the shift from industrial to service economies (Bramham & Wagg, 2009). The postmodern city, particularly its urban core, is characterized by diversity, individualized entertainment, hedonistic experiences, consumption and commercialization (Bramham & Spink, 2009; also see Hollands, this volume). During the 1980s and onwards Leeds established its reputation as a 24-hour-city, 'a city that never sleeps', by reinventing itself through extensive refurbishment, pedestrianization and construction of central shopping facilities (Bramham & Spink, 2009, p. 22). This reinvention can be seen as a form of affective engineering (Thrift, 2007) as cities are increasingly expected to have buzzes and atmospheres that make them sensually appealing. In Leeds, these sensual atmospheres are created and sustained by the smorgasbord of drinking establishments that cater to a large student population during the academic year. According to Adams, Moore, Cox, Crowford, Rafaee and Sharpies (2007, p. 201), the city is not merely a 'static visual object, it is a dynamic blend of the built, the demolished, the evolving, the remembered, the sensorial, responding to and changing according to the observer, or rather witness'. The Leeds' metal scene, which operates within the 24-hour city, is saturated with various sensual encounters and sensory opportunities that are highly significant to people's everyday urban experience.

For Jayne, Valentine and Holloway (2011) cities are sensuous, embodied sites of consumption and alcohol use further enhances the city's affective potentiality. Alcohol consumption has become part of the regeneration strategies of urban areas. The Leeds economy can be understood as an economy of hedonistic pleasure, or an 'entertainment economy', that is constantly saturated by emotion, movement and affect. Drinking and drunkenness should perhaps be considered in terms of the connectivities and belonging generated in public space, and as being grounded in pleasures, enjoyment and risk (Jayne et al., 2011; also see Wilkinson, this volume). Through embodied subcultural practices, female and male metal fans carve out spaces for themselves in the city and assert their identities as active, yet marginal, consumers in Leeds. In their research about women's drinking experiences, Jayne et al. (2011) found that the corporeal feelings induced by alcohol are one of the key attractors for women. Similarly, female metal fans find pleasure in the ways that alcohol 'amps' them up, allows them to be more outgoing and sociable, and provides an increase in adrenaline and confidence when participating in male-dominated subcultural practices. Despite the ubiquity of alcohol consumption in metal scenes, the ways in which women subvert traditional performances of femininity and transgress social and subcultural norms through drinking practices have not been examined.

Drinking and moshing can be understood as non-representational practices as they are both performative; they typically generate unpredictable and complex emotions, and the affective experiences they produce are often difficult to articulate. According to Thrift (2007), non-representational theory takes seriously social practices and the spaces which practices open up and acknowledges that the body is essential in understanding our social worlds and ourselves as complex entities. It emphasises practices that cannot adequately be spoken of, that words cannot capture, that texts cannot convey, on forms of experience and movement that cannot be understood in the moment. Using non-representational theory as an analytical and methodological lens is valuable when examining the affective fields of drinking and mosh pit practices because it acknowledges that meanings emerge out of practical contexts. It stresses the importance of practices that we take for granted, that we usually do not think about but always *do* (Anderson & Harrison, 2010). Metal venues, as affective spaces, are emotionally spatialised because they are spaces in which people are emotionally in touch with and open to the world and to the different ways it affects them (Simonsen, 2010). Demant (2013) argues that drinking spaces, like nightclubs or metal venues, should not be understood as stable entities but as assemblages and 'as-if' spaces, full of potentialities as they are continually being shaped and reshaped through affect and embodiment (Thrift, 1996). In this way not only is alcohol consumption performative but also it is an important affective characteristic that demarcates spaces, physical interactions and metal identities.

'Moshography': a sensuous exploration of Leeds' extreme metal scene

This chapter, which is part of a larger doctoral research project, draws upon ethnographic data gathered from 18 months of immersive ethnographic fieldwork in northern England. My research explored the role and significance that mosh pit practices play in the lives of female metal fans and although alcohol consumption was not the focus of the project it became apparent, as I analysed my field notes and transcripts, that drinking practices were central to not only my ethnographic experiences but also to the construction of affective relations within the metal scene. Being a white, heterosexual, single[1], non-British female academic and avid metal fan was advantageous in accessing participants and relevant information about extreme metal discourses and practices. In a male-dominated subculture I was considered 'one of the lads' because I frequently drank ale, enjoyed particular extreme subgenres of metal, engaged in mosh pit practices and dressed less feminine compared with other women in the scene (i.e., baggie hoodie, cargo trousers, un-altered metal shirts, no make-up). Although my Canadian accent and scholarly interests in metal practices exposed me as an 'outsider', my personal feelings about performing and being a metal fan positioned me quite clearly *within* the Leeds metal scene (Hodkinson, 2002). However, my 'outsiderness' and lack of membership affiliations enabled me to interview and interact with a variety of female metal fans who operated in different, and often isolated, social circles within the scene. Throughout my fieldwork I attended more than 100 metal gigs in and around Yorkshire, conducted in-depth, unstructured interviews with 13 male scene members and 26 female scene members between the ages of 21 and 55 years old[2], and spent extensive time with various metal fans and musicians on nights out in pubs, at metal festivals and at various metal venues in Leeds. Many of the interviews took place in well-known pubs within Leeds and I usually offered to buy participants a pint which worked as an incentive for participation and compensation for the interviewees' time and efforts. Furthermore, drinking is a shared practice within the Leeds extreme metal scene so in order to fit in, build rapport, immerse myself in mosh pit practices and gain the confidence to talk with complete strangers I chose to moderately consume alcohol at metal gigs.

Within the discipline of anthropology, interest is growing about the importance of drink to ethnographic experiences and practices. Wilson (2005, p. 6) explains that alcohol, as an elixir of verbosity, is one way in which researchers 'gain confidence, trust, information and access to wider networks through and with the use of alcohol' in different drinking spaces, with various people, and on numerous drinking occasions. For many ethnographic researchers alcohol is considered the most visible, corporeal, affective and significant way in which people express and perform their identities and cultures. It puts people at ease, enhances conviviality, and enables researchers to learn more about their participants (Palmer, 2010; Wilson, 2005). However, studies of male-dominated drinking (sub)cultures conducted by female researchers reveal that gaining access, information and legitimacy are not straightforward processes. Examining the role and importance of alcohol for Australian football fans Palmer (2010) claims that her visible consumption of alcohol, as a deliberate ethnographic strategy, was more important in securing her access to the field and garnering trust from her participants than negotiating with gatekeepers. Within highly intoxicated social environments where women were mostly absent, Palmer had to continually manage and accept sexist discourses and the continuing threat of aggressive male behaviour. For Overell (2014), a female metal music scholar, the choice to drink alcohol whilst conducting ethnographic research at extreme metal shows enabled her access to the affective qualities of 'brutal belonging' which necessitated the valuing and adhering to the ritualistic practices of drinking that male band members and fans engaged in. Both of these accounts illustrate the importance of engaging in the behaviours and practices within the field, even if it muddies the boundaries and roles between researcher and participant. Yet despite the pervasiveness of alcohol consumption within extreme metal scenes (Kahn-Harris, 2007; Overell, 2014; Weinstein, 2000), there have been very few in-depth ethnographic explorations into the ways in which heavy metal drinking practices affect the research process, facilitate access to the field, shape and blur researcher and participant relations, and are inextricably gendered.

For Wood (2012) thinking non-representationally requires the *active* engagement with specific, temporally and spatially defined, practices. Participating in mosh pit practices was an essential way to gain access to the field for both me and my female participants. Because drinking and moshing are both performative experiences, my ethnographic approach is both performative and sensuous. According to Morton (2005, p. 669) performance ethnography attends to the ways in which bodies and sensations reconfigure spaces and time and draws attention to 'the excessive parts of life, of social practices that happen in the *now*'. Spaces and embodied practices are sensual; hence, according to Stoller (1997), sensuous ethnography is about incorporating and being attentive to the smells, textures, tastes and sensations that are felt through the body and recognising that these sensual experiences are critical to our ethnographic understandings within the field. Considering that alcohol is a performative, sensual practice I used my body as a tool of inquiry so I could flesh out the ways in which alcohol, a sense-making practice, produces a sensuous self: 'a performative, reflex, perceptive, intentional, indeterminate, emergent, embodied being-in-the-world' (Vannini, Waskul & Gottschalk, 2014, p. 85). Furthermore, being attuned to all the senses has the potential to enrich our understanding of body-space relationships, and the bodily performances that occurred throughout the research process were significant and told me more than the transcribed interviews (Longhurst, Ho & Johnston, 2008). Similar to leisure practices and gender, drinking practices are learned through bodily and sensory interactions. In other words, the ways in which metal fans learn to behave at metal gigs, handle their drink, come to belong to the scene and negotiate mosh pit spaces are all acquired through the body's sensual repertoire (Evers, 2009). The ethnographic material presented in this chapter is a constructed patchwork of interview data, excerpts from my field notes, photographs and fictional writing which when merged together aim to capture the messy, busy, ephemeral aspects of scenic life in situ. This form of performative writing is a way to get beyond 'representation', a vehicle that offers the reader an entrance into other worlds that are otherwise intangible and inaccessible (Pollock, 1998). In the following sections I bring you, the reader, into the Leeds metal scene to explore how drunkenness works to expand women's spatial positionings within the scene, produces fleeting yet intimate encounters and becomes an important metaphor to articulate the taken-for-granted affective qualities of mosh pit and extreme metal experiences.

'It helps that everyone in the scene drinks': the role of alcohol in the Leeds metal scene

Under the dimly lit street lamp a group of young men gather outside the entrance of the Royal Park pub, cigarette smoke lightly resting above their heads as they chatter over their pints of ale.[3] I make my way into the pub and amongst the regular crowd I spot a few heavy metal fans, leaning over the bar ordering drinks. Their long hair concealing the bar rail as they shove their hands into their pockets to reveal an assortment of coins, the colourful tattoos imprinted on their skin, and their patched vests, studded belts, vulgar band t-shirts and leather jackets stand in stark contrast to the everyday embellishments of the patrons. I order a beer and the foam spills over the lip of the glass, coating my hand in a cold, sticky liquid. I walk towards the back of the pub where the Cellars venue[4] is located. Pulling back on the large black door adorned with metal gig posters, it is the symbolic entrance into the metal underground and before I enter I can already hear and feel the thumping of the kick drum and the electric roar of a guitar riff. Making my way down the narrow, steep, darkened flight of stairs I'm immediately confronted by the pungent stench of urine, beer, stale air and body odour. My shoes stick to the cement floor and the room is cloaked in darkness, with only the stage being illuminated by soft coloured lights which emanate warmth to the long-haired fans below. Suddenly a visceral cacophony of sound erupts, people start colliding into one another, bouncing from side to side, hair is whirling around me, the vibrations rattle my ribcage and I feel electrified. In front of me people hoist their pint glasses in the air, the hairs on the back of my neck begin to rise, my heart beats rapidly, and my clothes are sodden with sweat. Someone plunges their arms into me from behind and I bend sideways like a flower getting battered by the wind. After regaining my composure I look down and realise that half my pint has spilt all down the front of my new metal band t-shirt!

After the band finishes their set I head back upstairs to the bar where a group of metal fans are gathered in a semicircle. I recognise Curtis, who is a well-known promoter and musician within the metal community. He has organised the gig tonight and as a token of my appreciation I offer to buy him a pint. As we wait in the queue I ask him about his initial experiences of getting involved in the scene. Curtis, as he curiously surveys the room, admits that when he first got involved in the scene he would only converse with people he knew at gigs but as he attended and performed at more shows and mingled with a wider group of metal fans, which was facilitated by the consumption of alcohol, people began inviting him around to their houses, parties and other social events. Curtis explains how drinking facilitated opportunities for networking (particularly as a musician) and sociability within the metal scene: 'I think it helps that like everyone in the scene drinks so fucking much [laughs] it's such a social lubricant, you know, and so it's cool like that'. Within the Leeds extreme metal music scene alcohol is used as a tool to transcend social and bodily boundaries, a substance that heightens bodily experiences and facilitates social encounters within the context of the live metal gig. According to Jayne, Valentine and Holloway (2010) alcohol consumption and drunkenness offer ways to solidify a sense of collectivity through the way in which bodies of others are read and encountered. In the metal scene, subcultural legitimacy and collectivity is predicated by conspicuous drinking practices. Early on in my fieldwork I attended a gig at the Cellars and was questioned by two well-known male scene members about why I was drinking water at a gig; I replied shyly 'well, it's a Tuesday night'. They turned to each other with quizzical expressions and chortled, 'So, it's a *metal gig!*'.

For female metal fans, drinking practices take on a more complex role as they constitute performances of alternative femininity and the 'doings' of a metal identity. Paige, an avid thrash metal fan, explains that her identity as a legitimate metal member is closely tied to the fact that she drinks ales, actively listens to metal and confidently participates in mosh pit practices:

> . . . so the fact that, you know, that I drink ales and stuff when I go out and umm the music I like and how involved I get in pits and stuff . . . I sort of have no fear and the way that I talk I'm sort of a force to be reckoned with [laughs] (Paige)

Paige distinguishes herself as a more 'authentic' metal fan by embodying masculine norms such as drinking ale, which for Spracklen et al. (2013, p. 309) is 'still a marker of northern English masculinity', and having no inhibitions towards moshing. Within the context of extreme metal her drinking behaviours are not read as problematic but are essential ways of 'doing' metal fandom intelligibly.

Drunkenness also becomes a language that is used to describe feelings and emotions that are embedded in scenic participation. Mack, who has been a long-time member of the scene and played in punk bands in the late '80s, explains how feelings of drunkenness are not only created through the ingestion of alcohol but also through live musical performances:

> . . . even if you don't drink it's a bit bizarre because if you don't drink, like, I don't drink alcohol now at all and if you don't drink you can still get drunk on the atmosphere and that's a funny thing for people to understand who drink. If you don't drink, the atmosphere . . . it just makes you drunk if you get what I mean, it really does. (Mack)

Mack's statement illustrates the non-representational and affective qualities of the live metal experience, qualities that are considered quite 'bizarre' and 'funny' when one tries to articulate them but become tangible through the metaphor of drunkenness. As metal fans are introduced to new experiences and sensations it creates new embodied metaphors that transform the ways in which they speak about drinking and subcultural practices (Jackson, 2004). In fact, most of the metaphors that we utilise are derived from simple physical and spatial experiences such as drinking (Lackoff & Johnson, 1980). Wilson (2005) argues that because alcohol is one of the most noticeable, emotional and important ways in which people express and display their identities, it becomes a significant metaphor of cultures in which we study and afford a language to describe 'more-than' experiences that are beyond words. The 'more-than-ness' of mosh pit participation is further elucidated by Roxanne, whom I met in the mosh pit at a local gig, when she explains the metaphorical relationship between moshing experiences and feeling inebriated:

> Like, I come away from gigs and I am, I swear to God I'm higher than somebody on a load of ecstasy, like you can *feel* it . . . your heart's beating faster, everything's brighter and you can hear more and it's just you're more alert and you're on that like absolute high, but just from your own energy. (Roxanne)

Here Roxanne is drawing upon the physical metaphor of being 'high' in order to account for the ways in which she experienced different bodily states (i.e., increased heart rate, alertness, enhancement of the senses) almost simultaneously whilst being completely sober. The affective intensities that are felt when one emerges from a mosh pit are physical and emotionally similar to how the body is affected by the consumption of drugs and alcohol. In the next section I focus on the actual practices of consuming alcohol and how they are instrumental to a positive mosh pit experience for female metal fans.

'I just open myself up': female moshers and drinking practices

The clear 2-litre bottle of cheap cider is maladroitly being passed around to outstretched hands bursting forth from the mosh pit. I grab it and take a swig of the bitter warm liquid and pass it to the guy next to me. The band steps on stage and a roar of excitement emerges from the crowd. My head is feeling light and my heart beat quickens because of the increased adrenaline. The pain from the collisions and shoves is masked but I know the bruises will still appear the following day; the mild buzz overpowering my vulnerabilities making me feel confident of launching myself into the chaos, into the moving space of crashing male bodies. I spin around in the pit, oscillating from the edge to the centre. I move, almost weightlessly, around all the areas of the pit, in between all of the heaving, sweating bodies, exploring every spatial contour of the mosh pit. I am shoved into the middle; the venue became a blur as I am caught up in a human game of pinball, my long brown hair assaulting my face as I am pushed in different directions. Immediately the room is humid which heightens the smells of beer, sweaty leather and unwashed bodies. I feel deeply connected to the people around me as we all dance together. As I immerse myself in the turbulence of crashing bodies and take one last mouthful of the cider I allow myself to be moved by this fleeting moment.

I bump into Paige, and before I could even greet her she swiftly puts me into a friendly headlock and we charge around the pit in unison. After a couple of rotations we untangle ourselves and I ask her if alcohol ever affected her participation in mosh pits; she bursts out in laughter and replies:

> I don't think I've got into the pit fully sober! It's like the more you have the more sort of riled up you get, and you get in the pit and stuff. So definitely, the more you had [sic] the more free and easy or the less fear you have. (Paige)

Mosh pits, along with the broader Leeds metal scene, are predominantly male-dominated spaces whereby alcohol use and mosh pit participation enable female metal fans to carve out spaces where they are visible, central and assertive subcultural members. Notably, alcohol consumption expands female fans' spatial positionings within the scene because it allows women to feel invincible, confident and courageous within physically demanding spaces that are usually occupied by men. For female moshers such as Paige, the bodily feelings of being 'riled up' and having less anxiety about the physical impacts of the pit are pleasurable qualities of alcohol consumption that make mosh pit encounters meaningful for women. Most metal fans that I spoke with claimed that positive mosh pit experiences were associated with the *proper* amount of alcohol consumption. Bridget, a female fan from London whom I met at an all-day festival in Leeds argues: 'I think a little bit tipsy is like perfect [laughs] 'cause you know what's going on, you're not just gonna fall over if someone taps you, umm, so you're just kind of buzzing a bit'. Many female metal fans admitted that they actively monitor the amount they drink before entering into mosh pit spaces, which speaks to how moshing has been constructed and naturalised as a masculine arena which is incompatible with the feminine body. There is already an assumption that women do not have the physical capabilities to 'fully' engage in mosh pit practices in which case their presence within these spaces, especially when intoxicated, is seen as highly disruptive. When intoxicated male fans enter into a pit their clumsiness and drunken behaviour is considered a mild nuisance, but when women exhibit public drunkenness in mosh pits they are accused of killing the positive 'buzz' of the pit which strengthens dominant suppositions that women are not 'fit for pitting' because they are fragile, weak and physically inept. In other words, women who do not 'perform' their metal identities and handle their drink appropriately within hegemonic masculine spaces potentially open themselves up to other exclusionary practices that circumscribe their ability to garner subcultural recognition.

I turn towards the band and people suddenly start climbing onto the stage as the floor rumbles beneath us. They remain there for a few seconds, singing, dancing while scanning the crowd for a safe leap. I look over my shoulder and there is still a whirl of moving bodies circling the floor. I see Lottie getting up on stage. She squints, against the stage lights, to observe the formations of the crowd gathering towards the stage. She raises her arms to give the crowd the horns. Quickly she turns her back to the crowd, sticks her arms out to her side, places her feet together and allows herself to fall. As my hands stretch upwards towards the ceiling, I and a couple of others at the front catch Lottie as her feet leave the stage. As we carefully let her down I ask Lottie what it feels like to stage dive and to be in the pit; she responds:

> It's that feeling of [pause] you know that point when you've been drinking you get so drunk that you're completely reckless but not in a dangerous way, you're carefree, everything's fine, but you're still safe. It's [moshing] just like that but with the most brutal beat inside your ribcage that you can imagine. (Lottie)

Lottie's experience highlights how metal scene drinking practices create spaces that can be experienced in out-of-the-ordinary ways, safe spaces that are sustained through relations and sensations, acts and enactments of affective practices and embodiments (Jayne et al., 2010). According to Bissell (2010), affect is uncaptured, an unqualified intensity that pushes the threshold of signification; it goes beyond understanding and conceptualisation. To make sense of the complex and non-representational sensations produced in mosh pit spaces female metal fans draw upon common metaphoric discourses in the scene. The language of moshing often refers to a sense of moving beyond the mundane, and this idea of 'being carefree' and 'reckless' can be considered an expansion of that everyday reality through which metal fans begin to understand the socio-sensual limits of their reality (Jackson, 2004). Lottie's depiction of the mosh pit attends to the 'opening up' of complex spaces that allow for feelings of safety, risk, control and recklessness. Furthermore, alcohol and moshing are both practices that disrupt conventional gendered spatial patterns in metal venues whereby women are part of the action, centralised as active metal fans and thus challenging any peripheral relegations.

I crash into Rhea's tall, slender and heavily tattooed body, the sweat drips off of her skin onto mine; I feed off of her energy, her long black hair thrashes me in the eyes as she head bangs in the pit. I put my arm around her and she leans in to tell me she has not been drinking for more than 2 years and that it has influenced her way of engaging with the music:

> You don't have any reservations when you've been drinking, you just wanna, just like the same as if you went to a nightclub and your friend started dancing because she was the drunkest, it's exactly the same. It's umm [pauses] it's just a different form of movement, I think. But if you're sober, it's more as if the music is stirring up something inside you and you can't just stand still and listen to it, you have to *do* something. (Rhea, emphasis in original)

Rhea's description highlights how drunkenness can also act as an affective contagion in that one can feed on and consume other people's drunkenness and the buzz that that creates simulates the effects of intoxication. Her narrative also reveals the interconnections between affect, movement and sensations: 'Indeed it is often through this movement whereby meaning is coupled with and ascribed to such sensations that affects are felt most tangibly and made more present' (Bissell, 2010, p. 82). It was agreed among most female metal fans that sobriety was seen as a limitation to mosh pit participation and a constraint to intimate encounters with both strange and familiar people. Winona, for example, observes:

> I guess if I was so sober I would probably be more reluctant and I know a lot of people say that drinking plays a part and obviously you get hurt less, and you have less inhibitions, and you feel a bit more warm towards people. (Winona)

Winona's response speaks to the ways in which the effects of alcohol produce feelings of 'closeness' in multiple ways. Importantly, within a male-dominated subculture the ability to feel close and intimate with others is not restricted to male metal fans. When thinking about alcohol and moshing as affective, non-representational practices, it is the use of alcohol that enables a sense of 'openness towards the worlds of others, involving an interweaving of the personal with the social, and the affective with the mediated', providing opportunities for metal fans to intimately engage with friends and strangers in a manner that they may not do if they were sober (Ahmed, 2004, p. 28). Drinking practices unravel bodily boundaries that are perceived and negotiated in emotionally powerful ways. Winona demonstrates that alcohol not only makes her feel warm towards other people at live metal gigs but also alleviates concerns about her ability to mosh in a particular way. Consequently, the effects of alcohol enable her, along with other female metal fans, to 'lose herself' in the moment by transcending 'perceived' bodily limitations.

Last call!

There are diverse and heterogeneous feelings, sensations and experiences involved in the 'intoxicated geographies' of the Leeds extreme metal music scene. For female metal fans alcohol consumption is a way of engaging with different spaces and different bodily practices whilst experimenting with new performances of gendered identities. Not only is moshing a way to meet new people and build meaningful relationships with people in the scene, but also drinking played a role in cementing friendships. Feelings of belonging and social encounters were to a large extent facilitated by alcohol. The interplay between people's engagement in moshing and drinking practices enabled them to overcome social and bodily boundaries, leading to heightened corporeal encounters. According to Jayne et al. (2011), thinking of alcohol consumption in terms of a mode of embodiment and expressive practice transforms the ways bodies connect with other bodies and spaces and how alcohol consumption is an active search to experience certain affects and emotions in specific subcultural contexts. In relation to the Leeds metal scene, this affective sense of belonging is facilitated by bodily proximity in the mosh pit and heightened intensities through the ingestion of alcohol.

Understanding alcohol use through a non-representational lens affords a more nuanced understanding of the role alcohol plays in localised subcultural communities. By focusing on practice, affect and sensations, I was able to illustrate the multidimensional aspects of intoxicated experiences within the scene. It was crucial for me, as a researcher, to immerse myself in the localised drinking and moshing practices because sensuous research generates embodied knowledges. Incorporating my embodied accounts of drinking and moshing whilst highlighting women's experiences in the scene uncovers the ways in which alcohol and moshing are both bodily and collective experiences that have become accepted as social norms, common practices and ways of knowing in the scene. The research sought to address the multidisciplinary gaps by maintaining a gendered focus on the affective and embodied aspects of drinking practices within a subcultural context. Parallel to Jayne et al. (2011) assertion about paying attention to the connectivities and belonging that drinking generates, my research also takes seriously the pleasurable aspects of drinking practices and how drunkenness allows people to interact in ways that are usually deemed unacceptable. The research conceptualises mosh pits as affective spaces because they allow metal fans to experience the sense of being moved, 'riled up' and 'opened up' emotionally through bodily movements, while alcohol amplifies this excitement of encountering other bodies. Drinking and drunkenness within the Leeds metal scene were not confined to the literal but were used as important metaphors to describe the sensual aspects of mosh pit participation. Additionally musical performances, other people's inebriations and the atmospheres produced at gigs were other sources of intoxication. The negotiations made by metal scene members in terms of how much alcohol is suitable for positive mosh pit experiences is illustrative of a knowledge that is gendered, learned, and embodied. This form of embodied knowledge, however, does not immediately dissipate when people leave the metal venue but becomes embedded into the body over time and re-orientates the body's relationship to the everyday world (Jackson, 2004). In this way mosh pit spaces are significant research sites to study drinking practices as they are assemblages of music, movement, bodies and alcohol which produce meaningful corporeal experiences that create new configurations of sensations, social relations and performativities (Thrift, 2004).

Notes

1 I was considered 'single' in the scene, despite being in a long-distance relationship, because I was unaccompanied by a significant other at metal gigs, which helped position me as a more legitimate metal fan by both male and female fans.
2 To protect the identities of all the research participants, pseudonyms have been used.
3 My field notes and accounts of the field are written in the ethnographic present (Fetterman, 1998) in order to enliven and flesh out these ethnographic stories, and to illustrate the bodily and emotional proximity I had to my participants and the data.
4 At the time of the research the Cellars, which was in the basement of the Royal Park Pub, was an active venue but closed its doors at the end of August 2013.

References

Adams, M., Moore, G., Cox, T., Crowford, M., Rafaee, M. and Sharpies, S. 2007. The 24-hour city: Residents' sensorial experiences. *Senses and Society*, 2(2): 201–215.
Ahmed, S. 2004. Collective feelings: Or the impression left by others. *Theory, Culture and Society*, 21(2): 25–42.
Anderson, B. and Harrison, P. 2010. The promise of non-representational theories. In B. Anderson and P. Harrison (Eds.), *Taking place: Non-representational theories and geography* (pp. 1–34). Surrey, UK: Ashgate.
Bissell, D. 2010. Placing affective relations: Uncertain geographies of pain. In B. Anderson and P. Harrison (Eds.), *Taking place: Non-representational theories and geography* (pp. 79–97). Surrey, UK: Ashgate.
Bramham, P. and Spink, J. 2009. Leeds: Becoming the postmodern city. In P. Bramham and S. Wagg (Eds.), *Sport, leisure and culture in the postmodern city* (pp. 9–32). Aldershot, Surrey: Ashgate.
Bramham, P. and Wagg, S. 2009. Introduction. In P. Bramham and S. Wagg (Eds.), *Sport, leisure and culture in the postmodern city* (pp. 1–8). Aldershot, Surry: Ashgate.
Campbell, H. 2000. The glass phallus: Pub(lic) masculinity and drinking in rural New Zealand. *Rural Sociology*, 65(4): 562–581.
Demant, J. 2013. Affected in the nightclub: A case study of regular clubbers' conflictual practices in nightclubs. *International Journal of Drug Policy*, 24: 196–202.
Donze, P. L. 2010. Heterosexuality is totally metal: Ritualized community and separation at a local music club. *Journal of Popular Music Studies*, 22(3): 259–282.
Evers, C. 2009. 'The point': Surfing, geography and a sensual life of men and masculinity on the Gold Coast, Australia. *Social and Cultural Geography*, 10(8): 893–908.
Fetterman, D. M. 1998. *Ethnography: Step by step*. 2nd ed. Applied Social Research Methods Series, Volume 17. Thousand Oaks: Sage.
Frandsen, D. 2011. Living for music, dying for life: The self-destructive lifestyle in the heavy metal culture. In R. Hill and K. Spracklen (Eds.), *Heavy fundamentalisms: Music, metal and politics* (pp. 9–17). Oxford: Inter-Disciplinary Press.
Hodkinson, P. 2002. *Goth: Identity, style and subculture*. Oxford: Berg.
Holloway, S. L., Valentine, G. and Jayne, M. 2009. Masculinities, femininities and the geographies of public and private drinking landscapes. *Geoforum*, 40: 821–831.
Hubbard, P. 2005. The geographies of 'going out': emotions and embodiment in the evening economy. In Davidson, J., Bondi, L. and Smith, M, (Eds.), *Emotional geographies* (pp. 117–134). Aldershot: Ashgate.
Hutcherson, B. and Haenfler, R. 2010. Musical genre as a gendered process: Authenticity in extreme metal. *Studies in Symbolic Interaction*, 35: 101–121.
Jackson, P. 2004. *Inside clubbing: Sensual experiments in the art of being human*. Oxford and New York: Berg.
Jayne, M., Valentine, G. and Holloway, S. L. 2008a. Geographies of alcohol, drinking and drunkenness: A review in progress. *Progress in Human Geography*, 32(2): 247–263.
Jayne, M., Valentine, G. and Holloway, S. L. 2008b. The place of drink: Geographical contributions to alcohol studies. *Drugs: Education, Prevention and Policy*, 15(3): 219–232.
Jayne, M., Valentine, G. and Holloway, S. L. 2010. Emotional, embodied and affective geographies of alcohol, drinking and drunkenness. *Transactions of the Institute of British Geographers*, 35: 540–554.
Jayne, M., Valentine, G. and Holloway, S. L. 2011. *Alcohol, drinking, drunkenness: (Dis) orderly spaces*. Surrey, UK: Ashgate.

Kahn-Harris, K. 2007. *Extreme metal: Music and culture on the edge.* Oxford: Berg.

Lackoff, G. and Johnson, M. 1980. *Metaphors we live by.* Chicago: The University of Chicago Press.

Longhurst, R., Ho, E. and Johnston, L. 2008. Using 'the body' as an 'instrument of research': Kimch'i and pavlova. *Area,* 40(2): 208–217.

Malbon, B. 1999. *Clubbing: Dancing, ecstasy and vitality.* London: Routledge.

McCormack, D. 2008. Geographies for moving bodies: Thinking, dancing, spaces. *Geography Compass,* 2(6): 1822–1836.

Morton, F. 2005. Performing ethnography: Irish traditional music sessions and new methodological spaces. *Social and Cultural Geography,* 6(5): 661–76.

Overell, R. 2014. *Affective intensities in extreme music scenes: Cases from Australia and Japan.* Basingstoke: Macmillan.

Palmer, C. 2010. Everyday risks and professional dilemmas: Fieldwork with alcohol-based (sporting) subcultures. *Qualitative Research,* 10(4): 421–440.

Pollock, D. 1998. Performing writing. In P. Phelan and J. Lane (Eds.), *The ends of performance* (pp. 73–103). New York: New York University Press.

Simon, B. S. 1997. Entering the pit: Slam-dancing and modernity. *Journal of Popular Culture,* 31(1): 149–176.

Simonsen, K. 2010. Encountering O/other bodies: Practice, emotion, ethics. In B. Anderson and P. Harrison (Eds.), *Taking place: Non-representational theories and geography* (pp. 221–239). Surrey, UK: Ashgate.

Spracklen, K., Laurencic, J. and Kenyon, A. 2013. 'Mine's a pint of bitter': Performativity, gender, class and representations of authenticity in real-ale tourism. *Tourist Studies,* 13(3): 304–321.

Stoller, P. 1997. *Sensuous scholarship.* Philadelphia, PA.: University of Pennsylvania Press.

Thrift, N. 1996. *Spatial formations.* London: Sage.

Thrift, N. 2004. Intensities of feeling: Towards a spatial politics of affect. *Geografiska Annaler,* 86(1): 57–78.

Thrift, N. 2007. *Non-representational theory: Space, politics, affect.* London: Routledge.

Tsitsos, W. 1999. Rules of rebellion: Slamdancing, moshing, and the American alternative scene. *Popular Music,* 18(3): 397–414.

Vannini, P., Waskul, D. and Gottschalk, S. (2014). *The senses in self, society, and culture: A sociology of the senses.* New York and London: Routledge.

Weinstein, D. 2000. *Heavy metal: The music and its culture.* Chicago: Da Capo Press.

Wilson, T. M. 2005. Drinking cultures: Sites and practices in the production and expression of identity. In T. M. Wilson (Ed.), *Drinking cultures: Alcohol and identity* (pp. 1–24). Oxford: Berg.

Wood, N. 2012. Playing with 'Scottishness': Musical performance, non-representational thinking and the 'doings' of national identity. *Cultural Geographies,* 19(2): 195–215.

Chapter 8

'Never, ever go down the Bigg Market'

Classed and spatialised processes of othering on the 'girls' night out'

Emily Nicholls

Introduction

Traditionally, women's alcohol consumption has been portrayed through the media and safety campaigns as a threat to femininity (Day, Gough & McFadden, 2004), with excessive drinking in particular threatening women's respectability and positioning them as unfeminine and out of control (Measham, 2002). In more recent years, however, researchers have argued that drinking plays a key role in women's negotiations of pleasure, fun and sexual identities (Sheehan & Ridge, 2001). Women must manage these contradictions through their everyday drinking practices within a wider societal context where there may be tensions around the meanings and scope of respectable femininities and alcohol consumption. Existing research recognises the ways in which positioning themselves as moderate drinkers may allow middle-class young women to consume alcohol without threatening their respectability, while 'othering' the drinking practices of working-class women (Cullen, 2011). However, this chapter argues that the distinctions between respectable and deviant drinking practices are becoming increasingly blurred as young women experience an 'imperative to intoxication' (Griffin, Bengry-Howell, Hackley, Mistral & Szmigin, 2009), meaning they are expected to consume alcohol on a night out, and some degree of drunkenness is expected. Drawing on research comprised of qualitative interviews with 26 young women on the 'girls' night out' in Newcastle upon Tyne, this chapter explores the ways in which participants frequently felt they were treading a fine line between being 'tipsy' and 'drunk'. With the distinctions between respectable and unacceptable drinking more precarious, the data suggests that space has become highly important in managing processes of othering. The most out-of-control drinking practices and behaviour were spatially confined within the 'risky' spaces of the city centre's Bigg Market, and the local, working-class 'Geordie' woman was imagined to embody drunkenness and excess within these spaces. However, the self-identified Geordies frequently resisted these labels through distancing themselves from women who drink in the Bigg Market and engaging in their own processes of othering which distinguished themselves from an 'underclass' characterised by worklessness and violence.

Gender, femininity and respectability

Gender can usefully be theorised as something that women 'do' rather than something they 'are'. Bodies thus become gendered through social and cultural processes. Whilst dimorphic understandings around sex and gender – such as equating femininity with female bodies – have been challenged (Halberstam, 1998), it can be argued that individuals are still expected to perform the characteristics, behaviours and practices associated with 'doing' masculinity or femininity (Rahman & Jackson, 2010) in order to be successfully read as male or female. According to Butler (1990), gender is performative in that bodies become gendered through this continual 'doing' of masculinities or femininities, creating the false impression that gender is fixed and natural rather than something we 'do'.

It is widely recognised that some ways of 'doing' femininity have traditionally been deemed more 'appropriate' than others. Historically, femininity has been associated with passivity, fragility and respectability. Skeggs' (1997) pivotal work around gender and class in the UK explores the ties that have traditionally existed between femininity, sexuality, social class and respectability, where respectability can be associated with control over one's sexual reputation and behaviour (Lees, 1989). Respectable femininity is heavily tied to maintaining control over one's body as well as one's sexuality; as Bordo argues, the feminine body has traditionally been required to be a 'tight, controlled, "bolted down" form' (1993, p. 190).

Yet understandings of femininities and respectability have arguably become more complex in a contemporary British society characterised by supposed gender equality. In a so-called post-feminist society (Valentine, Jackson & Mayblin, 2014), women may more easily be able to access assertive sexual identities based on agency and empowerment (McRobbie, 2007). Whilst such subject positions may appear to mark a positive shift away from the constraints of traditional femininity, it is important to consider any continuities and explore the ways in which traditional conceptualisations may continue to limit the abilities of young women to redefine femininities. For example, Griffin, Szmigin, Bengry-Howell, Hackley and Mistral (2013, p. 186) argue that whilst 'respectability and the importance of maintaining a "good" sexual reputation remain as normative elements of contemporary femininity, this rests uneasily alongside a post-feminist discourse in which young women are also exhorted to be always "up for it"'. This is clearly supported by Jackson and Cram (2003, p. 114), who argue that the continued 'negative labelling of an active, desiring female sexuality' still makes it difficult for such an identity to be safely adopted. Clearly, such debates around contemporary understandings of respectable femininity demand further empirical investigation in terms of what this actually means for the lived experiences of young women within contemporary spaces such as the night-time economy (NTE).

Feminised spaces? The night-time economy

The term *night-time economy* was coined in the 1990s, and further defined in the early 21st century, to reflect the expanding number of bars and clubs concentrated in city centres and predominantly targeting 18- to 24-year-olds (Roberts, 2006). Participating in the NTE has long been recognised as an important component of the lives of many young women (Hollands, 1995), with research demonstrating that there has been an increase in alcohol consumption amongst young women in the UK during the 21st century (Plant, 2008)[1]. Yet such locations have been theorised as the site of a number of contradictory scripts surrounding the participation of women's bodies (Cullen, 2011). The NTE has been conceptualised as an increasingly 'feminised' space, where broader changes in their social positions have allowed women to enter this previously male space (Lyons & Willott, 2008), experiment with different feminine identities (Hutton, 2006) and re-write sexual scripts through shared embodied practices such as collective drinking (Waitt, Jessop & Gorman-Murray, 2011). Drinking has been theorised as a key component of female socialising and the negotiation of fun, sexual pleasure and desire (Sheehan & Ridge, 2001; Jayne, Valentine & Holloway, 2010), and it is increasingly recognised that alcohol consumption is normalised and expected on a night out (Griffin, et al., 2009).

Yet Day et al. (2004, p. 177) argue that the 'long-standing, traditional discourses around femininity and sexuality are still pervasive' and it is important to consider the ways in which the NTE can still be conceptualised as a site of control where young women are expected to conform to certain modes of respectable, heterosexual femininity. Drinking has long been intertwined with women's sexuality and respectability (Brooks, 2008), and excessive consumption has been seen as particularly damaging because it demonstrates a lack of restraint and may undermine women's embodied self-control. As Hey (1986, cited in Meyer, 2010, p. 27) reports, respectable, female identities are heavily tied to self-control, and the voluntary loss of control achieved through heavy drinking may threaten a woman's reputation.

As a result, alcohol can be conceptualised both as a tool to facilitate the construction of positive feminine identities, y*et al*so as a continued threat to respectability (also see Ross-Houle, Atkinson and Sumnall, this volume). It is important to examine the contemporary scripts of respectable femininity and drinking to which young women have access and the ways in which these are reworked through interactions and bodily practices in the NTE. This will aid understanding of the ways in which the embodiment of femininities across contexts might empower or constrain women in a supposed 'post-feminist' era, as well as contribute to knowledges around *who* can access these positive identities and which bodies become excluded or stigmatised. Moving beyond the theoretical debates, what might be the consequences for the young women who negotiate these contradictions in their everyday lives? And are some women more (or less) able than others to buy into different feminine identities in a 'post-feminist' society?

Class and 'othering'

It is widely recognised that respectable feminine identities are not equally available to all women, as processes of 'othering' have traditionally allowed some women to position themselves as respectable compared with others. Othering in this context can be understood as a process whereby some women are able to claim respectable feminine identities by distancing themselves from others who are pushed into 'deviant' categories (Skeggs, 1997). Class-based othering has long been used to maintain a distance from those who are seen as unrespectable (Walkerdine, Lucey & Melody, 2001), attaching negative values and categorisations to the working-class body in order to attribute value to the middle-class body and self. The working-class body is thus typically depicted as excessive (Skeggs, 2005), tasteless and lacking restraint (Lawler, 2005).

It is clear then that ideas of control and restraint – or lack thereof – are crucial in defining who can claim to be respectably feminine, and women's drinking identities are a case in point, with research suggesting that one strategy for managing the tensions around drinking as a threat to women's respectability is to self-identify as a responsible, controlled drinker. As Rolfe, Orford and Dalton, (2009, p. 333) argue, women who drink are required 'to perform a balancing act in order to protect against a stigmatized identity – particularly that of "manly woman", "unrespectable or irresponsible" woman, "addict" or more generally "woman out of control"'. For example, Lyons and Willott (2008, p. 705) report that in discussion groups with young women in New Zealand, the participants' own drinking was connected to fun and pleasure, but other women were positioned as 'problem' drinkers who violated appropriate feminine behaviour through their drunkenness and undermined their respectability through sexual promiscuity. Such processes are frequently classed, with research demonstrating that excessive drinking is often labelled as working-class behaviour (Brooks, 2011).

This chapter draws on qualitative research in the city of Newcastle to explore the ways in which young, middle-class women continued to engage in these classed processes of othering through self-construction as responsible drinkers against the drunken and excessive working-class body of the Geordie, whilst the local, working-class women engaged in similar processes directed against an imagined 'underclass'. However, with the young women often treading a fine line between being 'tipsy' and 'drunk' themselves, processes of othering were also highly spatialised, as participants confined the most problematic drinking practices and behaviours to certain areas.

The girls' night out project: situating the study

The 'Girls' Night Out Project' was a three-year PhD research project funded by the Economic and Social Research Council and based in the city of Newcastle upon Tyne in North-East England. This study involved in-depth interviews with 26 young women aged 18 to 25 who went on 'girls' nights out'[2] in the city, exploring their understandings of the boundaries of 'appropriate' femininity, the ways in which these boundaries were negotiated through embodied practices on the 'girls' night out', and the types of gendered, classed, sexualised and aged identities that were enabled or constrained as a result. Interviews were semi-structured, based around an interview schedule exploring a 'typical' girls' night out and discussing femininities in relation to appearance, drinking practices and risk management. Participants were recruited through a range of methods, including presentations at various university and college sessions, promotion on various Facebook pages and snowballing.

Feminist research calls for a reflexive awareness and recognition of the researcher's own presence within the project, including the way in which characteristics such as researcher gender, class and age may affect the research process (Letherby, 2002). My own position as both interviewer y*et al*so a middle-class young woman who engages personally with the NTE in Newcastle arguably helped to establish rapport and facilitated my position as a non-judgemental peer who could relate to discussions around drinking and dress and possessed relevant local knowledge regarding venues in the city. It could be argued that the more middle-class participants, particularly students, may have felt the most comfortable within the interview setting with a middle-class, university-educated interviewer. However, some of the most animated and in-depth interviews took place with working-class women who self-identified as Geordies. It may be that my participants were able to 'read' my middle-class background through cues such as my accent, but this did not appear to greatly affect my ability to build rapport with most of the young women.

The study's geographical location within Newcastle is of particular interest in relation to both its NTE and the city's classed dynamics. From a past shaped predominantly by industry, authorities in Newcastle have attempted to rebrand it as a cosmopolitan 'party city' and invested heavily in regenerating its NTE (Hollands & Chatterton, 2002). Yet Newcastle can be seen as a city of extremes where despite its attempted reinvention and high student population it remains tied to a strong sense of regional identity 'in the midst of the now decaying remnants of what was a massively productive industrial landscape' (Buckley & Fawcett, 2002, p. 131). This traditional identity is embodied in the local 'Geordie', who remains associated with the historical values of working-class life such as heavy industry, strong local communities and regional pride (Barton, 1990). Whilst prior research by Nayak (2003, 2006) has explored the ways in which Geordie men renegotiate their identities in the post-industrial city through the embodiment of spectacular masculinities defined by excess and heavy drinking, it is also important to examine contemporary feminine identities within this context, particularly as media representations of the Geordie have seen a recent resurgence with the MTV show 'Geordie Shore'. This reality television show following the exploits of a group of Geordie young people is one of a number of 'structured reality' television programmes depicting 'excessive' classed and regional femininities such as the 'Essex girl' or 'Geordie' (Woods, 2014, p. 197). The female cast members are depicted as regularly drinking to excess, displaying a hyper-sexualised femininity and engaging in what might be regarded as 'promiscuous' behaviour, and this may have implications in terms of how contemporary Geordie identities are managed by Geordie women and imagined by others.

In a move away from other research on young people's drinking that — according to Gill, Donaghy, Guise and Warner, (2007) — has tended to focus on heterosexual, student populations (although see Sheard, 2011 for a notable exception), the sample of women was diverse in terms of current circumstances, sexuality and education[3]. The sample was also reasonably diverse in terms of self-identified class background and exactly 50% of the participants were local to the North-East and 50% non-local. Whilst being local, of course, cannot be conflated with being working-class, those who identified as working-class *were* much more likely to be local to the area (75% of all working-class participants), and those identifying as middle class were predominantly from outside Newcastle (88%), possibly because the middle classes may be more likely to have the resources to move away from home for work or study. Participants were asked to self-identify their own class background in order to understand what class the participants *felt* that they identified with. Whilst it is recognised that self-identified class may not always reflect objective class position (Savage, Bagnall & Longhurst, 2001), *perceived* class identity was felt to be more relevant for this study because this factor may affect practices of labelling or othering others. All participants had consumed alcohol in the NTE, although some described heavier consumption levels than others.

Respectable drinkers: moderation and responsibility

Most participants said drinking was an important part of a girls' night out, with several positioning it as a priority. Lydia's reflections on the value of drinking were fairly typical:

> You can't *really* enjoy it unless you've had a couple of drinks. I mean, don't get me wrong, not wasted but, you know, tipsy. If you have to drive on a night out, oh god [sigh] . . . there's no point going, it's just so boring'. (21, middle-class student, straight)

The young women often echoed the idea that there is now an 'imperative to intoxication' (Griffin et al., 2009, p. 463), where *some* alcohol consumption is normalised and expected:

> I'd not say 'oh I'm *not* drinkin' tonight' or 'I'm only gonna have, like, two drinks tonight'. I'd never vocalise that, because then it's like you're not honouring a part of the agreement in going out, which is to get a bit drunk, because 'then you *will* be fun'. (Jessie, 21, working-class non-student, straight)

Here, Jessie argues that getting 'a bit drunk' is seen almost as a compulsory component of going out with female friends. Mirroring recent research, several participants saw alcohol as a tool that could – almost *should* – be used to boost confidence, lower inhibitions and encourage women to 'have a laugh' and 'loosen up' (Jayne et al., 2010). Jessie felt it was important not to draw attention to any attempts to minimise alcohol consumption, and this was echoed by other participants who described the ways in which non-drinking or even limiting consumption was often challenged by friends who pushed them to drink, suggesting that the female friendship group plays a role in policing alcohol consumption. Non-drinkers were often labelled as 'stuck-up' and 'boring' and could even be excluded from friendship groups:

> I've got a friend who doesn't drink as well – she doesn't really come out with wur[4] anymore, I wonder why(!)'. (Nicole, 24, working-class non-student, straight)

Nicole's sarcastic example of the exclusion of her non-drinking friend demonstrates that failure to comply with drinking norms can have real consequences, supporting Griffin et al.'s argument that non-drinking can be 'a source of social exclusion or marginality' for young people (2013, p. 188).

The data clearly suggests that women must manage a pressure to drink within the NTE and 'get a bit drunk'. Yet the young women frequently still had to work to resist some of the negative assumptions around women's drinking by positioning themselves as moderate and responsible drinkers who remained in control of their consumption. There was a general consensus that being 'tipsy', 'merry' or even fairly drunk was generally acceptable, whereas excessive consumption and extreme drunkenness was regarded as unattractive, risky and unfeminine. The need to present a controlled drinking identity was clearly demonstrated by Susie; she very much constructed herself as a moderate drinker who often took responsibility for looking after female friends. Here, she describes her own responsible behaviour in contrast to that of others:

> I just sort of think, you *know*, you get to that point where you think 'I'm really quite drunk, I'm gonna not have a drink for a bit, I'm just gonna dance, or I'll have some water or something'. But some people just don't seem to understand when to stop drinking. And they just keep drinking and drinking and drinking until they're in a pile on the floor. And you just think 'you're an idiot!' (22, middle-class student, straight)

As suggested by Susie – who regards drunken women as 'idiots' – there was a clear consensus that regulating drinking was the responsibility of women themselves, with some participants attributing blame to those who appear visibly drunk in public. Several other participants also positioned themselves as responsible drinkers who were aware of their own limits and knew when to slow down or stop drinking. Interestingly, there were no hard and fast 'rules' about where the limits of drinking should be, and drunkenness was never measured in terms of units consumed, rather through embodied cues such as feeling dizzy or sick, reduced awareness or losing control (see also Guise and Gill, 2007). For most participants, notions of control were absolutely essential in defining where the boundaries between acceptable and unacceptable levels of drunkenness might lie.

Drunkenness and lack of control

The loss of control associated with excessive or irresponsible drinking or drunkenness could continue to represent a threat to respectable, feminine identities, as the drunken female body was frequently depicted as beyond governance and control. Many of the young women recognised the need for the respectable feminine body to remain 'ladylike' and 'in control', arguing that the drunken female body subverts this:

> EN: So why do you think it's not seen as *feminine*, to be drunk?
> I think 'cause you sort of lose control of yourself, and you don't really *care*, you don't hold yourself together as much. And I think, being *feminine* is about being respectable and being *ladylike*. But obviously, when you're drunk, that all goes out the window. (Kimberley, 20, middle-class student, straight)

The drunken woman was frequently described as a 'mess' or a 'state', reinforcing the idea that she lacks control over her disorderly body. The drunken woman may also literally lose control of the boundaries of her own body; for example, through vomiting in the street, exposing herself or being unable to stand:

> I think it looks quite bad when you see young girls that are not in control of themselves whatsoever. And are just, sort of, *crawling* round the streets and being sick. (Jade, 23, working-class non-student, straight)

These bodily consequences of drunkenness were seen as particularly problematic for women; for example, some participants felt that women vomiting or urinating in the street were particularly distasteful and problematic, echoing Cullen's (2011) argument that the corporeality of drunkenness and associated bodily practices such as urinating in public places are seen as more acceptable for men than women (also see Thurnell-Read, 2011).

To a lesser extent, excessive drinking was also depicted by some women as a threat to sexuality and reputation. This functioned in two main ways. Firstly, promiscuous women were assumed to drink more heavily, because they were looking for sexual attention from men. For example, when asked who it was she tended to see who was drunk on a night out, Emma replied:

> ... people that have put themselves out there a bit more. Like, dressed more slutty and stuff.
> EN: So why do you think they tend to be the ones that are very drunk?
> Probably cause they're trying harder to get laid! [laughter]. (20, working-class student, bisexual)

Furthermore, some women argued that heavy drinking was likely to encourage women to engage in more promiscuous sexual behaviour. Most women also argued that drunken women were likely to be regarded as 'easy access' by men (either because they were actively looking for sex or less likely to resist sexual advances). Drunkenness could even be associated with looking 'slutty' or 'tarty':

> Other people definitely do see women, if they've drunk too much, as not feminine . . . sort of *tarty* looking. (Kimberley, 20, middle-class student, straight)

The data suggests that feminine drinking identities on a girls' night out continue to be shaped to an extent by understandings of the feminine woman as restrained and self-denying (Day, 2010), demonstrating the ongoing relevance of previous research suggesting young women do consciously limit and manage their alcohol intake in order to maintain control over their bodies and sexuality. For example, Measham's (2002) term *controlled loss of control* was coined more than a decade ago to describe the desired level of intoxication which many young women strive to achieve through their recreational drug use. The data suggests that this continues to represent the ideal state of intoxication, where drunkenness is acceptable but only up to a point; drinking is used strategically to achieve a desired mental and physical state of fun and relaxation but must still be regulated to avoid excessive drunkenness.

Balancing alcohol consumption levels: 'It could be me'

There was some recognition by the participants that women frequently negotiate a difficult boundary when attempting to position themselves as moderate drinkers, with participants arguing that it can be difficult to find the balance between being too sober and 'overshooting'. Crucially, with young women experiencing the pervasive 'imperative to intoxication' within the NTE, the majority recognised their own precarious position as just a drink or two away from the problem drinker. For example, some of the young women claimed they would not judge drunken women as they recognised that they themselves can find it hard to negotiate the line between being 'merry' and 'too drunk':

> I don't judge women as much, cause I know *I* could be in that situation . . . people buy you *drinks*, you can just . . . you talk about the *line* that you *draw* once you're really drunk. It can happen to anyone. (Christina, 20, working-class student, straight)

Even more commonly, a significant number of participants also claimed that they *had* been in a 'state' before, so would be less likely to be judgemental towards a drunken woman. For example, Joanna's comment of 'we've all been there' was fairly representative of the comments made by the participants in general:

> If somebody is absolutely storming drunk, and she's being sick, and she's all over the place, I think that looks absolutely horrendous. But then I also say to meself, *I* can't talk because that is me on a regular basis. (Nicole, 24, working-class non-student, straight)
>
> Ah, I would probably judge her, but I do it meself, so I've got no room to judge. It's just not attractive if somebody . . . like . . . slurrin' their words, or shouting, or being sick, or god forbid, anything like that! And I think when it's you, and your friends are there, you don't even notice, but when you see it on someone else, it does make you think 'oh my god, am I like that'?! (Megan, 25, working-class non-student, straight)

Both Megan and Nicole have negative reactions to seeing drunken women, describing it as 'absolutely horrendous' or unattractive. Yet both acknowledge that they themselves have been in similar situations. There was also a widespread recognition that a 'double standard' exists whereby women who are drunk are judged much more harshly by others than men:

> . . . you *do* get a lot of people being really *nasty* about women that are drunk and throwing up on the side of the road. Whereas if it's a guy, they're just like 'oh, never mind'
> EN: So why is there that gender difference, do you think?
> I guess it's not seen as very feminine, or it's not very classy, or ladylike, whatever . . .
> EN: So what about it, do you think, isn't seen as classy or ladylike?
> Hmm . . . it's that thing of, like, women are meant to maintain more control over their bodies and their actions in a public place. (Abigail, 24, middle-class student, bisexual)

The foregoing quote clearly establishes the link between the feminine, ladylike body and the maintenance of respectability and bodily control, whilst recognising the way in which a gendered double standard exists to police the drinking practices of women. These examples demonstrate that attempts to 'other' drunken women may not always be simple and clear-cut, as young women recognised the precariousness of their own drinking identities and also acknowledged the existence of a gendered double standard that may police women's drinking in particularly harsh ways. Yet the women still frequently talked about excessive drinking and drunkenness in negative terms themselves and engaged in what Piacentini, Chatzidakis and Banister (2012) term scapegoating to distance themselves from the potentially dangerous subject position of 'problem drinker'. Rather than simply positioning all drunken women as deviant, processes of othering often took place along both classed and spatialised lines. This allowed the young women to confine problematic drinking not just to risky bodies but also to risky spaces, allowing extreme drunkenness and associated behaviour to be contained within certain spaces in the city centre.

The classed and spatialised dynamics of drinking

Class was only sometimes explicitly referenced in the construction of the drunken body, with a small number of participants more openly contrasting the notion of middle-class respectability with the out of control, drunken working-class female body in attempts to distance themselves from undesirable drinking practices and associated behaviours such as being loud or 'rowdy':

> I've never *screamed* down the street. And when you do see that, I normally think it is mainly lower class people that do that. And start fights on the street. I hardly ever see girls fight that are students or my friends. My friends would never fight on a night out, like proper physical. (Alex, 19, middle-class student, straight)

The data supports other research suggesting that the working-class woman may continue to be positioned as potentially beyond the boundaries of respectable femininity by other women, embodying 'the folk devil of the rough, binge drinking woman exhibiting 'out of control' public behaviour' (Rolfe et al., 2009, p. 332). However, whilst class-based othering was overt in the above example, the processes of othering were often more subtle and heavily tied to dynamics of space as well as class. Several of the non-local students in particular tended to attribute heavy drinking to working-class, local women, despite research suggesting that female university students consistently consume more alcohol than their peers who are working (Kypri, Cronin & Wright 2005). 'Locals' or 'Geordies' were positioned as working-class and – crucially – associated with less desirable parts of the city:

> I think you get far less fighting between women in clubs, for example, that would be frequented by students, than down the Bigg Market, for example. Umm . . . and . . . I know I'm stereotyping massively here, but students tend to be . . . from a . . . better background [laughter] . . . than those who are down the Bigg Market. Ummm . . . that sounds kinda bad but [laughter] . . . ummm . . . so I guess . . . a lot of students would be far less inclined to punch someone because they've said something that they don't like. (Susie, 22, middle-class student, straight)

Susie does not mention class explicitly in this extract, although through her hesitations, laughter and the disclaimer of 'that sounds kinda bad' still expresses some discomfort in talking about class even in coded terms (see also Holt & Griffin, 2005). Despite this, class is alluded to in multiple ways here, firstly by the use of 'student' to implicitly represent middle classness. She then argues that students tend to be from a 'better background' than women 'down the Bigg Market', marking out class distinctions between different women. Crucially, a particular space within the NTE is used to reference working-class, local identities. The Bigg Market represents a small area within the city centre with a high concentration of what were widely perceived by most participants to be 'rough' bars and clubs (also see Hollands, this volume). Almost all of the young women mapped the Bigg Market as undesirable and frequented by women who drink too much and engage in violent or out-of-control behaviour, commonly using terms such as 'cheap', 'easy' and 'rough' to describe the venues of the Bigg Market or the people who frequent them. Ally's comment was fairly typical:

> I don't wanna sound really *bad*, that's where the locals tend to go. And the police will be just *all* around there. And you know there'll be *fights* breaking out. (21, does not identify with a class, student, bisexual)

Undercurrents of violence and aggression were almost universally associated with the Bigg Market by most of the participants. Notions of risk and the way in which they intertwine with respectability are key here. Green and Singleton (2006) observed in their own research on risk, safety and leisure with young women in the North-East that processes of othering allowed girl groups to distinguish themselves from others by labelling certain non-respectable young women as 'risky bodies' or 'slappers' who occupy risky spaces on the streets.

These processes also allowed the participants to 'contain' unrespectable and undesirable drinking practices within the Bigg Market; arguably this geographical containment may be particularly important when young women's own respectability is precarious and they risk at times being labelled 'too drunk' themselves. Confining extreme drunkenness and associated promiscuous or aggressive behaviour to these spaces allowed the middle-class drinker to position herself as able to consume alcohol responsibly outside of these risky spaces without threatening her respectability. The, at times intense, focus on the Bigg Market also drew attention away from deviant drinking in other areas, particularly the so-called Diamond Strip on Collingwood Street associated with more 'classy' bars and popular amongst most participants, regardless of class. Despite the local media naming Collingwood Street a 'crime hotspot' and the site of the highest reported number of violent and sexual crimes in the region in 2013 (Doughty, 2014), it is the supposedly problematic drinkers within the Bigg Market who are positioned as hyper-visible. For example, Lydia describes the drinking practices of local women as more 'obvious' and subject to scrutiny, in part because of the spaces they frequent. Abigail also argues that the drinking practices of the working-class woman might be much more visible than those of her middle-class peers:

> You *do* get this thing of 'oh yeah, working-class women go out and are really *messy* and get too drunk and sleep around and stuff'. And middle-class

women do it as well, they just do it in a *different* way. So I guess it's the way that what you're doing *looks*, rather than what you're *actually* doing.
EN: So how would middle-class women do that in a different way?
Going to different *places*, probably. (24, middle-class student, bisexual)

It may not even necessarily be that these women are doing anything differently; rather it is likely that there continues to be a discrepancy in the ways in which drunken women of different classes are judged. Griffin et al. (2013, p. 186) agree that 'the upper class as a whole is not subject to the same level of horrified moral outrage and disgust that has been directed at the drinking practices of white working-class youth'. As Abigail suggests, the working-class woman may remain highly visible in public space, particularly if she frequents some of the more scrutinised spaces of the NTE within the city. To an extent, the middle-class woman can escape this by 'going to different places'. With the drink prices on the 'Diamond Strip' higher than in many of the Bigg Market bars, it may be that some can afford to access particular venues whilst others are priced out of them.

The underclass

Depictions of the drunken Geordie woman frequenting the Bigg Market allowed several of the students to shift problematic drinking identities onto the bodies of others, supporting the idea that dimensions of class are often played out within the NTE through the tensions between locals and students (Holt & Griffin, 2005). The local women were very much aware of the negative connotations others – such as people from 'down south' – might make about their drinking levels and behaviour, which may to an extent reflect the 'Northernisation' of the working-class in popular media (Milestone, 2008). However, they too positioned the Bigg Market as a problematic space. The young women thus resisted constructions of their bodies as deviant through engaging in their own processes of othering. For example, Megan described the women who go out in the Bigg Market as 'rough', and this was very much echoed by other Geordie women, such as Kirsty, who described herself and her sister Nicole as 'working-class, down to earth Geordies'. Kirsty was adamant that she and her sister would never go out in the Bigg Market, establishing a sense of physical distance by claiming that 'they're not the types of people that we would wanna be hanging around with'. Similarly, Nicole claimed that:

> A lot of people I think – down south especially – will look at us and think we're all like the people who are down the Bigg Market . . . which, I'm not being funny but you can tell that a lot of them *don't* have jobs, just from the way they're behaving and what they're dressed in. They're what we would call the underclass. And they're all fighting, and they're all really drunk. I mean, yeah OK, not *all* of them, but I would say the vast majority, if you go down the Bigg Market, you know what you're gonna get. (24, working-class non-student, straight)

Here, Nicole positions women who 'go down the Bigg Market' as 'rough' and more likely to get involved in fights and be 'really drunk', as well as positioning them as visibly different from her friends through the way that they dress and their behaviour. Throughout the interview, she describes the 'underclass' or 'charvers' as defined by generations of worklessness in contrast to hard-working Geordies such as herself. Nayak (2006) reports similar findings in his work on working-class Geordie masculinities, where distinctions were made by participants between themselves as working-class and an underclass of 'charvers' characterised by unemployment and undercurrents of violence. This allowed young men to associate themselves with the 'respectable' rather than the 'rough' wedge of the working-class (Nayak, 2003). Interestingly, some of the most vocal critiques of the spaces of the Bigg Market were the women who identified as working-class Geordies such as Nicole, who often worked the hardest to differentiate themselves from the women who go there. This may be because such women are already positioned as on the boundaries of respectability, so it is more important for working-class women to distance themselves from the drunken female body and the spaces in which she consumes alcohol. Other, recent research in this area also recognises that the spatial dynamics of othering may be particularly important for working-class young women. For example, Griffin et al. (2013, p. 196) found in their pivotal work on young women's drinking practices that working-class women often othered particular localised groups of women who were associated with a particular suburb of the town. In this sense, while young white middle-class women may use classed disgust to distance themselves from non-respectable working-class others, working-class women may engage in similar processes targeted at particular local groups of 'cheap' and 'rough' working-class youth.

Conclusion

Clearly, as Rudolfsdottir and Morgan (2009) argue, alcohol may be a 'friend', but it can be a fickle one, and young women's relationships with drinking can be complex. The young women's accounts suggest that the notion of a 'controlled loss of control' continues to be relevant to female drinkers as they balance the pressure to consume alcohol with the need to present themselves as responsible drinkers (also see Smith, this volume). Thus, whilst *some* alcohol consumption was associated with facilitating fun, lowering inhibitions and 'loosening up', the ideal level of intoxication was very much framed in terms of getting 'tipsy' rather than 'wasted'. This balancing act may reflect wider tensions between more traditional theorisations of suitably feminine behaviour as passive, controlled and respectable and more recent 'post-feminist' arguments that position femininity as a space for agency and sexual assertiveness. In contrast, heavy drinking was positioned as unfeminine behaviour that threatened women's sense of embodied control. With feminine respectability ultimately tied to ideas of restraint and control over the body and sexuality, the voluntary loss of control associated with heavy drinking can still be seen as a threat to respectability brought about by young women as a result of their irresponsible choices.

The data also shows how othering continues to operate along classed lines that allowed some women to position themselves as respectable in contrast to the perceived unruly, drunken working-class women. However, the young women often recognised that they themselves may walk a fine line between being 'tipsy' and 'too drunk' with alcohol consumption now normalised and expected. This may be an example of what Skeggs (2005, p. 969) describes as part of the recent 'crisis' in the boundaries of acceptability, where shifts away from traditional conceptualisations of classed respectability muddy the boundaries of 'good' and 'bad'. Whilst for Skeggs, this crisis is materialised through the extension of sexuality to the middle-class, with middle-class women permitted to be more sexual and talk about sexuality, this 'crisis' could also be applied to shifting understandings in the acceptability of female public drinking. Skeggs argues that the crisis creates a level of ontological insecurity which means that the 'other' needs to be rendered clear and obvious, and the data suggests that processes of othering are taking on important meanings for contemporary young women along not just classed but also spatialised lines. When problematic drinking is largely depicted as confined to Bigg Market venues and the women who frequent them, this allows unrespectable feminine identities to be contained within these geographical boundaries. Such processes of spatialised othering may be particularly important for the working-class Geordie, as her claim to respectability may be more precarious than for her middle-class peers. Associating the Bigg Market with excessive drunkenness, rowdy behaviour and violence allows young women to transfer the label of 'other' onto the 'underclass'. The intense scrutiny of women's drinking practices and associated behaviours within these spaces may focus attention on certain locations whilst allowing women's negotiations of the fluid boundaries of respectability and drunkenness elsewhere in the city to go relatively unchallenged.

Notes

1 However, it is important to note that young women's rates of alcohol consumption may fluctuate, and appear to have plateaued in the early 2000s according to Measham and Østergaard (2009).
2 Characterised as nights out within an all-female friendship group. These typically involved some form of communal drinking at home whilst getting ready as a group, before visiting a few city centre bars and a club.
3 A third of the participants identified as non-heterosexual, including one transgender participant. All women identified as White-British, and two young women were mothers at the time of the study.
4 Geordie term for 'us'.

References

Barton, C. 1990. 'The Geordie joke: The role of humour in the reaffirmation of regional identity.' Master's thesis. Available at http://Etheses.Dur.Ac.Uk/6522/'. Durham University (accessed 12 December 2014).
Bordo, S. 1993. *Unbearable weight: Feminism, western culture, and the body*, London: University of California Press.

Brooks, O. 2008. Consuming alcohol in bars, pubs and clubs: A risky freedom for young women? *Annals of Leisure Research*, 11(3–4): 331–350.

Brooks, O. 2011. 'Guys! Stop doing it!': Young women's adoption and rejection of safety advice when socializing in bars, pubs and clubs. *British Journal of Criminology*, 51(4): 635–651.

Buckley, C. and Fawcett, H. 2002. *Fashioning the feminine representation and women's fashion from the fin de siecle to the present*. London: I. B. Tauris and Company, Limited, Macmillan Distributor.

Butler, J. 1990. *Gender trouble: Feminism and the subversion of identity*, London, Routledge.

Cullen, F. 2011. The only time I feel girly is when I go out: Drinking stories, teenage girls, and respectable femininities. *International Journal of Adolescence and Youth*, 16(2): 119–138.

Day, K. 2010. I. Pro-anorexia and 'binge-drinking': Conformity to damaging ideals or 'new', resistant femininities?. *Feminism and Psychology*, 20(2): 242–248.

Day, K., Gough, B. and McFadden, M. 2004. 'Warning! Alcohol can seriously damage your feminine health". *Feminist Media Studies*, 4(2): 165–183.

Doughty, S. 2014. 'Chronicle crime hotspots: City centre streets most violent in north east'. *Chronicle Live* [online]. Available at http://www.chroniclelive.co.uk/news/north-east-news/chronicle-crime-hotspots-city-centre-7217753 (accessed 27 August 2014).

Gill, J. S., Donaghy, M., Guise, J. and Warner, P. 2007. Descriptors and accounts of alcohol consumption: Methodological issues piloted with female undergraduate drinkers in Scotland. *Health Education Research*, 22(1): 27–36.

Green, E. and Singleton, C. 2006. Risky bodies at leisure: Young women negotiating space and place. *Sociology*, 40(5): 853–871.

Griffin, C., Bengry-Howell, A., Hackley, C., Mistral, W. and Szmigin, I. 2009. 'Every time I do it I annihilate myself': Loss of (self-)consciousness and loss of memory in young people's drinking narratives. *Sociology*, 43(3): 457–476.

Griffin, C., Szmigin, I., Bengry-Howell, A., Hackley, C. and Mistral, W. 2013. Inhabiting the contradictions: Hypersexual femininity and the culture of intoxication among young women in the UK. *Feminism and Psychology*, 184–206.

Guise, J.M.F. and Gill, J.S. 2007 'Binge drinking? It's good, it's harmless fun': A discourse analysis of accounts of female undergraduate drinking in Scotland. *Health Education Research*, 22(6): 895–906.

Halberstam, J. 1998. *Female masculinity*. London: Duke University Press.

Hollands, R. 1995. *Friday night, Saturday night: Youth cultural identification in the post-industrial city*. Newcastle: Newcastle University.

Hollands, R. and Chatterton, P. 2002: Changing times for an old industrial city: Hard times, hedonism and corporate power in Newcastle's nightlife. *City*, 6(3): 291–315.

Holt, M. and Griffin, C. 2005. Students versus locals: Young adults' constructions of the working class other. *British Journal of Social Psychology*, 44: 241–267.

Hutton, F. 2006. *Risky pleasures? Club cultures and feminine identities*. Aldershot, Hampshire: Ashgate.

Jackson, S.M. and Cram, F. 2003. Disrupting the sexual double standard: Young women's talk about heterosexuality. *British Journal of Social Psychology*, 42(1): 113–127.

Jayne, M., Valentine, G. and Holloway, S.L. 2010. Emotional, embodied and affective geographies of alcohol, drinking and drunkenness. *Transactions of the Institute of British Geographers*, 35(4): 540–554.

Kypri, K. Y. P., Cronin, M. and Wright, C. S. 2005. Do university students drink more hazardously than their non-student peers? *Addiction*, 100(5): 713–714.

Lawler, S. 2005. Disgusted subjects: The making of middle class identities. *The Sociological Review*, 53(3): 429–446.

Lees, S. 1989. Learning to love: Sexual reputation, morality and the social control of girls. In Cain, M. (Ed.), *Growing up good: Policing the behaviour of girls in Europe* (pp. 19–37). London: Sage Publications.

Letherby, G. 2002. Claims and disclaimers: Knowledge, reflexivity and representation in feminist research. *Sociological Research Online* [Online], 6, 4, Available: http://www.socresonline.org.uk/6/4/letherby.html (accessed 10 December 2014).

Lyons, A., C. and Willott, S. A. 2008. Alcohol consumption, gender identities and women's changing social positions. *Sex Roles*, 59: 694–712.

McRobbie, A. 2007. Top girls? Young women and the post-feminist sexual contract. *Cultural Studies*, 21(4–5): 718–737.

Measham, F. 2002. 'Doing gender' – 'doing drugs': Conceptualizing the gendering of drugs cultures. *Contemporary Drug Problems*, 29(1): 335–373.

Measham, F. and Østergaard, J. 2009. The public face of binge drinking: British and Danish young women, recent trends in alcohol consumption and the European binge drinking debate. *Probation Journal*, 56(4): 415–434.

Meyer, A. 2010. 'Too drunk to say no': Binge drinking, rape and the Daily Mail. *Feminist Media Studies*, 10(1): 19–34.

Milestone, K. 2008. Urban myths: Popular culture, the city and identity. *Sociology Compass*, 2(4): 1165–1178.

Nayak, A. 2003. Last of the 'real Geordies'? White masculinities and the subcultural response to deindustrialisation. *Environment and Planning D: Society and Space*, 21(1): 7–25.

Nayak, A. 2006. Displaced masculinities: Chavs, youth and class in the post-industrial city. *Sociology*, 40(5): 813–831.

Nayak, A. and Kehily, M. J. 2006. Gender undone: Subversion, regulation and embodiment in the work of Judith Butler. *British Journal of Sociology of Education*, 27(4): 459–472.

Piacentini, M. G., Chatzidakis, A. and Banister, E. N. 2012. Making sense of drinking: The role of techniques of neutralisation and counter-neutralisation in negotiating alcohol consumption. *Sociology of Health and Illness*, 34(6): 841–857.

Plant, M., L. 2008. The role of alcohol in women's lives: A review of issues and responses. *Journal of Substance Use*, 13(3): 155–191.

Rahman, M. and Jackson, S. 2010. *Gender and sexuality*. Cambridge: Polity Press.

Roberts, M. 2006. From 'Creative city' to 'no-go areas': The expansion of the night-time economy in British town and city centres. *Cities*, 23(5): 331–338.

Rolfe, A., Orford, J. and Dalton, S. 2009. Women, alcohol and femininity: A discourse analysis of women heavy drinkers' accounts. *Journal of Health Psychology*, 14(2): 326–335.

Rudolfsdottir, A. G. and Morgan, P. 2009. 'Alcohol is my friend': Young middle class women discuss their relationship with alcohol. *Journal of Community and Applied Social Psychology and Sexuality*, 19: 492–505.

Savage, M., Bagnall, G. and Longhurst, B. 2001. Ordinary, ambivalent and defensive: Class identities in the north-west of England. *Sociology*, (35)4: 875–892.

Sheard, L. 2011. 'Anything could have happened': Women, the night-time economy, alcohol and drink spiking. *Sociology*, 45(4): 619–633.

Sheehan, M. and Ridge, D. 2001. 'You become really close . . . you talk about the silly things you did, and we laugh': The role of binge drinking in female secondary students' lives. *Substance Use and Misuse*, 36(3) 347–372.

Skeggs, B. 1997. *Formations of class and gender: Becoming respectable*. London; Thousand Oaks, Calif.: Sage Publications.

Skeggs, B. 2005. The making of class and gender through visualizing moral subject formation. *Sociology*, 39(5): 965–982.

Thurnell-Read, T. 2011. Off the leash and out of control: Masculinities and embodiment in eastern European stag tourism. *Sociology*, 45(6): 977–991.

Valentine, G., Jackson, L. and Mayblin, L. 2014. Ways of seeing: Sexism the forgotten prejudice?. *Gender, Place and Culture*, 21(4): 401–414.

Waitt, G., Jessop, L. and Gorman-Murray, A. 2011. 'The guys in there just expect to be laid': Embodied and gendered socio-spatial practices of a 'night out' in Wollongong, Australia. *Gender, Place and Culture* 18(2): 255–275.

Walkerdine, V., Lucey, H. and Melody, J. 2001. *Growing up girl : Psycho-social explorations of gender and class*. Basingstoke: Palgrave.

Woods, F. 2014. Classed femininity, performativity, and camp in British structured reality programming'. *Television and New Media*, 15(3): 197–214.

Chapter 9

Young people's alcohol-related urban im/mobilities[1]

Samantha Wilkinson

Introduction

Drawing on mixed methods qualitative research I conducted over the course of a year (September 2013–2014) in Wythenshawe and Chorlton, suburban areas of the city of Manchester, UK, this chapter explores young people's alcohol-related im/mobilities in, and through, various non-commercial spaces. Such analytical foci are needed because, as Holloway, Jayne and Valentine (2008) contend, the contemporary geographical imaginary of drinking is predominantly one of a city center issue – typified by a large body of work on the night-time economy. Prolific writers on the night-time economy, Hollands and Chatterton (2003), argue that many young people's desires for fun, hedonism and predictability are fulfilled through themed, mass, commercially oriented nightlife. Elsewhere, Chatterton and Hollands (2002, p. 95) explore 'urban playscapes'; that is, young people's activities in bars, pubs, clubs and music venues in the night-time economy. According to Hollands and Chatterton (2003), this mass provision of mainstream venues offers a safe, predictable space which is therefore popular with young people.

Academics, then, have been somewhat fixated with drinking practices and experiences in specific venues (Holloway, Valentine & Jayne, 2009). However, researchers have begun to engage with drinkscapes young people carve out for themselves. For instance, in a review of the effectiveness of street drinking bans in the UK, New Zealand and Australia, Pennay and Room (2012) contend that young people may prefer drinking in streets, perceiving licensed premises to be restricting in multiple ways relating to size, smell, noise, permissible behaviour and type of entertainment provided. Moreover, based on research conducted into the influence of marketing and subculture on young people's street drinking behaviour in Scotland, Galloway, Forsyth and Shewan (2007) argue that street drinking is less physically and socially restricting than consuming alcohol in commercial premises. Further, Townshend (2013, p. 158) explores young people's experiences of drinking in parks in North-East and South-East England. The author contends that whilst drinking in parks is a widespread practice amongst young people, many young people disapprove of this behaviour, labelling it 'trampy' or 'chavvy'.

Moreover, it is worth acknowledging Robinson's (2009) ethnographic study into young people's use of free space for alcohol and other drug use. The author contends that the appeal of the street lies in the fact that it is free in commercial terms and free in terms of close control.

It is not only outdoor spaces that young people create as drinkscapes, but also indoor spaces. For instance, Barton and Husk (2014) move towards an understanding of pre-drinking beyond cost as the single explanatory factor. Pre-drinking (also termed *pre-loading, pre-gaming, front-loading* or *prinks*, see Gee, Jackson & Sam, 2014) is the practice of intensive drinking in a pair or group preparatory to a night out, often involving drinking games (Bancroft, 2012). Barton and Husk (2014) seek to promote some of the more sociable and convivial aspects of pre-drinking sessions. The authors contend that young people enjoy pre-drinking at home because they can shape the affective atmospheres of the drinking space, for instance, by manipulating the soundscape through the type of music played (for the role of music also see Riches, this volume).

Whilst praising the above-mentioned work for going some way towards redressing the academic preoccupation with pre-formed drinking venues, I agree with Jayne, Valentine and Holloway (2008) who suggest that the ways in which spaces and places are fundamental constituents of experiences of alcohol, drinking and drunkenness have largely operated in a theoretical vacuum. I echo Jayne, Gibson, Waitt and Valentine's (2012) contention that drinking spaces have largely been treated as static, fixed, bounded terrains, thereby failing to engage with young people's movements in, and through, drinkscapes. This chapter therefore makes two notable contributions. First, it seeks to enhance understandings of the spaces within which young people consume alcohol, with a focus on the suburban micro-geographies of streets, parks and homes. Second, it draws on mobilities theory to elucidate young people's alcohol-related movements, in and through, such spaces. Before doing so, however, I outline the context of the research, geographically and methodologically.

Research context

I now provide a brief overview of the case study locations. Wythenshawe, a district eight miles south of Manchester city centre, was created in the 1920s as a Garden City in an attempt to resolve Manchester's overpopulation problem and 'depravation' in its inner-city slums. Wythenshawe continued to develop up to the 1970s. However, the 1980s and 1990s saw steady decline, high unemployment, decaying infrastructure, crime and drug abuse problems (Atherton, Baker & Graham, 2005). The population of Wythenshawe increased from 66,000 in 2001 to more than 70,000 in 2007 (Wythenshawe Town Centre, 2013). Wythenshawe has commonly been labelled one of the largest council housing estates in England (The Guardian, 2012). Wythenshawe wards have a resident White population that is above 90%; this compares with 23.2% of the population being from Black and minority ethnic communities across Manchester as a whole (Manchester City

Council, 2011). The area is thus dominated by White working-class drinking cultures. There are distinct neighbourhoods within Wythenshawe, along with a town centre with various shops, supermarkets, hairdressers, pubs and a club. Wythenshawe is several miles from Manchester city centre, and faced with relatively poor transportation links (Lucas, Tyler & Christodoulou, 2009).

Chorlton is a residential area approximately five miles from Manchester city centre, with a population of circa 13,500 people (Manchester City Council, 2012). It is described by Manchester City Council (2014) as a cosmopolitan neighbourhood with traditional family areas alongside younger, vibrant communities. The area has good road and bus access to, and from, the city centre, and is situated within easy access to the motorway network (Manchester City Council, 2014). Drawing on Manchester City Council's (2012) data: in 2011, pupils living in Chorlton achieved much higher educational results than the Manchester average. The percentage achieving five GCSEs A*-C was 69.5% in Chorlton, compared with 57% for Manchester's average. Chorlton has a higher proportion of minority ethnic residents compared with Wythenshawe, and compared with the national average (19.1% compared with the national average of 11.3%). As of November 2011, private residential property in Chorlton accounted for 90.3% of all property in the ward, much higher than the city average of 68.7%. In 2009, Chorlton had a much lower proportion of children under the age of 18 in poverty than the Manchester average (10.3% compared with 39.9%). However, Chorlton still has pockets of deprivation which are often underestimated by the council (Chamberlain, 2012). Because of the increasing number of bars and restaurants in Chorlton, a pub watch scheme has been initiated (Young, 2011).

These two case study locations were chosen because the differing socio-economic status of Wythenshawe, compared with Chorlton, and the varying micro-geographies within the wards, was intended to provide an interesting comparative analysis. Notably though, whilst young people from Wythenshawe and Chorlton often differ in the types of commercial spaces they frequent, non-commercial spaces seemed to be equally important to young people living in both case study locations and seemed to transcend class and other demographic differences. That said, young people from Wythenshawe and Chorlton sometimes articulated different reasons as to *why* these spaces were important for their drinking experiences.

In total, 24 young people were recruited for multi-stage qualitative research. In some respects, the sampling strategy was purposive, as I aimed to recruit 20 young people from each case study location, and aimed for an equal gender distribution. I recruited most participants through gatekeepers at local schools, community organisations, youth clubs and universities. To reach potential participants, I also: distributed flyers and business cards to houses and businesses in both case study locations; posted on discussion forums concerning both areas; used Twitter and Facebook to promote my study to locals from each area; and arranged to be interviewed by the host of a local radio station. Some young people were initially cautious about participating in my study, because of worries about others finding out about their drinking practices. By building trust and friendship with participants (Valentine, 2013), these participants could then tell their friends about the study and, from their first-hand experience, reassure friends that confidentiality and anonymity are strongly abided by. This is recognised as a snowballing sampling technique.

I had a palette of methods to utilise, and made it clear to the young people that they could 'opt in' to whichever method(s) they wished. As Holland, Renold, Ross and Hillman (2008, p. 19, emphasis in original) argue: 'by enabling young people to choose *how* they wish to communicate with us we recognize them as social actors and begin to move our practice away from adult-centric procedures'. The methods included in-depth interviews, peer interviews, written drinking diaries and drawing elicitation interviews. Many of these methods are deemed to be 'child-friendly' (Punch 2002, p. 321) and are commonly employed in research with young people (see, for instance, Harris, Jackson, Mayblin, Piekut & Valentine, 2014), perhaps reflecting that the terms 'children' and 'young people' are often used interchangeably (Weller, 2006). However, I assert that this conflation is problematic as it overlooks that young people have different experiences of space and place compared with children. The uniqueness of young people's lives means, just as with children, a special suite of methods should be in place to explore their lives.

Recognising this, I complemented the previously mentioned methods with: 1) text messaging (whereby I asked participants to send me text messages during the course of their nights out/in involving alcohol, thereby providing a present-tense snapshot of their alcohol-related im/mobilities) and 2) 'go along' mobile phone interviews (which involved asking young people to take photographs and videos during their nights out/in using their mobile phones, and, at a later date, to navigate through their mobile phones using photographs and videos as oral catalysts to tell me about their drinking experiences). These novel and fun methods were positively received by young people, and proved to be a culturally credible means of researching their alcohol-related geographies. Further, I conducted 'go along' mobile (auto)ethnographic participation, in which I accompanied young people on their nights out/in involving alcohol as they accessed drinking venues, outdoor drinkscapes and homes. During ethnographic participations, I consumed a small amount of alcohol; this 'true participation' enabled me to gain 'corporeal knowledge' (Joseph & Donnelly, 2012, p. 364) of young people's alcohol consumption experiences. I speculate that being a young researcher (in my twenties) may have been advantageous in some respects. To explain, my age relative to those participants younger than myself is lower than that of an older researcher, and participants perhaps perceived me as being more 'like them', and thus were possibly more willing to divulge their drinking experiences and practices.

With regard to analysing interviews, peer-interviews, diaries, text messages and ethnographic field diaries, I adopted the manual method of coding by pen and paper, perceiving that computer-assisted qualitative data analysis distances researchers from the data (Davis & Meyer, 2009). Initially, following Miles and Huberman's

(1994) three-stage model, a process of data reduction occurred, whereby I organised the mass of data and attempted to meaningfully reduce this. Second, I undertook a continual process of data display in the form of a table. Third, I undertook a process of conclusion drawing and verification. With regard to analysing sketch maps/photographs/videos, emphasis was placed on the narratives of participants accompanying their products, in the form of drawing elicitation interviews, and 'go along' mobile phone interviews. This chimes with Barker and Smith's (2012) contention that the interpretation of images should be undertaken with participants to ensure that their intended meanings are explored, rather than interpretive meanings given by the researcher. These data forms were thus also analysed utilising Miles and Huberman's (1994) aforementioned procedure. Participants are featured in this chapter through pseudonyms, so as to conceal their identities. Yet, in order to contextualise quotations, ages and locations are given.

Diversity of drinking spaces

According to Townshend and Roberts (2013), the success of government measures prohibiting young people under age 18 from entering pubs, bars and clubs means that, whilst underage drinking in licensed premises is not so much of a prevalent issue, unsupervised alcohol consumption by young people is now more concealed, occurring either in parks or private homes. Along similar lines, Valentine, Holloway and Jayne (2010) briefly note that young urbanites consume alcohol in arenas in which adult rules can be transgressed with greater ease, including church yards, bus shelters, outside of youth clubs, parks and streets. Importantly, through an exploration of alcohol consumption in informal spaces in rural Cumbria, UK, Valentine, Holloway, Knell and Jayne (2008) make it clear that drinking in informal public spaces is not only something done by underage drinkers; those over 18 years old who live in small towns and villages and have negligible access to commercial premises after the pubs close also consume alcohol in spaces such as scenic view shelters, cemeteries and parks. Throughout my research, young people, from both Wythenshawe and Chorlton, spoke of three non-commercial spaces that are particularly important to their drinking experiences. These included streets, parks and homes. Each of these spaces is now explored, respectively.

As Gough and Franch (2005) recognise, for many young people, the street is an important meeting space, and often the only autonomous space they are able to carve out for themselves (see also Bonte, this volume). Indeed, the street was an equally important drinking space for young people in my study, from both research sites. Coinciding with findings from Galloway et al.'s (2007) study, whilst exclusion played a role in decisions to drink outside, my findings show that the street has a distinct allure over commercial premises for some young drinkers. This can be seen through the contentions of Richard and Jake below:

> If you drink out on the street and that you can see new people and ask them to join . . . There's no closing times. You can do what you want, when you want. (Richard, 15, Chorlton, drawing elicitation interview)

> It was just obviously, that's where you used to like being when you were younger, it was good, you had fun. You can throw up wherever you want innit, just do what you want. (Jake, 18, Wythenshawe, peer interview)

For Richard, the attraction of the street is due to the potential it offers for serendipitous encounters, and also the flexibility afforded because, unlike commercial premises, the space is open 24/7. For Jake, one of the appeals of drinking in streets is due to the freedom it affords to show tangible evidences of embodiment, by being physically sick. Further, ethnographic participations showed me that the street is popular for young people's experimentations with alcohol because it is a relatively casual drinking space; that is, some young people spend all night there, whilst others may 'pop along' for a few minutes. This notion of flexibility lends credence to the appeal of the street noted by Lieshout and Aarts (2008). The authors contend that streets are spaces where 'no strings are attached' (Lieshout & Aarts, 2008, p. 501). Following on from this, the street is appealing for young people because they can leave whenever they wish, without offending someone; they can move to another spot if the space is no longer fun or exciting, or if they do not like the people there.

Additionally, consuming alcohol on the streets offers an alternative to other more costly socialising opportunities (see Elsley, 2004), such as drinking in bars, pubs and clubs. On this point, Galloway et al. (2007) make evident that many young people cannot afford to spend an entire evening drinking in commercial premises. This was the case for participants in my study, from both Wythenshawe and Chorlton:

> Getting towards the end of the month so won't go to a club or anything tonight as I'm skint[2]. Probs just hang around the streets? (Olly, 17, Wythenshawe, text message)
>
> Yeah, it's really bloody expensive drinking in pubs all the time. That's why I'd rather just drink around here. The streets are cheaper and some of the best times I've had. (Amy, 18, Chorlton, interview)

For Olly and Amy, the appeal of street drinking seems, in part, to lie in its cost-effectiveness. This resonates with findings from other studies. For instance, Galloway et al. (2007) found that drinking in outdoor spaces allows drinkers a chance to pre-drink on relatively cheap alcohol prior to entering pre-formed drinking venues later in the evening. Further, Demant and Landolt (2014), in the context of Zurich, Switzerland, explore alcohol consumption on the street within the vicinity of nightclubs. The authors recognise that, during a night out, young people frequently exit and (re)enter clubs to drink the less expensive alcohol they have hidden outside on the streets. Further, something not typically recognized in the extant literature, is the rhythmic nature of the street as a drinking space. Yet, from Olly's comment, one can see that drinking spaces have rhythms. That is, commercial premises are popular with young people when they have recently been paid from their jobs. Yet, throughout the month, streets may increase in popularity as young people's disposable income decreases. As the comments from Olly and Amy illustrate, far from 'transgressing the moral geography of everyday behavior' (Dixon, Levine & McAuley, 2006, p. 197), young people sometimes drink in streets because of being priced out of commercial venues.

As with streets, my findings showed that parks were popular drinking spaces for young people from both research sites. Interestingly though, for young people from Wythenshawe, drinking seemed to be the main reason why they frequented parks, whilst for young people from Chorlton, drinking was part of a broader repertoire of activities they engaged in. This can be gleaned through the comments from Jim and Max below:

> The park is good because you can get loads of people in there, there used to be like hundreds of people who go there, so they all use to go there, in one big park, at night drinking. (Jim, 15, Wythenshawe, peer interview)
>
> In the summer we'd meet up on the weekends, and people would like bring a barbeque and drink a bit then, just with music and hanging out, maybe play football, stuff like that, so it was just part of a big day out at the park. (Max, 23, Chorlton, drawing elicitation interview)

Whilst alcohol can be seen to play a predominant role in Jim's decision to drink in the park, for Max alcohol has more of a peripheral role. More than this, and as the quotations just presented intimate, there are temporal differences: For young people in Chorlton, drinking in parks is something they do not solely undertake in darkness; they also consume alcohol in such spaces in broad daylight. By comparison, for young people in Wythenshawe, drinking in parks was something almost unanimously undertaken at night-time, away from the policing gaze of the public. Nonetheless, despite these differences, the quotations have in common the fact that parks seem to facilitate social situations that commercial premises may not offer. For instance, Jim indicates the spatiality of the park is significant in enabling hundreds of people to gather together. Meanwhile, Max, in line with Galloway et al. (2007), contends that park drinking enables young people to feel socially and physically unrestricted, for instance, by playing football, whilst consuming alcohol.

Further, ethnographic participations showed me that, consistent with Galloway et al.'s (2007) findings, drinking in outdoor locations enables young people the opportunity to have a cigarette, or take drugs, alongside drinking. This supports Lieshout and Aarts' (2008) contention that, whilst there are rules in public spaces, they are not as strictly or rigidly enforced (again, see Bonte, this volume). More than this, young people are, to an extent, able to make their own rules and try new things; young people have a certain anonymity in public spaces (White, 1993), 'being able to disappear into the mass' (Lieshout & Aarts, 2008, p. 504). Some young people, supporting findings in the extant literature, drank in marginal spaces in order to escape the gaze of others (Trell, Hoven & Huigen, 2013; Townshend & Roberts, 2013; Valentine et al., 2010). However, against this grain, for some young people in my study, the distinct thrill of drinking in the park is partially due to the possibilities of being seen, and 'getting caught'. Consider the comments below:

> It's a bit more of a rush [drinking in the park] cos it's like 'what if we get caught?' That's good to know in a sense, it makes you more excited. It makes you wanna do it more so I dunno, if feels more out of order than drinking in a house. It's fun running away from police. (Oliver, 16, Wythenshawe, peer interview)
>
> You coming out tonight? We're going park, gunna bring speakers and get some tunes blasting. Show off and have a party. (Sarah, 18, Chorlton, text message)

Oliver's contention highlights the thrill he gets from the perceived risk of getting 'caught' by the police when consuming alcohol, under the legal drinking age, in marginal spaces. This coincides with the findings from Townshend's (2013, p. 158) study, which showed that some young people enjoy the 'cat and mouse' aspect of being displaced. Further, as both Oliver and Sarah make evident, the park allows for what Leiberg (1995, p. 722) terms 'places of interaction', which provide young people with an opportunity 'to meet and confront the adult world, to put oneself on display, to see and be seen'. Indeed, Sarah articulates purposefully crafting a soundscape in the park in order to 'show off' and make her presence felt. Whether aiming to drink in a relatively anonymous manner, or aiming to visibly perform drunkenness, it is indisputable that parks are an important social forum for young people.

Thirdly, young people from both Wythenshawe and Chorlton recounted the home to be an important drinking space. Indeed, the home as an important site of drinking for both working and middle-class young people renders inaccurate and unhelpful the stereotypical dichotomy whereby pub culture is a commonly cited component of working-class culture (Richardson, 2014), whilst domestic drinking is thought to be a predominantly middle-class pursuit (The Guardian, 2013). John (22, Wythenshawe, interview) is quoted at length here, as he identifies a myriad of reasons why young people choose to consume alcohol at home prior to accessing other drinking spaces:

> It's good in the sense that it gets you pissed quicker, cheaper, and it just gets you in the mood because it tends to be in a room, say you're drinking at someone's house, you'd all just be in one room, there could be 8 to 10 of us . . . to be fair you can probably have more fun doing that, than on an actual night out, because you've still got music on, except you get to choose the playlist so, that is quality. It's just in that sense you can have a nice relaxed beer before, like calm before the storm, you know what's going to happen later on, but for now you just want to have a beer, you just want to sit back, have a relax, just have a chat first before you go out and get shitfaced.

As John's account attests, space is both sensually and emotionally apprehended (Middleton, 2009); home is a 'relaxing' drinking space. More than this, John recounts that the home provides a space for young people to cement and enhance social bonds, as they would 'all just be in one room'. Supporting this notion, other young people commented that pre-drinking provides opportunities to enhance social bonds which could be threatened in the club space (see Bancroft, 2012) because, as Fraser (24, Chorlton, interview) says, 'you sort of lose people really quickly'. This is qualified by Pennay and Room's (2012) assertion that, as licensed premises are open to the public, young people cannot be selective about who they are drinking with, and may find it difficult to remain together as a group with their chosen companions. Further, in line with the findings from Barton and Husk's (2014) study, John favours the ability to tailor the drinking environment to his tastes. For instance, the music he plays and the volume at which he plays it ensures that he and his friends can 'have a chat first'. Indeed, it is not only the soundscape that I saw young people attempt to manipulate on their nights in involving alcohol, but also the lightscape.

As Shaw (2015) puts it, because of familiarity with the micro-geographies of the space when at home, one is potentially able to control their experience of darkness. According to Shaw (2015), this ability to control dark and light is at the heart of domestic relaxation. To elaborate, when at home, one is able to decide whether to experience complete or partial darkness, and thereby have control over when and how bodies are opened up towards the affectivity of the space. Indeed, during ethnographic participations, I witnessed candlelight being utilized to mould atmospheres that pull people towards particular affective states (see Sumartojo, 2014):

> When I arrived at Kirsty's at 8.00 p.m., lights were turned off, yet candles were lit. The candles, and slow-paced music, contributed towards the creation of a calm atmosphere. The candles set the tone that this would not be a 'big night out', but rather a relaxing night in over a few glasses of wine. (Field notes)

As Bille (2015) says, light is continuously being turned on, off or adjusted, dependent upon the activity and atmosphere desired. Indeed, my account just presented suggests that candlelight was used by Kirsty (24, Chorlton) to indicate a particular mood that is sought (see Bille, 2015). Here, Kirsty's manipulation of sound and light was used to generate an affective atmosphere that primes her friends to perform their drinking practices in a particular way. The space of Kirsty's home, then, was shaped through sound and light to evoke intimacy and cosiness, quite distinct feelings to what some may desire prior to gearing up for a 'big night out'. This correlates with Kirsty's comment, 'I just thought it would be nice for me and my friends, you know, a nice chilled environment' (text message). Light therefore can be seen to have agency in shaping social relationships through material qualities that assist in constituting spatial experiences (Sumartojo, 2014). The central point to take away from this is that the drinkers can manipulate the physical layout and atmospheric qualities of the home to create their desired drinkscape, in a way they are unlikely to achieve in commercial premises.

Drunken Im/mobilities

The importance of mobility has been recognised within the social sciences, leading Sheller and Urry (2006) to declare that a 'new' mobilities paradigm has been formed. Recent work within the apparent 'mobile turn' has made clear that young urbanities are of an age where mobility is crucial in order to take advantage of the resources, recreation and sociality offered by urbanscapes (Skelton, 2013a). Indeed, Skelton (2013a) proclaims that this is an important aspect of 'growing up', and identity formation. As McAuliffe (2013) insists, young people are subject to manifold micro-politics of mobility and immobility that differentiate their experiences of urban spaces from the experiences of adults. Mobilities research then, echoing Sheller (2011), should not only take seriously physical movement, but also potential movement, blocked movement and immobilisation. This section provides a much needed response to Jayne et al.'s (2012) claim that the extant alcohol studies literature has largely rendered drinking spaces fixed, bounded terrains, thereby failing to engage with young people's alcohol-related im/mobilities.

There are a few examples in the literature whereby authors have engaged with the notion of alcohol-related im/mobilities. Duff and Moore (2015) explore the affective atmospheres of spaces of mobility in Melbourne's night-time economy and how these atmospheres shape the experience of alcohol-related problems. Inner-city participants described 'comfortable' or 'fun' journeys on the tram, walking or cycling whereas participants from periurban communities spoke of 'boring' or 'unpleasant' journeys via train, night-bus or taxi. Moving beyond reports of the 'priming' effects of affective atmospheres, Duff and Moore (2015) conclude that affective atmospheres are enacted and transformed in encounters in, and through, spaces of mobility. Whilst urban space is not the focus of the chapter, Jayne et al.'s (2012) research into the im/mobilities and experiences of young backpackers relating to alcohol consumption, drinking practices and performativities of drunkenness, seeks to redress the academic preoccupation with mobilities to, and from, pre-formed drinking establishments in the night-time economy. The authors provide an in-depth consideration of the embodied aspects of alcohol-related im/mobilities, contending that alcohol can help to soften a variety of (un)comfortable embodied and emotional materialities linked with budget travel; act as an aid to 'passing the time' and 'being able to do nothing'; and heighten senses of belonging with other travellers and the 'locals'.

As Spinney (2009, p. 819) convincingly argues, 'movement strait-jacketed as transport is overwhelmingly utilitarian in nature and consequently there is an enormous expanse of lived experience that such an approach fails to make visible'. I would similarly echo such an exhortation to promote the conceptualisation that travel entails a lot more than simply a means of getting from A to B as quickly as possible (Sheller and Urry, 2006). Ethnographic participations, in which I often travelled with young people from the pre-drinking space, to their next drinking destination, showed me that young people often seek a seamless transition between the home space and the pub/club space. To achieve such a transition, young people request taxi drivers to play music. If a taxi driver refuses, or is unable, to play music, young people often use their mobile phones to perform this function, thereby crafting their own affective soundscapes. This was confirmed by several participants:

> See here [pointing to photograph] we're in the taxi and we're all on our phones. Pretty anti-social when you think of it. Sofia's probably texting her ex; Allie's taking a selfie; Alana is playing some tunes to keep us in the mood, and I'm taking a snap of us all. (Holly, 18, Chorlton, 'go along' mobile phone interview)
>
> Last night was so fun!!! Bus to the city was probably the best bit to be honest, playing tunes from our phones and having a few sneaky drinks. (Melissa, 24, Wythenshawe, diary)

As Berry and Hamilton (2010) propose, the multifunctionality of mobile phones offers different types of social activities that may be undertaken on the move that, in turn, can reconfigure spaces. In other words, the mobile phone is a place-making device (Berry & Hamilton, 2010), a means in which individuals manage their moods and orientations to space, giving them greater control over their experiences (Wilson, 2011). Here then, both bus and taxi journeys illustrate that young people temporarily dwell within these mobilities (Urry, 2002); that is, young people co-opt the spatial and temporal affordances of buses and taxis and make something with them (Vannini, 2011). To explain, travelling in taxis and buses becomes an opportunity to steal time and place (Vannini, 2011); and an occasion to engage in activities carved out from the space, including texting, drinking, taking photographs and listening to music. This transforms the travelling experience from the 'in-between' feeling of being neither here nor there, to one of connectedness and belonging (Berry & Hamilton, 2010). To sum up, then, taxis and buses become what Vannini (2011, p. 292) may describe as an 'extension of the home'.

It is important to recognise that the alcohol-related im/mobilities of young people are often at odds with the im/mobilities that are defined and normalised as 'appropriate'. Consequently, young people are not always mobile through their own volition (Hannam, Sheller & Urry, 2006). Take the comments for Siena and Rik:

> We're in the park just hanging, but I've just checked Facebook and adults are going mad saying there's groups of teenagers in park doing bad things, so going to go home now. (Siena, 16, Chorlton, text message)
>
> We'd probably go to like, a park. And then, the police would end up coming, and then we'd go, and we'd go to a different park. And if the police come

there again, we'd all just split up and go different places. (Rik, 15, Wythenshawe, peer interview)

According to young people from both Wythenshawe and Chorlton, the clashing mobilities of young people with adults/police require young people to sculpt new geographies through what Skelton (2013b, p. 463) terms 'forced and adaptive mobilities'. By keeping mobile, young people are able to 'jump scales' and avoid confrontations with adults/police (Beazley, 2003). When drinking in outdoor public spaces, young people are characterised by high mobility (see Beazley, 2003). Here then, young people face a politics of mobility which resonates in some ways with that experienced by the homeless, as they become 'fixed in mobility' (Jackson, 2012, p. 725). Importantly, to echo Dee (2013), such continual displacement may diminish young people's sense of place and belonging.

As Cresswell (2012) asserts, when theorising movement, it is important not to downplay the significance of stuckness and stillness. However, as Bissell and Fuller (2009) note, a focus on the dialectic of statis and movement neglects other registers and modalities which are not necessarily reducible to the dialectic of mobility and immobility. With this in mind, Bissell (2007) thinks through the event of waiting from the perspective of embodied corporeal experience. Along similar lines, Anderson (2004) argues that, even as boredom stills and slows time-space, movement always accompanies boredom. Whilst much of the extant literature focuses on alcohol-related experiences in pre-formed drinking spaces, queuing in the streets prior to accessing bars/clubs has gone relatively unexplored. Whilst queuing may be dismissed as a period of relative im/mobility or boredom, the process was not conceptualised as such by young people in my study. Young people, predominantly males, from both Wythenshawe and Chorlton, described tensions with bouncers as a common feature of their queuing experiences:

A lot of bouncers, especially in town, are quite rude, it's annoying, especially if you're not a girl, if you're a bloke and you know, you're queuing to get in, they can be quite rude to ya. (Theo, 19, Chorlton, interview)

We were trying to get into this club and the queue was all the way round, and the bouncers kind of went "no, no, no, no, no more, full capacity", and this drunk lad kind of walked up, and the bouncers just went, pushed him on the floor, so I kind of went "was there any fucking need?" and he just looked at me and walked off. (Sam, 21, Wythenshawe, interview)

As Theo and Sam's comments suggest, events of corporeal stillness, such as waiting or boredom, should not be conceptualised as dead periods of statis. In line with Bissell's (2007) argument, my findings show that each of these processes is alive with the potential of being other than this. To explain, for Theo, the process of queuing was overlaid with feelings of annoyance at the apparent gender discrimination against males practiced by bouncers. Meanwhile, for Sam, queuing is a time when arguments and fights may break out. Paraphrasing Adey (2006) then, I argue that there is never any absolute immobility, only mobilities which get mistaken for immobility. The embodied, emotional and affective experiences of queuing indicate that, when conceptualising young people's alcohol-related mobilities, it is important not to downplay the importance of stillness for identity construction (see Collins, Esson, Gutierrez & Adekunle, 2013).

Conclusion

When surveying the literature on alcohol consumption practices and experiences, several authors found a paucity of material (Holloway et al., 2009; Jayne et al., 2008; Jayne et al., 2012). Consequently, I opened this chapter by suggesting two caveats it was necessary to take on board in contemporary alcohol studies research. One was that there has been an empirical pre-occupation with the pre-formed drinking spaces of bars, pubs and clubs, and thereby a dearth of research conducted into a range of spaces young people carve out for themselves as drinkscapes (Holloway et al., 2009). The second caveat was that drinking spaces have been treated as bounded, static terrains, with a lack of appreciation of young people's alcohol-related im/mobilities in, and through, drinkscapes (Jayne et al., 2012). This chapter sought to address these deficits through research conducted in two suburban locations, Wythenshawe and Chorlton, Manchester. I complemented existing methods with novel techniques that are culturally credible to young people (text messaging and 'go along' mobile phone interviews). From my wider research, young people from Wythenshawe and Chorlton often differed in the types of commercial spaces they frequented. However, whilst young people from Wythenshawe and Chorlton occasionally articulated different reasons as to *why* non-commercial spaces are important to them, my contention in this chapter is that streets, parks and homes seem to be equally important drinking spaces to young people living in both case study locations, and, in this respect, transcend class and other demographic differences.

In this chapter, young people from both Wythenshawe and Chorlton articulated that they consume alcohol in parks and streets, not solely because they are excluded from drinking in pubs, bars and clubs. To explain, for some young people, parks and streets have a distinct appeal over drinking in commercial premises or homes. However, reasons given for liking outdoor marginal spaces to experiment with alcohol varied by case study location. For instance, a temporal difference was evident. Alongside drinking in parks at night-time, young people in Chorlton also spoke about consuming alcohol in such spaces during the day – something not typically recounted by young people in Wythenshawe who preferred darkness to perform drunkenness. Further, whilst for young people in Wythenshawe consuming alcohol was a key reason why they visited parks, for young people in Chorlton, alcohol had a more peripheral role and was one element amongst a much broader range of activities, for instance, playing football and having barbeques. Houses were also highlighted as significant drinkscapes for young people from both research sites. Young people reported pre-drinking at home, not solely because of cost-effectiveness (Barton & Husk, 2014), but also because of opportunities the home affords for sculpting the drinking space, for instance, by deciding who is present and absent and crafting affective soundscapes and lightscapes. This led me to contend that the stereotype of pub culture as a working-class pursuit, and home drinking as a middle-class one, is an inaccurate and unhelpful dichotomy.

Then, through the young mobilees' eyes (Skelton, 2013a), we gained insight into young drinkers' complex im/mobilities. I contended that, when travelling in taxis or on buses, young people in both Wythenshawe and Chorlton seek to extend pre-drinking beyond the realm of the home, and dwell within their mobilities, for instance, through playing music from their mobile phones. This chapter then turned to illustrate that young people are not always mobile through their own volition (Hannam et al., 2006). Consequently, I asserted that young people's alcohol-related mobilities are typically characterised by high levels of forced mobility. Finally, the importance of stillness was highlighted as being equally as important for identity construction as young people's alcohol-related mobilities. Young people, from both research sites, intimated that queuing to access clubs was far from a dead period of statis, but rather an embodied, emotional and affective experience.

On a final note, whilst my research has gone some way towards addressing a range of spaces in which young people consume alcohol, there are numerous spaces which remain underexplored. Future research then, should fruitfully engage with a host of spaces within, and through which, young people consume alcohol which have not garnered sufficient academic attention. These include casinos, cinemas, restaurants, woods, fields, bus stops, public toilets and cemeteries. This is important because, to date, the lived experiences of young people's drinking have not been fully represented in the world of young people's geographies.

Notes

1 This work was supported by the Economic and Social Research Council [ES/J500094/1] and Alcohol Research UK [RS 12/02].
2 *Skint* in an informal way of someone saying they have little or no money available.

References

Adey, P. 2006. If mobility is everything then it is nothing: Towards a relational politics of (im)mobilities. *Mobilities*, 1(1): 75–94.
Anderson, B. 2004. Time-stilled space-slowed: How boredom matters. *Geoforum*, 35(6): 739–754.
Atherton, J., Baker, C. and Graham, E. 2005. A 'genius of place'?: Manchester as a case study in public theology. In Graham, E. and Rowlands, A. (Eds.), *Pathways to the public square: Proceedings of the 2003 IAPT Conference, Manchester UK* (pp. 63–83). London: Transaction Publishers.
Bancroft, A. 2012. Drinking with and without fun: Female students' accounts of pre-drinking and club-drinking. *Sociological Research Online*, 17(4): 11.

Barker, J. and Smith, F. 2012. What's in focus? A critical discussion of photography, children and young people. *International Journal of Social Research Methodology*, 15(2): 91–103.

Barton, A. and Husk, K. 2014. 'I don't really like the pub . . .': Reflections on young people and pre-loading alcohol. *Drugs and Alcohol Today*, 14(2): 1–12.

Beazley, H. 2003. The construction and protection of individual and collective by street children and youth in Indonesia. *Children, Youth and Environments*, 13(1): 105–133.

Berry, M. and Hamilton, M. 2010. Changing urban spaces: Mobile phones on trains. *Mobilities*, 5(1): 111–129.

Bille, M. 2015. Lighting up cosy atmospheres in Denmark. *Emotion, Space and Society*, 15: 56–63.

Bissell, D. 2007. Animating suspension: Waiting for mobilities. *Mobilities*, 2(2): 277–298.

Bissell, D. and Fuller, G. 2009. The revenge of the still. *M/C Journal*, 12(1). [Online], Available: http://www.journal.media-culture.org.au/index.php/mcjournal/article/viewArticle/136

Chamberlain, V. 2012. *Council putting Chorlton to the back of the queue*. [Online], Available: http://victorchamberlain.blogspot.co.uk/2012/04/council-putting-chorlton-to-back-of.html (27 February 2015).

Chatterton, P. and Hollands, R. 2002. Theorising urban playscapes: Producing, regulating and consuming youthful nightlife city spaces. *Urban Studies* 39(1): 94–116.

Collins, R., Esson, J., Gutierrez, C. O. and Adekunle, A. 2013. Youth in motion: Spatialising youth movement(s) in the social sciences. *Children's Geographies*, 11(3): 369–376.

Cresswell, T. 2012. Mobilities II: Still. *Progress in Human Geography*, 36(5): 645–653.

Davis, N. W. and Meyer, B. B. 2009. Qualitative data analysis: A procedural comparison. *Journal of Applied Sport Psychology*, 21(1): 116–124.

Dee, M. 2013. Public space and the marginalisation of children and young people. In *Conference Proceedings: The Inaugural European Conference on the Social Sciences 2013*, IAFOR (International Academic Forum), Brighton, United Kingdom. [Online]. Available: http://eprints.qut.edu.au/66830/ (27 February 2015).

Demant, J. and Landolt, S. 2014. Youth drinking in public places: The production of drinking spaces in and outside nightlife areas. *Urban Studies*, 51(1): 170–184.

Dixon, J., Levine, M. and McAuley, R. 2006. Locating impropriety: Street drinking, moral order, and the ideological dilemma of public space. *Political Psychology*, 27(2): 187–206.

Duff, C. and Moore, D. 2015. Going out, getting about: Atmospheres of mobility in Melbourne's night-time economy. *Social and Cultural Geography*, 16(3): 299–314.

Elsley, S. 2004. Children's experience of public space. *Children and Society*, 18(2): 155–164.

Galloway, R., Forsyth, A. J. M. and Shewan, D. 2007. *Young people's street drinking behaviour: Investigating the influence of marketing and subculture*. [Online], Available: http://www.sccjr.ac.uk/wp-content/uploads/2008/11/Young_Peoples_Street_Drinking_Behaviour.pdf (27 February 2015).

Gee, S., Jackson, S. J. and Sam, M. 2014. Carnivalesque culture and alcohol promotion and consumption at an annual international sports event in New Zealand. *International Review for the Sociology of Sport*, 1–19.

Gough, K. V. and Franch, M. 2005. Spaces of the street: Socio-spatial mobility and exclusion of youth in Recife. *Children's Geographies*, 3(2): 149–166.

Hannam, K., Sheller, M. and Urry, J. 2006. Editorial: Mobilities, immobilities and moorings. *Mobilities*, 1(1): 1–22.

Harris, C., Jackson, L., Mayblin, L., Piekut, A. and Valentine, G. 2014. 'Big brother welcomes you': Innovative methods for research with children and young people outside of the home and school environment. *Qualitative Research*. [Online], Available: http://eprints.whiterose.ac.uk/81351/1/BigBrotherChildhood_revisions_CLEAR%20(1).pdf (27 February 2015).

Holland, S., Renold, E., Ross, N. and Hillman, A. 2008. The everyday lives of children in care: Using a sociological perspective to inform social work practice. *Qualitative Working Papers*, 1–27. [Online], Available: http://www.cardiff.ac.uk/socsi/qualiti/Working Papers/Qualiti_WPS_005.pdf (27 February 2015).

Hollands, R. and Chatterton, P. 2003. Producing nightlife in the new urban entertainment economy: Corporatization, branding and market segmentation. *International Journal of Urban and Regional Research*, 27(2): 361–385.

Holloway, S. L., Jayne, M. and Valentine, G. 2008. 'Sainsbury's is my local': English alcohol policy, domestic drinking practices and the meaning of home. *Transactions of the Institute of British Geographers*, 33(4): 532–547.

Holloway, S. L., Valentine, G. and Jayne, M. 2009. Masculinities, femininities and the geographies of public and private drinking landscapes. *Geoforum* 40(5): 821–831.

Jackson, E. 2012. Fixed in mobility: Young homeless people and the city. *International Journal of Urban and Regional Research*, 36(4): 725–741.

Jayne, M., Gibson, C., Waitt, G. and Valentine, G. 2012. Drunken mobilities: Backpackers, alcohol, 'doing lace'. *Tourist Studies*, 12(3): 211–231.

Jayne, M., Valentine, G. and Holloway, S. L. 2008. The place of drink: Geographical contributions to alcohol studies. *Drugs: Education, Prevention and Policy*, 15(3): 219–232.

Joseph, J. and Donnelly, M. K. 2012. Reflections on ethnography, ethics and inebriation. *Leisure*, 36(3–4): 357–372.

Leiberg, M. 1995. Teenagers and public space. *Communication Research*, 22(6): 720–744.

Lieshout, M. and Aarts, N. 2008. Youth and immigrants' perspectives on public spaces. *Space and Culture*, 11(4): 497–513.

Lucas, K., Tyler, S. and Christodoulou, G. 2009. Assessing the 'value' of new transport initiatives in deprived neighbourhoods in the UK. *Transport Police*, 16(3): 115–122.

Manchester City Council. 2011. *Manchester City Council: Childcare Sufficiency Assessment District Report*: Wythenshawe. [Online], Available: http://www.manchester.gov.uk/downloads/download/4352/childcare_sufficiency_assessment_2011_-_wythenshawe_district_analysis (27 February 2015).

Manchester City Council. 2012. *Chorlton Ward Profile*. Manchester: Manchester City Council.

Manchester City Council. 2014. *Chorlton*. [Online], Available: http://www.manchester.gov.uk/directory_record/115641/chorlton (27 February 2015).

McAuliffe, C. 2013. Legal walls and professional paths: The mobilities of graffiti writers in Sydney. *Urban Studies*, 50(3): 518–537.

Middleton, J. 2009. 'Stepping in time': Walking, time, and space in the city. *Environment and Planning A*, 41(8): 1943–1961.

Miles, M. B. and Huberman, A. M. 1994. *Qualitative data analysis*. 2nd Ed. California: Sage Publications.

Pennay, A. and Room, R. 2012. Prohibiting public drinking in urban public spaces: A review of the evidence. *Drugs: Education, Prevention and Policy*, 19(2): 91–101.

Punch, S. 2002. Research with children: The same or different from research with adults? *Childhood*, 9(3): 321–341.

Richardson, M. 2014. Intergenerational relations and Irish masculinities: Reflections from the Tyneside Irish, in the north-east of England. In P. Hopkins and A. Gorman-Murray (Eds.), *Masculinities and place* (pp. 255–268). Farnham: Ashgate Publishing Limited.

Robinson, C. 2009. Nightscapes and leisure spaces: An ethnographic study of young people's use of free space. *Journal of Youth Studies*, 12(5): 501–514.

Shaw, R.E. 2015. Controlling darkness: Self, Dark and the Domestic Night. *Cultural Geographies*, 22(4): 585–600.

Sheller, M. 2011. Mobility. *Sociopedia.isa*. [Online], Available: http://www.sagepub.net/isa/resources/pdf/Mobility.pdf (27 February 2015).

Sheller, M. and Urry, J. 2006. The new mobilities paradigm. *Environment and Planning A.*, 38(2): 207–226.

Skelton, T. 2013a. Young people's urban im/mobilities: Relationality and identity formation. *Urban Studies*, 50(3): 467–483.

Skelton, T. 2013b. Introduction: Young people's im/mobile urban geographies. *Urban Studies*, 50(3): 455–466.

Spinney, J. 2009. Cycling the city: Movement, meaning and method. *Geography Compass*, 3(2): 817–835.

Sumartojo, S. 2014. 'Dazzling relief': Floodlighting and national affective atmospheres on VE Day 1945. *Journal of Historical Geography*, 45: 59–69.

The Guardian. 2012. *On the white bus to Wythenshawe: Council housing by design*. [Online], Available: http://www.theguardian.com/commentisfree/2012/may/22/white-bus-to-wythenshawe-council-housing (27 February 2015).

The Guardian. 2013. *Public health teams are overlooking middle class alcohol dependency*. [Online], Available: http://www.theguardian.com/local-government-network/2013/oct/18/middle *class-alcohol-dependency-councils* (27 February 2015).

Thompson, L. and Cupples, J. 2008. Seen and not heard? Text messaging and digital sociality. *Social and Cultural Geography*, 9(1): 95–108.

Townshend, T. G. 2013. Youth, alcohol and place-based leisure behaviours: A study of two locations in England. *Social Science and Medicine*, 91: 153–161.

Townshend, T. G. and Roberts, M. 2013. Affordances, young people, parks and alcohol consumption. *Journal of Urban Design*, 18(4): 494–516.

Trell, E., Hoven, B. V. and Huigen, P. P. P. 2013. 'In summer we go and drink at the lake': Young men and the geographies of alcohol and drinking in rural Estonia. *Children's Geographies*, 12(4): 447–463.

Urry, J. 2002. Mobility and proximity. *Sociology*, 36(2): 255–274.

Valentine, G. 2013. Using interviews as a research methodology. In R. Flowerdew and D. Martin (Eds.), *Methods in human geography: A guide for students doing a research project*. 2nd Ed. (pp. 110–127). New York: Routledge.

Valentine, G., Holloway, S., Knell, C. and Jayne, M. 2008. Drinking places: Young people and cultures of alcohol consumption in rural environments. *Journal of Rural Studies*, 24(1): 28–40.

Valentine, G., Holloway, S. L. and Jayne, M. 2010. Generational patterns of alcohol consumption: Continuity and change. *Health and Place*, 16(5): 916–925.

Vannini, P. 2011. Mind the gap: The tempo rubato of dwelling in lineups. *Mobilities*, 6(2): 273–299.

Weller, S. 2006. Situating (young) teenagers in geographies of children and youth. *Children's Geographies*, 4(1): 97–108.

White, R. 1993. Youth and conflict over urban space. *Children's Environments*, 10(1): 85–93.

Wilson, H. F. 2011. Passing propinquities in the multicultural city: The everyday encounters of bus passengering. *Environment and Planning A*, 43(3): 634–649.

Wythenshawe Town Centre. 2013. *Real community — real lives Wythenshawe: Wythenshawe town centre making a forgotten dream a reality.* [Online], Available: http://www.wythenshawetowncentre.co.uk/news-and-events/index.php/2013/10/real-community-real-lives-wythenshawe-wythenshawe-town-centre-making-forgotten-dream-reality/ (27 February 2015).

Young, H. 2011. *Manchester: Responsible alcohol sales project.* [Online], Available: http://www.alcohollearningcentre.org.uk/LocalInitiatives/projects/projectDetail/?cid=6495 (27 February 2015).

Chapter 10

Parenting style and gender effects on alcohol consumption among university students in France

Ludovic Gaussot, Loïc Le Minor and Nicolas Palierne

Introduction

During the second half of the 20th century, both family configurations and gender relations have undergone deep changes in France. These changes have given rise to a tension between the role of individuals and processes at work within families, between increasing individualism on the one hand and the family as an institution on the other (Giddens, 1992; Déchaux, 2007; 2010). Yet new ways of parenting have not made a clean break with the past, as the education of children still often remains the mothers' prerogative (Ricroch & Roumier, 2011; Cromer, 2008). While the child's sense of fulfilment has been seen to replace authoritarian practices in family education (Attias-Donfut, Lapierre & Segalen, 2002), the relationships between the parents and the children are still rooted in an asymmetric structural relation. Thus, while the increase of children's autonomy could have attenuated the traditional differences in the family configuration and socialisation, and specifically in the development of educational parenting styles (EPS), these changes have not been entirely dissolved in regards to both the uneven involvement of fathers and mothers and the style of education received by girls and boys. Further, as in the early work of Kohn (1963) on social class and styles of parenting in the United States, there appears to be an opposition between the liberal educational style of the middle and upper social classes and a more authoritarian parental education style favoured in working-class families. This distinction made a significant impact on 1980s sociological work on parenting and the family. Thus, while according to Combessie (1969) this opposition is modified by the weight of income and the parents' social trajectory and position, according to Lautrey (1980), it is the living conditions of the family that are more likely to determine the educational values adopted by parents. However, for Kellerhals and Montandon (1991), first, there is more than one style of education by social background and second, belonging to a social class cannot fully explain the variations of EPS. Others would also put forward the impact of the place where people live and the number of children within the family unit as being important influences on the parenting styles adopted by any particular family (Le Pape, 2008).

In France, particularly since the 1970s, research on EPS has particularly been developed along two main lines, with one line on educational processes within families and another related to the development of family education as a sub-discipline of science education (Durning, 1995). In the 1980s and 1990s, analysis of EPS focusing on the effect of social origins changed and the debate on the existence of educational styles of classes seemed to reach an impasse (Segalen, 2006). Afterwards, researchers started to raise the questions of the child's development of autonomy and the recognition of children's rights, and the democratisation of the family environment. However, some researchers still continue to emphasise the impact caused by social background on variations in family education and parenting practices (Le Pape, 2009; Lareau, 2011). If family education has evolved and diversified following changes in family configurations (Saint-Jacques, Turcotte & Oubrayrie-Roussel, 2012), it has not necessarily been freed from normative and moralistic conceptions. Family dysfunction and lack of proper family education is still often cited as a cause of social problems encountered or triggered by youth, such as underperformance at school, delinquency or, as this chapter explores, dangerous alcohol consumption practices (Gayet, 2004). Evidently, these dysfunctions cannot be understood without an understanding of the political, economic and cultural context and specific family histories which provide the social and cultural context for parent-child relationships.

In the field of addictions, while prevention and care professionals constantly emphasise the importance of parents, sociological studies tend to exclude them from their research to focus on intra-generational consumption practices. The various connections that young people have with alcohol (and also, as we consider in other publications, psychotropic substances) are frequently viewed as a simplistic confrontation between the two which too readily sets aside the probable involvement of the upbringing and family background, thus marginalising the impact of their parents' educational but also emotional behaviours (Kellerhals & Montandon, 1991). Even though certain practices of consumption grow in the interstices of parental supervision or knowledge (Le Garrec, 2002), or in opposition to them, it is not a sufficient reason to remove the family, the relationship between parents, children and young adults from the analysis. Because the issue of young people's alcohol consumption is evidently intertwined with a wider set of social issues embedded within family practices and structures, it is difficult to understand the question of youth alcohol consumption 'objectively' without nuanced understandings of parenting and familial attachments (Peretti-Watel, Beck & Legleye, 2007). Indeed the mindset we usually have on juvenile consumption conveys a set of alarming representations and is associated with moral judgements which point out the failure of parental authority. However, in the French context, few studies try to actually measure these phenomena, and this is why this research, in this particular context, focuses on young people's consumption in relation to family risk and protective factors. Indeed, a previous study on alcohol consumption practices among children and young adults aged 13–24 (Gaussot, Le Minor & Palierne, 2011b) has highlighted the protective effect of 'demandingness', stating that there are more non-users and consumers without risk amongst the authoritarian and authoritative parental style categories. The same study has also highlighted the potential moderating effect of responsiveness together with demandingness to deal with heavy chronic drinking.

The current research looked at drug and alcohol consumption practices among students although, in this chapter, alcohol use is our exclusive focus. Our analysis is taken from a survey, conducted during the 2011–2012 academic year, on the effect of EPS on student consumption of alcohol in the region of Poitiers in central France (MILDT, INCa, IREB[1]). The survey was distributed to all the students through the university's mailing list, which constitutes approximately 25,000 students. In total, we collected 2,364 completed questionnaires about the variations on the perceptions of EPS within this population, according to the gender of the parents and of the children, and their social class (*Professions et Catégories Socioprofessionnelles*, PCS[2]). Our sample therefore represents 11% of the whole student population of the region of Poitiers. To make it as representative as possible of the students of Poitiers, we have weighted the data with regards to the distribution by sex and educational stream of the students supplied by the services of the university. After weighting, our sample includes 45% of men (1,059) and 55% of women (1,305). A total of 13% are 18 years old or younger, 18% are 19 years old, 18,5% are 20 years old, 17% are 21 years old, 12% are 22 years old, 8% are 23 years old and 14% are 24 years old and older. Our students' mothers are 33% lower-level service and administrative occupations; 23% supervisory, clerical and junior managerial, administrative, professional occupations; 18% higher and intermediate managerial, administrative, professional occupations; 11% persons without professional activity/unemployed; 5% semi-skilled and unskilled manual occupations; 5% skilled manual occupations and small business owners; 4% retired people; and 2% agricultural labourers. The social categories of the fathers divide up as follows: 30% are higher and intermediate managerial, administrative, professional occupations; 17% supervisory, clerical and junior managerial, administrative, professional occupations; 15% semi-skilled and unskilled manual occupations; 12% lower-level service and administrative occupations; 10% skilled manual occupations and small business owners; 7% retired people; 5% agricultural labourers; and 4% persons without professional activity/unemployed.

Data sets were generated by the execution of two quantitative tests. The first, the Authoritative Parenting Index (API), is based on 16 questions measuring two dimensions of parent-child interaction, demandingness and responsiveness. Alongside this, the research used the Alcohol Use Disorders Test (AUDIT)[3] to measure students' alcohol consumption patterns and practice. Participants also completed a set of demographic questions relating to topics such as academic attainment, social class characteristics and, crucially, parent's professions. Finally, 63 semi-directive interviews with students were also conducted in order to qualitatively determine the evolutions of the EPS they received, their 'careers' of consumption of alcohol and general attitudes towards alcohol and drunkenness.

The combination of these two dimensions reveals four educational parenting styles: a strong presence of both responsiveness and demandingness defines the *authoritative* style; a strong presence of demandingness but a low level of responsiveness refer to the *authoritarian* style; a strong presence of responsiveness and a low level of demandingness correspond to the *indulgent* style; and finally, a relatively low presence in both dimensions characterises the *uninvolved* style. The API does not construct *absolute* parenting styles, but *relative* ones, that depend on the population being studied. The lowest level of demandingness and the lowest level of responsiveness in the 'uninvolved style' does not mean the total absence of those dimensions (Figure 10.1, A&B), but these parents are less involved than others. After introducing the measure of the parenting style and the results obtained, we study its effects on alcohol consumption.

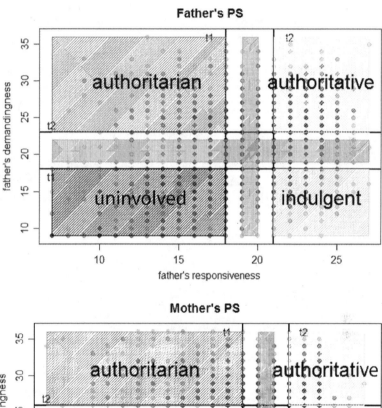

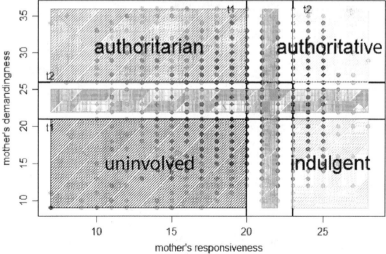

Figure 10.1 Structure of the educational parenting styles of the father and mother.

The structure of educational parenting style

Evaluating educational parenting style on the basis of the authoritative parenting index

The API test was developed to measure the connection between young people's behaviours such as school achievement, delinquency and risky behaviours such as alcohol and drug consumption, and the educational style of their parents (Maccoby & Martin, 1983; Steinberg, Mounts, Lamborn & Dornbusch, 1991; Jackson, Henriksen & Foshee, 1998; Jackson, 2002). The API test therefore measures two dimensions seen as central to varying parenting styles. 'Demandingness' relates to parental supervision of activities, assertive control, permissiveness and monitoring of child behaviour, whereas 'responsiveness' incorporates parental warmth, acceptance and involvement of parents in children's daily lives:

> The demanding behaviors characteristic of authoritative parenting include setting and enforcing clear standards of behavior, actively monitoring and supervising a child's activities, maintaining structure and regimen in a child's daily life, and making maturing demands consistent with the developmental phase of a child. The responsive behaviors characteristic of authoritative parenting include being affectionate and accepting, providing comfort and support, being involved in children's academic and social development, and recognizing children's achievements.
> (Jackson et al., 1998, p. 319)

The test, administered to children or young adults, therefore measures young people's perceptions of their familial parenting styles. Predictive influence of education by young people would be difficult to assess without studying its receipt by the young. Taken once in relation to each parent, the test determines the paternal and maternal educational styles through eliciting responses to nine items of demandingness and seven items of responsiveness. Students had to answer questions about the parenting style they received when they were in high school and living with their parents (equivalent to 16–17 years of age; see box in appendix).

It should be mentioned that we tried to rectify some limits related to the API. This test evaluates all individuals and all educational practices according to the same standard, without detailing the forms of communication used between parents and children, and without taking educational practices within the framework of a more general attitude towards the social world and others (Le Pape & Van Zanten, 2009). For example, the API does not take into account the fact that the distance or (educational) absence of fathers may be culturally assumed and to some extent normalised. Thus, what is seen as almost a 'failure' in the 'uninvolved' style can result from gendered division of the educational practices, especially in popular backgrounds where fathers are not always involved in educational issues handed down to mothers (Le Pape, 2006). Consequently, these results must be handled with care. While noting that we should not forget that the results come from a variability of social configurations, the test nonetheless provides us with a useful means to differentiate educational styles according to the sex of the parent and that of the child.

The four educational parenting styles

In accordance with research on this issue (Jackson et al., 1998; Jackson, 2002), scores of the 'demandingness' and 'responsiveness' dimensions have been the subject of a 'trichotomy', that is, broken down from the calculation of the 'tertiles' which divide the sample into three equal parts for each dimension. To keep only the most pronounced EPS measures, the answers included in the central tertile of each dimension were eliminated in order to provide clear ideal-types of the four main parenting styles (see Figure 10.1, A&B). One third of the whole sample has been excluded and EPS therefore display comparable proportions and numbers.

As can be seen in Figure 10.1, tertiles of responsiveness and demandingness are not the same for fathers and mothers, with scores of responsiveness and demandingness notably higher among mothers, reflecting the greater educational investment of mothers from the perspective of youth survey participants which, as we will see, is associated with less risky alcohol consumption. While sharing the same denomination, the EPS of fathers and mothers do not exactly represent the same reality. The divisions previously noted show the following distribution of the EPS of mothers and fathers (Table 10.1).

The API test builds relative, rather than absolute, parental styles. EPS are subject to historical developments, and outcomes would differ according to the various generations studied. Similarly, demandingness appears to be more frequently perceived among younger respondents and decreases with age, reflecting the development of increasing autonomy from parental authority with age (Gaussot et al., 2011a). Therefore, variations in the demandingness and responsiveness scores according to the sex of the parent and that of the child demonstrate the

Table 10.1 Distribution of educational parenting styles (EPS) of mothers and fathers

A total of 334 mothers of the sample's students have an authoritarian PS that represents 25% of the sample.

	Mother		Father	
Authoritarian EPS	334	25%	257	19%
Indulgent EPS	265	20%	174	13%
Uninvolved EPS	345	26%	466	34%
Authoritative EPS	399	30%	454	34%
Totals	1,343	100%	1,351	100%

continued importance of gender in relation both to family educational style and alcohol consumption.

Gender and educational parenting style

Parental education is not a naturally uniform set but the result of maternal and paternal educational work. In our study – after removal of the central tertile – 840 students, or 35.5% of the sample, are retained, because both parents are retained in the built sample. For 67% of them, the paternal EPS is identical to the maternal EPS. However, for almost all of the items, fathers get lower scores than mothers, which means that, even when EPS of mother and father are aligned, the perceived investment of fathers is lower than that of mothers. Further, while the level of education of the mother does not appear to influence their role as educators and the parenting styles adopted, that of fathers means that those with the highest academic levels are the most involved in their children's education and their risky behaviours. Furthermore, as regards socioeconomic professional categories, parents belonging to higher social classes are described as the most committed ones. Couples with the most significant disparities in EPS show a pronounced asymmetry, with fathers appearing largely withdrawn from parental education.

Parental investment is not expressed in the same manner according to the gender of the child; there are thus differences between classes which are strongly modulated by gender. This is important to understand variations of the alcohol consumption and risky behaviour of the young. Gendered education seems to be more given by the father in the lower categories and by the mother in the middle professional categories. Among executives, both parents give a gendered education of equal intensity, on the same number of items. Generally speaking, gender differences mainly appear on the demandingness dimension of the EPS. During the period of high school, we can see that there is a stronger parental control over when and where girls can go out on the one hand, and on the other hand, over boys' homework and activities with peers. Whatever parent or social category, this more intensive control over girls going out can also probably be related to the fears linked with female sexuality (Bozon & Villeneuve-Gokalp, 1994). The reception of the **exercise of authority**[4] is also particularly gendered with the more restrictive and authoritarian forms of authority (such as imposing rules without consulting children, constant reminder to follow rules) more felt by boys, especially by those whose fathers are skilled manual occupations and small business owners, semi-skilled and unskilled manual occupations and higher and intermediate managerial, administrative, professional occupations. Girls are more related to with 'softened' forms of authority, especially in supervisory, clerical and junior managerial, administrative, professional occupations. With regards to the **supervision of homework**, we generally see that boys are more subject to parental supervision and that this supervision comes mainly from the mother, which reinforces the research on the subject (Baudelot & Establet, 1992, 2007; Guyon, 2004; Guyon & Guérin, 2006).

Regarding the responsiveness dimension, girls perceive significantly more **testimonies of affection** than boys, except for children of executive mothers who are better 'graded' by their sons than by their daughters. Conversely, regarding the **availability of listening**, boys seem to be more privileged than girls, especially by their mother (amongst agricultural labourers, lower-level service and administrative occupations and higher and intermediate managerial, administrative, professional occupations) or sometimes by their father (amongst skilled manual occupations and small business owners and skilled manual occupations and small business owners). However, for the item stating 'My mother/my father was too busy to talk to me', the interpretation of significant differences is difficult: these differences may as well show a more important effective listening to the benefit of boys as the feeling experienced by girls who think that they are not sufficiently listened to (the one not excluding the other). Regarding the **management of the difficulties faced** by young people, boys report that they are generally less comforted than girls by their father and/or their mothers. Girls declare that they are less questioned about their problems than boys, especially by fathers of semi-skilled and unskilled manual occupations.

To summarise, girls are more supervised when it comes to their outings and enjoy a more flexible authority than boys, whose scholarly investments and activities with peers are more supervised. In terms of responsiveness, boys generally say that they receive less emotional testimony and support. Although it seems that boys benefit more from the availability and responsiveness of the parents than girls, this remains uneasy to interpret. However, beyond these differences related to gender and social category, we must now understand the influence of educational parenting style on the different practices of alcohol consumption.

The consumption of alcohol

Gendered practices

Drinking seems to be a highly gendered practice. The differentiation of accepted practices reflects hierarchical inequalities between men and women (Douglas, 1987; Scott, 1986; Delphy, 2001; Gefou-Madianou, 2002). Indeed, alcohol appears to be a product already historically and culturally gendered or even itself a symbol of gender (Eriksen, 1999). Concurring with this, the boys of our population record more pronounced alcohol consumption, both in terms of quantity and frequency, than that of girls. However, the Alcohol Use Disorders Test (AUDIT) reveals that heavy occasional drinking (Figure 10. 2) amongst girls (30.3%) does in fact approach that of boys (37.3%).

These data support the results of other studies (Legleye, Beck, Peretti-Watel & Chau, 2008) that highlight a lesser sex differentiation among alcohol-consuming students than among other young people aged 18 to 25 (either in work or

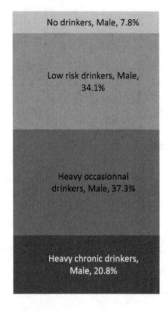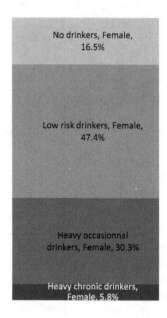

Khi² ***

Figure 10.2 Distribution of types of alcohol consumers (AUDIT) by sex (chi-square test***).

A total of 7.8% of males are not drinkers.

unemployed). Female students reported a higher frequency of heavy drinking than non-student females, whereas male students reported frequencies similar to those of other young men (Legleye et al., 2008). However, despite this comparison, there are in our sample twice as many abstainers among female students as among male students (16.5% compared with 7.8%) and 3.5 times fewer females than males in the heavy chronic drinker category (5.8% compared with 20.8%). Consequently, gender gaps appear more pronounced at either end of the modes of drinking.

Mary Douglas (1987) questioned the origin of the 'happy convergence' of the women's greatest biological vulnerability and the social prohibition hanging over their alcohol consumption. Today, the GENACIS[5] Group's international surveys emphasize the universality of the prevalence of men as regards to drinking. But the gendered variations between cultures, societies and eras remain important. However, neither this universality nor variations are still sufficiently explained today (Bloomfield, Gmel & Wilsnacks, 2006), nor are they widely accepted. Thus, women's alcohol consumption, when they drink or drink too much, is still the subject of questioning, surprise and concern in line with prevailing gender

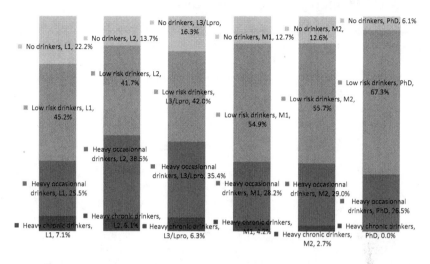

Khi² ***

Figure 10.3 Distribution of the types of alcohol consumers (AUDIT) among female students, by the level of study (chi-square test***).

A total of 22.2% of L1's women are not drinkers.

stereotypes. It is therefore important to analyse the practices of consumption and their variations within the different social settings in which they can be found.

The necessity to understand the consumption of alcohol as a process is reinforced by the developments linked to the level of university studies. However, only alcohol consumption, and only that of girls, seems to be modulated by the years of study (Figure 10.3). Female student consumption develops towards more controlled alcohol consumption since the rates of female consumers at risk and abstainers tend to decrease while they reach higher levels of studies, especially after the bachelor's degree (L3/Lpro).

Female students who have been questioned when reaching an advanced stage of their academic careers during our interviews are anxious to distinguish their current drinking habits from their former alcohol consumption practices. Thus, they negatively judge the juvenile consumption, characterised by 'drink to drink' and instead foreground a greater interest in more 'mature' forms of drinking practice based on sociability (slower paced, without misbehaviour or more focused on dancing) and responsibility (during events framed by school or academic and professional constraints). The choice of products, modalities and scale of consumption must be understood as a social learning object which undergoes fluctuations. This learning occurs in the articulation of the different contexts that students experienced (family, school, professional, friendly, associative, sports). Our purpose here is to understand the influence of family background, as it is less studied particularly in France.

Parental influence on alcohol consumption

Parental influence on alcohol consumption is estimated from the parental occupational category, from the educational level of parents and more generally from the EPS, as previously outlined, while also considering changes linked to the gender of both parents and children within these different relationships. Significantly, the alcohol consumption of female students is significantly more related to parental characteristics than that of male students.

Mothers' and fathers' socio-professional categories

In our findings, only the EPS of the mother has a significant link (Khi^2 **) with young people's alcohol consumption. Children of mothers in agricultural occupations have quite atypical characteristics: They have the highest rate of both non-drinkers (19.1%) and heavy chronic drinkers (19.1%) but the lowest rate of heavy occasional drinkers (21.3%). Children of workers mothers have the highest rate of heavy occasional drinkers (42.4%) but the lowest rate of heavy chronic drinkers (7.8%). Children of women working in higher and intermediate managerial, administrative, professional occupations have the second highest rates of heavy chronic consumption (11.9%) and heavy occasional consumption (37.4%). Risky alcohol consumption (heavy occasional and heavy chronic) are thus the most common in children of mothers in higher and intermediate managerial, administrative, professional occupations (49.5%) and the least common in children of non-working mothers (37.8%).

Educational level of parents

The level of education of parents affects the consumption of female students but not that of the male students. As such, with higher parental educational levels female experimentation, consumption and risky consumption increase. Educational level has been classified into three categories: below baccalaureate, baccalaureate to a degree equivalent to two years of graduate study, and higher levels that of baccalaureate equivalent to more than two years of graduate study. The number of female consumers (78.8%, 87.1% and 87.3%, respectively) and female consumers in heavy occasional and heavy chronic categories (32.5%, 31.9% and 42.5%, respectively) increases with the father's diploma (Khi^2 ***).

Family educational styles

EPS are generally significantly associated with different types of drinking (Table 10.2). While relations may vary according to the sex of the parent and the young, several recurrences can still be found. The authoritative style appears to be the most 'protective', according to the literature (Jackson et al., 1998). Here, whether exercised by the mother or father or both parents, the authoritative style appeared to limit the chronic drinking among both female and male students.

Table 10.2 Distribution of alcohol consumption among female and male students by the educational parenting style (EPS) of the father and mother

A total of 6.4% of the students who have an authoritarian mother are not drinkers.

	Khi² AUDIT	No drinkers	Low-risk drinkers	Heavy occasional drinkers	Heavy chronic drinkers
EPS of the mother for male students					
Authoritarian	*	6.4%	40.9%	33.6%	19.1%
Indulgent	*	8.9%	35.7%	39.3%	16.1%
Uninvolved	*	10.0%	26.5%	36.5%	27.1%
Authoritative	*	6.5%	36.4%	47.7%	9.3%
EPS of the mother for female students					
Authoritarian	**	14.7%	46.3%	30.7%	8.2%
Indulgent	**	24.4%	39.0%	30.8%	5.8%
Uninvolved	**	20.2%	41.8%	28.2%	9.9%
Authoritative	**	13.3%	28.2%	9.9%	2.4%
EPS of the father for male students					
Authoritarian	NS	8.2%	31.6%	37.8%	22.4%
Indulgent	NS	5.8%	42.0%	37.7%	14.5%
Uninvolved	NS	13.0%	29.0%	33.7%	24.3%
Authoritative	NS	9.3%	35.3%	41.3%	14.0%
EPS of the father for female students					
Authoritarian	***	19.2%	45.1%	25.3%	10.4%
Indulgent	***	23.7%	42.0%	30.5%	3.8%
Uninvolved	***	17.5%	44.3%	31.1%	7.1%
Authoritative	***	11.3%	56.3%	29.6%	2.9%

For both parents, the responsiveness dimension, more present in the indulgent and authoritative styles, has a limiting effect on youth alcohol consumption by reducing the occurrence of heavy chronic drinking in both male and female students. This more protective effect of responsiveness on consumption is supported by other studies (García & Garcia, 2009; Calafat, García, Juan, Becoña & Fernández-Hermida, 2014). Finally, the protective effects of responsiveness and authoritative style are more important when it comes to female students' consumption of alcohol. The stronger presence of responsiveness among female students limits risky alcohol consumption practices in the heavy chronic drinking and heavy occasional drinking categories. Similarly, the authoritative style records the lowest rate of alcohol consumer at risk amongst female respondents and producing a tendency towards moderation by reducing both abstinence and risk practices.

The data shows that the influence of parents (occupation category, educational level and EPS) appears to be more significant on the side of female than that of male students. Gendered norms of alcohol consumption can develop themselves within family socialisation, through the control of outputs and activities between peers, or by developing some capacities to overcome difficulties. As we have previously seen, male students tend to have been less comforted by parents when they were upset and have received less testimonies of affection than female students.

During qualitative research, it was apparent that there are many heavy chronic drinking males who seemed reluctant or ill at ease with the parental communication:

> I have the impression that when they [his parents] ask me a question, even if it is banal or if it is normal . . . er . . . I have the impression that they try to nose about my life and I hate that. When I don't want to speak, I don't speak anyway. You can put me so much pressure as you want, I don't speak! (Yohan, 22 y.o., L3 SFA, single).
>
> I have never spoken spontaneously . . . They [his parents] always blamed me for this kind of thing. I have never spoken a lot to my parents about myself (Benjamin, 21 y.o., L2 Law, single).

This lack of intimacy in the communication with parents seems to be counterbalanced by a more important investment with peers. The distance in communication from parents, characterised by a lack of communication between sons and parents, means not talking about themselves, about their emotions and problems, and seems to be characteristic of adolescence, especially for boys and young men who may place more value than young women on emotional independence and the withholding feelings. Thus, one male student responded:

> But yes, I tried rather early to avoid having to deal with my parents. Bah, I felt better with my groups of peers. Thus yeah, er . . . distancing with my family unit. (John, 34 y.o., M1 IUFM, couple)

The gender norms developed within the family refer more broadly to those that affect health, sexuality and self-control, as they can be actualised within peer groups. In all these domains, moderation appears to be the most emphasised drinking style for girls. Further, the female students tend to get closer to the family 'culture of wine' (Palierne, Gaussot & Le Minor, 2015) and to drop out more quickly from the excessive consumption developed among peers than male students (see Figure 10.3). So if parental influence may help explain the keeping of the double gendered standard in attitudes to acceptable alcohol consumption, it cannot do it on its own. It is necessary to analyse the different articulations between gender norms that exist within the family and those which take place among peers.

Family and peer: The double standard of gender in alcohol consumption standards

The female students interviewed for this research were quick to link their drinking patterns with the parenting style they received. For example, concerning moderate drinkers (low-risk and non-drinkers), we observe an asymmetry in parental expectations. Within many families this 'low'-level drinking goes without saying for daughters yet sons spoke of the disappointment of their fathers, uncles or grandfather evoked when they state that they do not appreciate alcohol. Thus, many described a more or less gentle but constant and insistent familial pressure to drink alcohol as part of a handing down of a masculine code of conduct (Gaussot et al., 2015). While drinking is seen as an appropriate marker of masculinity there is no such pressure for younger females to drink in order to establish their own gender role. Further, this absence of pressure on younger females to drink reflects parental fears, shared by girls, concerning their sexuality and possible vulnerability (Herman-Kinney & Kinney, 2013). Some parents tended to control the alcohol consumption of the girls in the family, even when they reached legal drinking age and achieved greater independent:

> Last summer, we were with cousins, in a holiday shack near the Arcachon Basin, and we spent the day doing fairly little, and it's a large meal for lunch. It finishes at 5 pm, and *apéro*[6] is at 6 pm and so on. And there, I know if I drink two glasses for the aperitif, still today, they *[her parents]* say to me: "Oh, you go too far!", all of this, and I'm not allowed to help myself again, while I leave alone, and that . . . So there! *[laugh]* (Anne-Laure, 18 y.o., L2, HSS, single)

Concerning heavy chronic drinkers, some female students link their heavy drinking to a clash with one of their parents. For example, Juliette reflected on her heavy drinking during high school as being a way of gaining compensatory support within her peer group:

> Yeah, we are still a good group of misfits, on the family front, there are many who have some hard times. So we are already able to talk about this, it helps, well I think it helped me to get some thoughts out, to talk about family problems, to have a good chat while drunk. (Juliette, 24 y.o., L3, HSS, couple)

Similarly, Mélodie explained her consumptions as being in opposition to her mother and to the heavy atmosphere of her family:

> If I had a problem, I couldn't talk to her *[her mother]* . . . She didn't realise that by demonising . . . cigarettes, alcohol and beyond, psychoactive substances, that, that as a result, gives me the desire to do it, and the more she tells me not do something, the more I have the desire to do it. . . . Somewhere

along the line, everybody is opposed to their parents, everybody needs to cut the cord, and for me, that has almost gone through a "kill the mother". I have absolutely done everything that she didn't want me to do. . . . The autarky in which my family lived . . . but for me, it was like a cave, I can't get into this, for me, it's toxic, it's locked, it's . . . it's rotten. (Mélodie, 20 y.o., L3, Letters and Languages, couple).

They are strongly different from male students who, unlike female students, mostly evoke their drunkenness through the positive register of sociability with peers, without any reference with personal trouble, or even to parenting. In this way, two heavy male drinkers appeared not to understand the purpose of our interviews that combined interrogations about family and parenting linked to alcohol consumptions:

In fact, I don't quite understand, you try to link my family life and my drug consumptions like if this had something in common? . . . I'm sorry, I don't have unhappy childhood with an alcoholic father. (Philippe, 18 y.o., L1 Law, single)

I don't think there is a strong link with family, but er, no, yeah right. (Damien, 20 y .o., L2 HSS, single)

However, if heavy drinking mainly takes place outside the family environment, it can never be purely external to a certain relationship with parents and parenting. Thus, alcohol consumption is often hidden or disclosed in partial and selective ways to parents and, further still, the need to return to the parental home influences drinking practices during adolescence. Therefore, we might better explain the misunderstandings of Damien and Philippe with the fact that their early and frequent alcohol consumption during secondary and high school, took place within peer groups yet was more or less tolerated by parents. If certain drinking practices (Le Garrec, 2002) develop in the interstice of parental supervision or knowledge, or even in opposition to parents, this is not sufficient, on the contrary, to exclude the family and the parent-young people relationships from the analysis.

The kind of reflexivity that female students develop about their excesses, and informs their efforts to reduce them (see Figure 10.3), relates to the close proximity they exhibit with their parents, and in the double standard of gender that continues to be expressive among young people. Beyond the family, girls can be encouraged to drink, especially by boys, seeing a drunken girl as likely to be much more susceptible to their attempts at seduction or to initiate sex (Lyons & Willot, 2008). Within peer groups, gender norms can mean that girls who drink do so under the threat of sarcasm or other pressures. As in Herman-Kinney and Kinney's (2013) research, there is some indication that non-drinking girls are at risk of being laughed at and being labeled 'sissy', 'a bit uptight' or even 'saintly hypocrite'.

However, amongst the student research participants, a clear disparity in the drinking practices of male and female students emerged, especially in relation to opportunities to drink in public spaces, the frequency of drinking and the degree of social acceptance apparent when female students drink. Standards that affect food and sexuality, attention to health, bodily and academic success even encourage female students to further limit their consumption and drunken behaviour. Thus, drinking remains a way of *doing gender* (Measham, 2002). Thus, risks and consequences of intoxication, particularly those relating to embodied gender standards relating to physical appearance and control of the body, appear to go against normative femininity while they can, particularly for young male drinkers, support normative masculinity when related to conceptions of fun, bravado and homosocial bonding (Thurnell-Read, 2011). While standards of alcohol consumption are therefore still structured by the asymmetry of gender, young women are no longer strictly prohibited from heavy alcohol consumption by gaining a degree of permissiveness in alcoholic *public* drinking and often claim the use of alcohol to be an adjuvant to the party. However, female students' alcohol consumption remains indexed to that of the boys whose standards would reflect 'universal neutrality' (Mathieu, 1991). Boys continue to drink more often, and in a more excessive manner than girls, meaning these spaces of excess remain largely a space of male privilege (Meidani, Dany & Welzer-Lang, 2005) that women enter only problematically and at the risk of social prohibitions. Evidently, then, alcohol consumption practices, and the meanings associated with them, remain heavily gendered. Female excess remains stigmatised by male students. Typically, seeing anxiety in the opposite sex, female students try to demonstrate their moderation while male students take pride in their excesses. These excesses can be prominent in the stories involved in the boys' identity construction (Peralta, 2007). Thus, Murielle drew a clear link between excessive drinking and masculine identity by saying that:

> For me it seemed obvious that when you drink a bottle, a bottle and a half of whiskey all by yourself, it's not good for you, there is always a danger you know. And seeing that you hold your liquor that you're happy to hold it, and that you're proud to hold it, it's . . . I think it's a shame. I told them "But you're fucking nuts, that's tough to hold so much hey". Just that. So maybe they saw it as "Oh yeah! See that? I hold!" Because you're a man, you hold whiskey hey. (Murielle, 23, L3, Literature and Language, single).

Conclusion

The research results presented here do not tend to lead to the same conclusions about the effects of EPS on alcohol consumption as those more generally measured. Demandingness does not seem to bring the protective effect that we found ourselves in the previous study on young people in France (Gaussot et al., 2011b) and which was confirmed by other research on the subject. Within the student population, responsiveness appears to play a greater protective effect against heavy chronic consumption, whether it comes from the father or the mother and is applied to girls or boys. This effect is also found in other studies (García & Garcia, 2009; Calafat et al., 2014). The protective effect of the parents' responsiveness is reinforced even with the girls since it appears to reduce the risks in their consumption of alcohol. The authoritative style that scores highly in measures of both demandingness and responsiveness appears to offer the most pronounced influence in reducing levels of heavy chronic drinking. Like responsiveness, its effectiveness in terms of preventing risky consumption is more significant in relation to female student alcohol usage.

These differences in the results find an explanation first in the effects of the EPS measure and second, in the effect of the composition (including age) of the surveyed population. It must be remembered first that the EPS test is a measure relative to each population: the levels of demandingness and responsiveness that separate the different styles remain dependent on their distribution in the population. Thus, we see an age effect: control is more perceived to a greater extent by the youngest people, the ones who are likely to have regular alcohol consumption. This relativity of EPS depending on the sample also invites us to broadly question the results presented here. If responsiveness seems to supplant demandingness among our young participants, it is probably because at their age, young people are less in demand for interdictions and strict rules as for listening and exchange.

However, if we do not observe any radically different educational parenting styles between female and male students, the 'mark of the gender' still exits, even in the populations which provide the most egalitarian education. In future research, it would be more relevant to measure gender disparities in the effects of EPS on the consumption of alcohol in a more socially and culturally diversified population. Through the highlighting of the structure and differentiated effects of family socialisation, sociology should then be committed to restore the complexity of the social world, without participating in any moral familialism on the consumption of alcohol.

Importantly, parenting has been shown to contribute to explanations of the upholding of gendered norms in drinking. On one hand, parental influence (socio-professional categories, educational level, parenting style) is more correlated with girls' alcohol consumptions than boys. On the other hand, even after an experience of heavy drinking in the early years at the university, female students appear to turn more quickly towards moderate drinking, and more readily conform with parental drinking norms (Palierne et al., 2015). Further, the peer influence, or more precisely, juvenile sociability is more significant among boys as the pressure to construct their masculinity calls for a greater emancipation from family norms and, as a result, seems to increase the intensity and duration of social pressures to drink to excess.

Appendix

The authoritative parenting index

Interviewed students had to answer questions about the parenting style they received when they were in high school, living with their parents (16–17 years old). Students had to complete an attitude scale for each item. First, they completed the scale about their mother and then about their father, in order to investigate a potential differentiation between their parents.

1: Strongly disagree 2: Somewhat disagree 3: Somewhat agree 4: Strongly agree

Categorisation of demandingness items and responsiveness items in thematic areas

Demandingness

Exercise of authority

a. Item: *My mother/my father was always telling me what to do.*
b. Item: *My mother/my father made rules without asking what I thought.*
c. Item: *My mother/my father had rules that I had to follow.*

Supervision of outdoor activities

d. Item: *My mother/my father told me times when I came home.*
e. Item: *My mother/my father made sure I told her/him where I was going.*
f. Item: *My mother/my father asked me what I did with friends.*
g. Item: *My mother/my father knew where I was after school.*

Supervision of homework

h. Item: *My mother/my father checked to see if I did my homework.*

Monitoring of lifestyle

i. Item: *My mother/my father made sure I went to bed on time.*

Responsiveness

Availability of listening

a. Item: *My mother/my father was too busy to talk to me.*
b. Item: *My mother/my father listened to what I had to say.*

Management of the difficulties faced by young people

c. Item: *My mother/my father wanted to hear about my problems.*
d. Item: *My mother/my father made me feel better when I was upset.*

Testimonies of affection

e. Item: *My mother/my father liked me just the way I was.*
f. Item: *My mother/my father told me when I did a good job on things.*
g. Item: *My mother/my father were pleased with how I behaved.*

Items have been sorted according to the thematic areas we have built for our study. Items scheduling is different during the assessment process. This sorting in coherent categories allows a more detailed analysis of parenting variations.

Notes

1 Respectively: Inter-ministerial Mission for Combating Drugs and Addictive Behaviors, National Cancer Institute, Institute for Scientific Research on Beverages.
2 See correspondence between *Professions et Catégories Socioprofessionnelles* defined by INSEE (National Institute of Statistics and Economics Studies) and OSC (Occupation and Socioeconomic Class) in Pevalin and Rose (2002). Given the differences between the French and English terminologies commonly used to define socioeconomic categories, throughout the chapter we use the following as approximate equivalents: *Cadres et professions intellectuelles supérieures* as 'higher and intermediate managerial, administrative, professional occupations'; *Artisans commerçants et chefs d'entreprise* as 'skilled manual occupations and small business owners'; *Professions intermédiaires* as 'supervisory, clerical and junior managerial, administrative, professional occupations'; *Employés* as 'Lower-level service and administrative occupations'; *Ouvriers* as 'semi-skilled and unskilled manual occupations'; *Agriculteurs exploitants* as 'agricultural labourers'; *Retraité* as 'retired people'; and, finally, *Personnes sans activité* as 'persons without professional activity/unemployed'.
3 This test was developed by the World Health Organization (Saunders et al., 1993). It had been validated in both the general population and specific populations. The AUDIT explores the past 12 months of consumption. Its aim is to detect people with alcohol consumption problems.
4 Terms in boldface type refer to the thematic areas of responsiveness and demandingness dimensions underlined in the box in the appendix.
5 Gender, Alcohol and Culture: An International Study.
6 *Apéro* is a French social custom of taking an early evening drink with friends and/or family.

References

Attias-Donfut, C., Lapierre, N. and Segalen, M. 2002. *Le nouvel esprit de famille*. Paris: Odile Jacob.
Baudelot, C. and Establet, R. 1992. *Allez les filles! Une révolution silencieuse*. Paris: Seuil.
Baudelot, C. and Establet, R. 2007. *Quoi de neuf chez les filles?: Entre stéréotypes et libertés*. Paris: Nathan.

Bloomfield, K., Gmel, G. and Wilsnacks, S. 2006. Introduction to special issue. Gender, culture and alcohol problems: A multi-national study. *Alcohol and Alcoholism*, 41(1): 13–17.
Bozon, M. and Villeneuve-Gokalp, C. 1994. Les enjeux des relations entre générations à la fin de l'adolescence. *Population*, 6: 1527–1555.
Calafat, A., García, F., Juan, M., Becoña, E. and Fernández-Hermida, J.R. 2014. Which parenting style is more protective against adolescent substance use?: Evidence within European context, *Drug and Alcohol Dependence*, 138: 185–192.
Combessie, J. C. 1969. Education et valeurs de classe dans la sociologie américaine. *Revue Française de Sociologie*, 10(1): 12–36.
Cromer, S. 2008. Les suppléments Parents des magazines jeunesse: Un outil de 'domestication' des mères? *Recherches et Prévisions*, 93.
Déchaux, J. H. 2007. *Sociologie de la famille*. Paris: La Découverte.
Déchaux, J. H. 2010. Ce que l''individualisme' ne permet pas de comprendre: Le cas de la famille. *Esprit*, juin, 94–111.
Delphy, C. 2001. *L'ennemi principal. 2. Penser le genre*. Paris: Syllepse.
Douglas, M. 1987. *Constructive drinking: Perspectives on drinking from anthropology*. New York: Cambridge University Press.
Durning, P. 1995. *Education familiale: Acteurs, processus et enjeux*. Paris: PUF.
Eriksen, S. 1999. Alcohol as a gender symbol: Women and the alcohol question in the turn-of-the century Denmark. *Scandinavian Journal of History*, 24: 45–73.
García, F. and Garcia, E. 2009. Is always authoritative the optimum parenting style? Evidence from Spanish families. *Adolescence*, 44(173): 101–131.
Gaussot, L., Le Minor, L. and Palierne, N. 2011a. Les styles éducatifs parentaux et la consommation d'alcool des jeunes. *Alcoologie et Addictologie*, 33(3): 205–214.
Gaussot, L., Le Minor, L. and Palierne, N. 2011b. Influence du style éducatif sur les pratiques de consommation d'alcool des jeunes de 13 à 24 ans. *Les Cahiers de l'Ireb*, 20: 129–135.
Gaussot, L., Palierne, N. and Le Minor, L. 2015. Les jeunes 'non-buveurs' au prisme du genre et de l'éducation familiale: Enquête en population étudiante. In M.-T. Déroff and T. Fillaut (Eds.), *Boire: une affaire de sexe et d'âge* (79–92). Rennes: Presses de l'EHESP.
Gayet, D. 2004. *Les pratiques éducatives des familles*. Paris: PUF.
Gefou-Madianou, D. 2002. *Alcohol, gender and culture*. London: Routledge.
Giddens, A. 1992. *The transformation of intimacy: Sexuality, love and eroticism in modern societies*. Cambridge: Polity Press.
Guyon, M. 2004. L'aide aux devoirs apportée par les parents. *Insee première*, 996.
Guyon, M. and Guérin, S. 2006. L'implication des parents dans la scolarité des filles et des garçons: des intentions à la pratique. *Economie et Statistique*, 398–399, 59–84.
Herman-Kinney, N. and Kinney, D. 2013. Sober as deviant: The stigma of sobriety and how some college students 'stay dry' on a 'wet' campus, *Journal of Contemporary Ethnography*, 42(1): 64–103.
Jackson, C. 2002. Perceived legitimacy of parental authority and tobacco and alcohol use during early adolescence. *Journal of Adolescent Health*, 31(5): 425–432.
Jackson, C., Henriksen, L. and Foshee, VA. 1998. The authoritative parenting index: Predicting health risk behaviours among children and adolescents. *Health Education and Behaviour*, 25(3): 319–337.
Kellerhals, J. and Montandon, C. 1991. *Les stratégies éducatives des familles*. Paris: Delachaux et Niestlé.

Kohn, M. L. 1963. Social class and parent-child relationships: An interpretation. *American Journal of Sociology*, 68: 471–480.

Lareau, A. 2011 [2003]. *Unequal childhoods: Class, race and family life*. Berkeley: University of California Press.

Lautrey, J. 1980. Classe sociale, milieu familial, intelligence. Paris: PUF.

Le Garrec, S. 2002. *Ces ados qui en « prennent »: Sociologie des consommations toxiques adolescentes*. Toulouse: PUM.

Le Pape, M. C. 2006. Les ambivalences d'une double appartenance: Hommes et femmes en milieux populaires. *Sociétés Contemporaines*, 62: 5–26.

Le Pape, M. C. 2008. La famille risquogène? Enjeux de recherche en sciences humaines et sociales: Une revue de littérature pluridisciplinaire. *Notes et Documents*, OSC/CNRS, n° 4.

Le Pape, M. C. 2009. Être parent dans les milieux populaires: Entre valeurs familiales traditionnelles et nouvelles normes éducatives. *Informations Sociales*, 154: 88–95.

Le Pape, M. C. and Van Zanten, A. 2009. Les pratiques éducatives des familles. In M. Duru-Bellat and A. Van Zanten (Eds.), *Sociologie du système éducatif: Les inégalités scolaires* (185–205). Paris: PUF.

Legleye, S., Beck, F., Peretti-Watel, P. and Chau, N. 2008. Le rôle du statut scolaire et professionnel dans les usages de drogues des hommes et des femmes de 18 à 25 ans. *Revue d'Epidémiologie et de Santé Publique*, 56: 345–355.

Lyons, A. C. and Willott, S. A. 2008. Alcohol consumption, gender identities and women's changing social positions. *Sex Roles*, 59: 694–712.

Maccoby, E. E. and Martin, J. A. 1983. Socialization in the context of the family: Parent-child interaction. In *Handbook of child psychology, socialization, personality, and social development*. 4th ed. (pp. 1–101). New York: Wiley.

Mathieu, N. C. 1991. *L'anatomie politique: Catégorisations et idéologies du sexe*. Paris: Côté-femmes.

Measham, F. 2002. 'Doing gender' – 'doing drugs': Conceptualizing the gendering of drugs cultures. *Contemporary Drug Problems*, 29: 335–373.

Meidani, A., Dany, L. and Welzer-Lang, D. 2005. Manière de boire et rapports sociaux de genre chez les jeunes (18–25 ans). *Les Cahiers de l'Ireb*, 17: 67–70.

Palierne, N., Gaussot, L. and Le Minor, L. 2015. Le genre de l'ivresse: Evolution des consommations d'alcool des étudiant-e-s. *Journal des Anthropologues*, 140–141, 153–172.

Pevalin, D. and Rose, D. 2002. The national statistics socio-economic classification: Unifying official and sociological approaches to the conceptualisation and measurement of social class in the united kingdom. *Sociétés Contemporaines*, 45–46: (1): 75–106.

Peralta, R. L. 2007. College alcohol use and the embodiment of hegemonic masculinity among European American men. *Sex Roles*, 56: 741–756.

Peretti-Watel, P., Beck, F. and Legleye, S. 2007. *Les usages sociaux des drogues*. Paris: PUF.

Ricroch, L. and Roumier, B. 2011. Depuis 11 ans, moins de tâches ménagères, plus d'internet. *INSEE Première*, 1377.

Saint-Jacques, M. C., Turcotte, D. and Oubrayrie-Roussel, N. 2012. L'éducation familiale à l'heure des compétences parentales. *Enfances, Familles, Générations*, 16: 1–16.

Saunders, J. B., Aasland, O. G., Babor, T. F., de la Fuente, J. R. and Grant, M. (1993). Development of the Alcohol Use Disorders Identification Test (AUDIT): WHO collaborative project on early detection of persons with harmful alcohol consumption. *Addiction*, 88, 791–804.

Scott, J. W. 1986. Gender: A useful category of historical analysis. *American Historical Review*, 91(5): 1053–1075.

Segalen, M. 2006 [1981]. *Sociologie de la famille*. Paris: Armand Colin.
Steinberg, L., Mounts, N., Lamborn, S. and Dornbusch, S. 1991. Pattern of competence and adjustment among adolescents from authoritative, authoritarian, indulgent and neglectful families. *Child Development*, 62(5): 1049–1065.
Thurnell-Read, T. 2011. Off the leash and out of control: Masculinities and embodiment in Eastern European stag tourism. *Sociology*, 45(6): 977–991.

Chapter 11

Growing up, going out
Cultural and aesthetic attachment to the night-time economy

Oliver Smith

Introduction

The night-time alcohol-based leisure economy has served as the backdrop for numerous pieces of work considering youth identities and consumer culture (Hollands, 2002; Winlow & Hall, 2006; Hayward & Hobbs, 2007) alongside broader considerations of youth transitions (Engineer, Phillips, Thompson & Nicholls, 2003) and cultural infantilisation (Hall, Winlow & Ancrum, 2008, Smith, 2014). Despite the fact that the night-time economy (NTE) is dominated by consumers under the age of 25 (Engineer et al., 2003; Winlow & Hall, 2006; Plant & Plant, 2006), there does not appear to be an overwhelming amount of evidence to suggest that individuals simply 'grow' out of their relationship with the alcohol-based night-time leisure economy, despite the assertions of a number of commentators (see Wright, 1999; Maggs & Schulenberg, 2004; Seaman & Ikegwuonu, 2010). In fact, data appears to suggest that excessive drinking behaviours are lingering further into adulthood for a greater proportion of the population than some might assume, contradicting what we assume to be true with regard to deviance and drift (Matza, 1964). The Office for National Statistics (2013) reports that 25% of men and 20% of women between the ages of 25 and 44 drank 'heavily' on at least one day in the previous week, compared with 22% of men and 17% of women aged 16 to 24 (Health and Social Care Information Centre, 2012). The documented rise in adult drinking (Smith & Foxcroft, 2009), combined with aggressive marketing and social positioning of alcohol and its imagery (Chatterton & Hollands, 2003; Hastings, Anderson, Cook & Gordon, 2005; Plant & Plant, 2006) suggests a problem that shows little sign of receding, despite reported closures of pubs, indicating an apparent contraction of the industry over recent years.

This chapter aims to present data collected through a range of ethnographic methods from a hitherto neglected population within the NTE, arguing that for some individuals, the aging process and associated 'markers of adulthood' (Blatterer, 2007) are insufficient to dislodge them from a deep commitment to the pleasures of alcohol-based leisure. As the NTE expands to cater for a broader demographic, the perceived identity gains associated with a presence in urban drinking environments are available further into the life course. If these shifts were accompanied by real and lasting opportunities for the creation and maintenance of identity beyond those available off-the-peg in the consumer market place, then this may well be cause for celebration. However, as the following pages suggest, the reality is that many committed adult consumers are faced with anxiety at the prospect of the cultural inconsequentiality that looms should the individual fail to avail his or herself of the opportunities offered by the NTE. Recent shifts in labour markets, changes to the system of higher education and altered landscapes of interpersonal relationships that characterize Bauman's notion of Liquid Society have drawn young people and the adults they become away from a traditional form of maturation, instead allowing consumer culture to provide alternative ways of being, through conforming with the ideologically dominant and ultimately infantilising processes of competitive individualism. It is here that the application of Slavoj Žižek's interpretation of cultural infantilisation allows a more nuanced understanding of the socio-symbolic status associated with certain forms of consumer items and the desire to avoid missing out on opportunities for hedonistic excess.

Becoming adult

Youth studies literature has long been concerned with transitions to adulthood (see, for example, Coles, 1995). Recent literature appears to be moving away from a notion of a categorical concept of youth, and a staid and logical progression toward the end 'goal' of adulthood (Currie, 2005; Winlow & Hall, 2006). Transitions are increasingly viewed as necessarily imbued with a degree of fluidity and non-finality. Traditional markers, such as leaving home, employment and, increasingly, marriage, are all transitory and reversible, serving as unsatisfactory milestones by which to measure movement towards adulthood. Even Arnett's (2000, 2001) assertion that more internalistic and individualised criteria for adulthood, such as independent decision making and financial independence from parents, should replace traditional markers results in non-milestones, since they can be blocked or even reversed by the vagaries of global capitalism.

Furthermore, while we might assume that the expansion and promotion of further and higher education and the increasingly fluid nature of culture (Bauman, 2005) has created a largely positive experience of increasing levels of upward mobility and equality of opportunity, it appears that, in fact, the converse is true. There is now a surfeit of literature that suggests that recent history has witnessed growing forms of inequality, despite a dominant ideological discourse that rests upon the image of freedom, openness, democracy and meritocracy (Young, 1999; Žižek, 2009; Dorling, 2010; Wilkinson & Pickett, 2010). Indeed, recent changes in the way university places are funded are likely to result in increased levels of social inequality and an increased widening of the chasm between rich and poor. Further still, large numbers of graduates today are failing to achieve the employment opportunities that match their expectations or qualification-based skill set, not forgetting, of course, that the three or four years spent in higher education serve to further fragment the transition to adulthood. With the prospect of unfulfilling, insecure jobs within the service industries beckoning (Lloyd, 2013), large numbers may be expected to fall under the influence of the infantilising aspects of consumer capitalism (Barber, 2007), becoming, perhaps irreversibly, enveloped in the sign-value system of consumerism (Baudrillard, 1983).

Cultural Infantilisation and the NTE

The process of infantilisation (Barber, 2007) essentially provokes a level of childish puerility in adults, while maintaining elements of childishness within children who are 'growing up' and becoming empowered to consume. Furthermore, it succeeds in preventing individuals from taking on traditional adult concerns in order to retain them in stasis, the pause button pressed during a period in which they are most susceptible to consumer symbolism and marketing messages. Emphatically more nuanced a notion than its everyday understanding as an insult denoting the subject as childish and immature, *cultural* infantilisation ensures that certain features of childhood affect adult culture, becoming transformed and reintegrated into mature behaviour in such a way that retains childish aspects within a mature adult setting. Adults are henceforth likely to think nothing of being seen engrossed in a Harry Potter book on the bus on the way to work, drinking their morning coffee from a mug denoting their preferred sports team or using a cartoon-themed mouse mat. Additionally, the adult attachment to electronic gadgets can be viewed as representative of a broader slide into commercialised abstraction, with the aim of soothing the anxieties and dissatisfactions that are bound up with real adulthood in the formal economy and culture more generally. This appears to exemplify Virilio's (2005, p. 94) analysis of the pathological dimension of infantile narcissism – the creation of 'false adults or false children' – which serves to extend narcissism across the life course within consumer capitalism. More specifically, within the NTE, alcopops and drinks such as *Corky's* shots, which revolve around flavours of recognizable confectionary such as *Skittles, Kola-Kube* or *Crème Egg*, should be viewed as appealing to the 'cult of the child' (Barber, 2007) as much as they are accused of being marketed toward under-age drinkers.

Nowhere within the marketised environs of the NTE is this exemplified more overtly than in the hyper-real bar chain Reflex (a chain of more than 40 establishments which each promise 'the ultimate '80s party'), as the following field notes imply:

> There is the unmistakeable sickly smell in the air of stale alcohol, a smell synonymous with an establishment, where drinks are spilt often and floors cleaned less so. The bar itself occupies a central position directly in front of me as I enter, its glittered surface winking lewdly, and has an array of chrome beer dispensers along its length, each of which proclaims proudly which global corporate brand name it is allied to. *Stella Artois, Foster's* and *Strongbow* all feature. The back of the bar is heavily mirrored, with a predominance of *Corky's* vodka shots. The brightly coloured bottles stand three deep at the

bar in order to make the transition from empty to full bottle as quick as possible. The bottles contain a variety of coloured, almost glutinous liquid, the hues highlighted by the lighting from behind and underneath the bottles. The possible flavours to tempt the drinker are plentiful, and include apple sour, blueberry, cappuccino, cherry, chocolate orange, cola cube, cream egg, mint cream, strawberry and cream, toffee and white chocolate. According to their website, *Corky's* shots are 'a true game changer . . . creating never before seen theatre of serve, boosting interest and excitement, (globalbrands.co.uk 2014). This, however, is not enough to convince me, and I order a bottle of *Beck's*.

Above the regiment of *Corky's* shots run a fairly standard selection of spirits, some of which are available as a double measure for an extra pound, indicated by a garish star in neon card and glitter. In addition to alcohol, the bar offers a number of items for sale that could be considered loosely in keeping with its 1980s theme. This includes oversized and glittery sunglasses, wigs, candy necklaces, 'Madonna-style' conical brassieres and Reflex-branded sweatbands and T-shirts. Bar staff wear bright coloured T-shirts, laden with '80s references to the cult film *The Goonies* and Liverpool band Frankie Goes to Hollywood, whose 'Relax' motif is ubiquitous as far as any homage to the decade is concerned.

The '80s theme is rammed down the throats of the drinkers everywhere I look; indeed, the place resembles a poorly thought-out museum. From the ceiling hang glitterballs, oversized Rubik's Cubes, and huge, square television sets playing videos that sometimes match the tune being played by the garrulous DJ. A cardboard David Hasselhoff, leaning on his iconic car, looms over the revolving dance floor, while brightly coloured posters inform us of the drink deals on offer tonight. The fonts used on posters and on the TV screens have been liberated from classic '80s cultural heavyweights such as *The A-Team* and the Tom Cruise film *Cocktail*. Ascending the stairs to the lavatory I am accompanied by a barrage of familiar faces from the 1980s, leering out from the walls, before being faced with the option of entering a door titled 'East End Boys' or 'West End Girls', a nod in the direction of The Pet Shop Boys' 1985 hit. Inside the gents, the music from downstairs is piped through, complete with the DJ's less than intelligent or intelligible commentary. Above the trough urinal is a mural in graffiti art style, as perhaps you might see sprayed on the side of a New York subway train in an Eddie Murphy film. Closer inspection reveals that the 'art' is in fact little more than a short section of print, duplicated several times along the length of the wall.

Finding something real or authentic in this establishment is impossible, with everything presented as a cut-price parody of a corporate perception of a moment in time.

As is clear upon spending any time inside one of the culturally homogenous night-time drinking venues on the high street of any British city, drinking cultures appear to be inseparable from a variety of childish motifs, from drinking games to the legitimisation of childish behaviour and separation from the emotional and mental demands of more formal culture. This necessitates a closer examination of the broader socioeconomic context of consumer symbolism, and its effects on the individual.

As Bauman (2005) suggests, the uncertainty and anxiety resultant from neo-liberal market principles appear to have had the unsettling effect of rendering long-term planning not only undesirable but also difficult. The low-paid nature of many service industry jobs in call centres or faceless offices, regardless of whether they are seen by many graduates as temporary or some kind of 'stepping stone' to something better (Winlow & Hall, 2006), has a number of knock-on effects. The lack of financial reward and the cautious nature of the mortgage market following the recent economic crisis places gaining a foot on the property ladder beyond the reach of all but a minority of individuals (Bone & O'Reilly, 2010). A number of respondents expressed concern at their inability to access the housing market and highlighted the debilitating hangover of forays into the world of consumer credit. One such person was Rob, 33, a 'relationship manager' for a large credit-card processing company. Rob left university with a lower second-class honours degree in history, spent five years working on the shop floor for a chain of booksellers both in London and his current city, before taking agency-based office work. Here he describes the ontological fear and existential vulnerability (Southwood, 2011) at being left behind, mired in debt and facing an unedifying future:

> When I came back, everything was fine, a lot of my old friends were here, and there were a really good bunch of people working at the bookshop. After a while though, things began to change . . . Alan left to go and live in Manchester, Brendan trained as a policeman and Charlie and a couple of others left the bookshop to get proper jobs at the council or [a large insurance firm]. As everyone else started earning more money I realised I was getting left behind with no chance of getting a house, going on holiday or anything else like that . . . everything I earned was going on rent, credit card bills and paying back my loans.

Rob equates leaving minimum-wage employment at a bookshop to the process of becoming adult. The purchase of a house, the financial ability to go on holiday and 'everything else' are viewed as indicative of a competency in the role of 'adult', and his statement is tinged with an acknowledgement that his previous inability to defer gratification, existing in the hedonistic moment and drawn to the carnival of consumer experiences offered by the NTE is in danger of rendering him unable to competently participate in consumer markets – in effect he is suffering anxiety at the possibility of becoming a 'flawed' consumer (Bauman, 1998). His concerns are echoed by Steve, 36, who has spent the past 10 years working on a string of temporary contracts arranged through an employment agency:

> I really need to get two things sorted out this year – a pension and buying a flat. I mean, for fucks sake I'm 36 years old. I can't live in rented accommodation for the rest of my life, and I don't want to be working in *B & Q* to

pay off my mortgage when I'm 70. I've never got round to getting a pension either so I really need to start thinking about that.

Steve appears to be acutely aware of his age and the possibility that his commitment to consumer symbolism and a sustained attachment to maintaining a presence within the NTE have had the effect of essentially de-railing his progress through the more traditional life course. Pensions, owning property and progression up the career ladder are, for him, all factors that contribute to the process of 'becoming' adult. However, it is not enough for the individual to *believe* they are 'an adult'. As Žižek (1999) suggests, the Big Other – the communal network of law, custom and social institutions that provides a framework for society – must know it too, through monthly deductions from the pay packet in mortgage payments, pension contributions and subscriptions to the Sunday Times wine club. It is the Big Other that confers an identity upon the fragmented, decentred individual (Žižek, 1999). For Rob and Steve it appears their status as adult is not confirmed by the Big Other because of a lack of trappings associated with being 'grown up'. Perhaps one of the most striking features of the data is that many people entering this life-phase fill the gap by utilising the symbolism of contemporary consumer capitalism, which renders the properties of youth, vitality and perpetual adolescence a more easily attainable identity while the markers of traditional adulthood remain unachievable and for some untenable. Status as young and 'cool' is confirmed through possession of certain clothes, belongings and trinkets that may be considered superfluous or indulgent to the traditional social order.

A characteristic that may yet prove to be distinct to this generation is the challenge found in the necessity to balance two opposing yet insistent forces – they are more than aware of what makes up a 'responsible' adult lifestyle, yet are unable to ignore the siren song of consumerised hedonism. This results in a complex plate-spinning exercise that is managed with varying degrees of success by the individuals observed here.

For some respondents, the pressures of a traditional notion of adulthood are experienced from family members, as Andrea, a 35-year-old office worker notes:

> A lot of my friends are starting to get married and have kids . . . having their lives completely altered, and that makes me think that maybe it is better to fit it in as much as possible now while you still have time. I know they wouldn't want to swap their children for the world, but I know they would like to still have the freedom that I have . . . We have so many choices and there is so much going on, getting married and losing independence and so on . . . I don't see it as a good thing. Having the kind of networks of friends and the girls and that, it's the way to go. My mum and dad nag at me about the fact I haven't got a husband, brood of kids and all that. Family parties and all that, and my auntie will whisper in my ear – don't leave it too late, and I'm like fuck off, I'm only in my thirties. All my cousins are married and have kids, so it's a bit of an issue.

Although clearly aware of the societal factors existing to draw her back into a more traditional life course, such as familial pressure exuding the expectation that she settle down with a man and set up home, Andrea is seduced by the promises of the NTE. The excitement it offers, and potential to push away from the dull actuality of her life, as well as the attraction of portraying herself as young and free, continue to push her towards another big night out (also see Hollands and Nicholls, both this volume). Her explanatory mechanism appears to consist of positioning herself as the discerning consumer who makes a calculated and fully rational decision to 'leave behind' the mediocrity of career building and prime-time television viewing, applying value to more rewarding and pleasurable pastimes. She locates the drudgery and constraint of marriage and breeding as hampering her liberty and creativity, expressed, of course, by her dedication to the consumer economy. This is actually a viewpoint that is clearly in harmony with many other academic accounts (see, for example, Skelton & Valentine, 1998; Malbon, 1999). However, while failing to give her any real sense of satisfaction, this explanation also negates to adequately justify her current approach to consumerised leisure. In many ways her account is similar to some of the street criminals interviewed by Hall et al. (2008), who appear to construct these positive narratives as an ideological fallback position, a means of momentarily convincing the self and others that the future is bright and the subject remains in control of their own destiny. Andrea actually appears to show little commitment to this narrative, and it is possible to discern an undercurrent of bleak nihilism, a depressive hedonia (see Fisher, 2009), that increasingly seems to characterise a culture at the end of history (Žižek, 2010).

Work – (night) life balance

Compounding the ontological precarity (Virno, 1996; Southwood, 2011) associated with the psychosocial tug-of-war described previously, many respondents appear to be caught in something of an ideological impasse. On the one hand, they are aware that marriage, property, family holidays and other ideological milestones of what Young (1999) might call the 'socially included' are, broadly speaking, an inevitable feature of their life course, but they are also deeply ensconced within the youthful consumer culture that necessitates their continued participation within the NTE. While there is a sense that they are merely staving off the inevitable conclusion of 'settling down' into adult conformity, there is also a feeling that such amounts to a rejection, no matter how temporary, of traditional elements of consumer capitalism, the rat race, the mill and so on. While this may be conceived as motivation for perpetual presence in the pubs, bars and clubs across the country, there exists a broader problem, in that their involvement and consumption within the NTE serves to power many of the instruments of capitalism against which they believe they are rebelling. This research tends to show that interviewees believe that they are the 'winners' in the game, working to live, making their job serve their own enjoyment while their place within the Symbolic

Order is cemented through the completion of their roles within it. For example, Steve knows that he has to go to work in order to be able to go out at the weekend, buy the clothes that he believes speak volumes about his tastes, interests and style. While he would rather not work in his administrative role, to give up work would relegate him to a much lower level of socioeconomic standing, not through the loss of status conferred as a member of the labour force, but through his inability to display ownership of material goods (see Baudrillard, 1983; Bourdieu, 1984).

Many of the respondents that I spoke to suggested that participation within the NTE is to be kept rigorously separate from their working lives, with some appearing wary of mixing their out-of-the-workplace identity with their workplace identity. Sally, a 32-year-old health professional is one such example:

> I have to be pretty careful about being seen out and about in town. It didn't matter so much when I was working [in Bradford] but now there is a chance that I might see someone out in town when I'm drunk who I have been treating earlier or, say, the son or daughter of a patient. It looks totally unprofessional, but they could also put in a complaint to my supervisor, and I could probably get struck off.

The desire to maintain a professional façade within working hours was repeated by a number of respondents, most of whom tended to be in jobs that had a much more defined 'career path' or were in positions of more responsibility. Other respondents tended to display a much more casual attitude towards comportment at work and while socialising with work colleagues. Ellie, for example, has worked in administrative positions since leaving school at age 18. She currently works within the administrative arm of a government department, based in the city centre. A large core of their lower-level employees are sourced from recruiting agencies, before being offered more permanent contracts after a period of approximately a year, a fairly common practice among large corporations who may have a fast turnover among positions of this nature:

> At work, in the office it is kind of divided up into groups of people who like to go out for a drink after work or whatever, and those who don't. It's mostly an age thing I would say, but there are a couple of guys who are in their 50s who love to come out for a couple. They tend to go home in time for their tea, whereas the rest of us might stay out later. Sometimes it turns into a proper session, staying out 'til last orders, which means going into work the next day with a hangover [laughs]. The pissheads in the office are the ones who are sitting with their sunglasses on like this [uses her hand to prop up and shield one side of her head] and trying not to be noticed, just drinking Lucozade.

For Ellie, work is clearly there to be endured, not enjoyed (Winlow & Hall, 2006). Her employment to date has been concerned with earning enough money to pay rent, buy clothes and maintain an active presence within the NTE. There is no vocational quality to her mode of employment, and up until the past couple of years it has been transitory and unstable, arranged through agencies or on temporary contracts. Membership of a union, or contributing to a pension are not priorities, because they divert money from the circuits of consumption. Her present contract allows for flexi-time, a valuable tool in terms of heavy heads and late starts that go hand in hand with weekday drinking sessions. Her accommodation too is in a state of fluidity. She appears to move house on average every 18 months, but never far from the city centre, where again her desire to be close to the action is palpable, and the fear that failure to partake in the continual flow of cultural symbolism orbiting the NTE will result in cultural anonymity, rendering her inconsequential maintains a perpetual state of anxiety.

A continual theme with regard to paid employment tended to be that its importance was greatly diminished in favour of participating within the consumer market, and the activities and cultural signifiers that this entails. A sense of ambivalence towards work was recurrent, with some respondents acutely aware of what Virno (1996) might call the precarity of their employment status in the shadow of the 'credit crisis' austerity synonymous with the end of the first decade of the century. Sam provides a concise example of this:

> I'm waiting to see what happens with my job at the moment. The contractors that I work for are looking like they are going to lose the contract, which means that my job will go, and I will be made redundant. There is a chance that [the company] will take me on either in the same job I am doing now, or somewhere else . . . I'm not bothered though really, if I get made redundant, I might just go travelling for a while or something, blow all my redundancy, sublet and just fuck off to America and travel around for a few months.

To what extent Sam's nonchalance is affected is hard to discern, but his words accentuate the acknowledgement among individuals within this age bracket of the isolating and transitory nature of employment. Under these conditions, the friendships, group identity and shared biographies that made no little contribution to the culture of the working-class, (see Willis, 1977) fail to materialise, and rather than the camaraderie of the shop floor or production line that we would have witnessed within the traditional working environments, the working lives of many respondents reflects isolation, and a feeling of disjointedness or alienation. As such, work is viewed in purely instrumental terms, lacking a larger symbolic meaning or significance (see Lloyd, 2013).

Further to the concept of instrumentalism that appears to be established within the social and working lives of many of the individuals recorded here, most individuals participating within this research project can be seen to be actively treating identity creation as a vocation, facilitated by the seemingly vast array of tools at their disposal thanks to global consumerism. Commercialised leisure, not least in the guise of the pubs and bars of the night-time high street, is grounded into everyday life and laden with meaning, becoming central to their sense of self and belonging (also see Ross-Houle, Atkinson and Sumnall and Thurnell-Read, both this volume). As their bodies start to visibly age, and a realisation dawns that other aspects of their life are underdeveloped and stunted, we can discern a complex array of anxiety, tension and pressure that hold a mirror up to the fragmented, individualised and increasingly isolated aspects of society. These identities that come to the fore within the context of the NTE have been years in the making, and for some are too valuable to be simply discarded as the pressures and expectations of the culture in which they were primarily socialised attempt to drag them away from the pull of commodified hedonistic excess.

Friends, family and the NTE

As has been intimated earlier, the consensus within the academic literature around alcohol consumption within the night-time leisure economy appears to be that as individuals age, they drift away from the youthful excesses of the NTE as their attention and finances become diverted onto more mature concerns (Power, 1992; Moore, Smith & Catford, 1994; Wright, 1999). While it is possible to view these new distractions as simply a further incarnation of the narcissistic progression of the wider consumer economy, we can take the individuals presented within this research as indicating that, for some, the allure of the NTE remains strong. Indeed, we could go so far as to say that older drinkers who are more likely to be at work during the day, or at home caring for children, invest very specific meaning into participation in the NTE.

While entrance into the full-time labour market, home ownership and the general trappings of 'settling down' may temper the individual's ability to while away evenings within the NTE as frequently as in their early twenties, it is clear that most respondents held a clear level of compartmentalisation between work life and leisure life, an observation that will be explored further in this chapter. This delineation, however, appears to blur once children enter the equation. Michelle is a 35-year-old single mother to a four-year-old girl. She has studied away at university, and worked in low-level management jobs in London and New York. Since returning, she has returned to study a degree at the Open University, a decision made after the breakup of her relationship with her child's father. She does not get to go out drinking as often as other respondents in this study, and opportunities are dictated by her child's routine and the availability of her parents to help out with childcare. She values being surrounded by her friends, and appears to fear that if she fails to maintain an appearance within the NTE then they – or she – will simply evaporate into nothingness:

> I don't see going out as needing a break from responsibilities, unwinding or any of that – in fact the opposite, because I sometimes feel guilty for going out. But people drop off the radar if they don't go out. There's the fear that if you keep saying no to people then they stop asking. If you keep turning people down, they will assume you are going to say no every time and you drop out of the loop. I think I've got the balance just about right.

Michelle displays a level of concern at being left 'out of the loop' if she does not go out every weekend but also has a very clear set of ideas about what her role as a mother should constitute, which results in a more traditional arousal of guilt surrounding the conflict of going out and maintaining an active presence in the consumer playing field of the NTE, and the awareness that she is perhaps contravening a social norm by leaving her daughter in pursuit of her own hedonism (see Parsons, 1954, 1955; and Cheal, 1991, p. 6). However, it is likely that this period of abstinence serves to make the attraction of the eventual and inevitable hedonistic excess that will accompany her re-entrance into the NTE all the more potent. Michelle's particular position of being a single mother to a young child makes her acutely aware of a number of elements surrounding socially sanctioned responsibility, while her embryonic relationship with a man who is very much embedded within the NTE forces her to confront the power and importance of youthful consumerism. She thereby occupies a particularly narrow cultural peninsula from where she both consciously and subconsciously attempts to deny a number of social processes that may drag her further from the 'ideal' of youthful and hedonistic independence and towards middle-age mediocrity and anonymity:

> When I started going out again [after the birth of her child and breakdown of her relationship] it was odd. I used to go out once a fortnight, just because I didn't want to go out more often, just didn't want to be away from her. I wouldn't go out unless there was a reason, like a birthday or celebration you know, but I was having more and more of a laugh and now usually the weekend is reason enough. It's such a social thing, Belle [daughter] wasn't at school, all my friends were at work, so I could be in all day and not see another adult all day, and not even be able to go to the shop if Belle was asleep or whatever.

Michelle is not alone in framing the experience of participating within the NTE as something other than the normal routine. The pubs and bars of the high street are the spaces in which relations and friendships are sought, developed and maintained as well as offering refracted images of the Real. For Michelle and other respondents who had family responsibilities, the NTE offers an opportunity to return or perhaps regress to forms of behaviours that would have been far more commonplace in the years before having children.

The illusory nature of youth and vitality within the sphere of the night-time leisure economy is hit upon by Andrea as she recalls thinking that drinkers of around her own age, when she was younger, were 'sad' or 'embarrassing', although she deflects any uncomfortable feeling that this might evoke through a thin veil of selective feminism:

> I'm happy doing this until I settle down and have a family, but then again when I was younger I would be sitting in a bar and see people not a lot older than we are now, mid to late 30s or something, and I would think to myself 'there is no way I'm going to be doing that when I get to your age because

it's just like embarrassing' and I'm still doing it now and can't see that it is embarrassing. I guess I'm not married or have kids, so my lifestyle fully allows it. The more acceptable it becomes for women to be single and not married off with children I think the more normal that this becomes.

Andrea, despite her protestations to the contrary, is still committed to indulgence and captured by the spectacle of consumer excess. The bottles of wine after work are not the epitome of the socially constructive café culture ostensibly sought after by the Labour government of 1997–2010 (see Lovatt & O'Connor, 1995; O'Connor & Wynn, 1996; Hadfield, 2006), and while Andrea may believe that she has full creative control over her social engagement, it is clear that she is in fact bound by a number of complex psychosocial factors that are shaping her identity and perpetually propelling her back to the market in search of something more.

Conclusion

The night-time economy provides us with an unparalleled opportunity to view the state of work, friendship and relationships within the context of contemporary adulthood. The data presented within this chapter reveals a high degree of instrumentality in the ways in which these individuals approach most of their friendships and indeed intimate relationships. Friendship bonds appear often fairly tenuous or, to use Bauman's terminology, 'liquid' compared with more traditional friendships that would be bound in a sense of communitas or shared experiences (Winlow, 2001). The shared experiences that people had under modernist conditions, however, would have consisted of a much higher degree of gravitas, sharing key moments in each other's closely parallel lives; births, deaths, the perils of capitalist exploitation, all of which would have served to forge tight bonds (see Willis, 1977). The data presented in the preceding pages illuminates a much weaker valency among friendship groups, as we witness bonds that exist only within the context of the consumerised NTE. Friendship is to some extent distilled down to its use-value, as respondents talk of 'dropping off the radar' in instances when they fail to maintain a presence in the bars and pubs of the city centre. Geographic mobility as well as events such as childbirth, illness or enthusiasm for a new relationship can all sever the bonds of friendship, if only temporarily, as for many individuals a case of 'out of sight, out of mind' ensues.

While success in entering the spheres of paid employment is viewed as a necessary route into the hedonistic playgrounds and stages of identity provided by global developments in the nature of liberal capitalism, more traditional markers of adulthood such as marriage and property ownership are still held as desirable goals, a hangover from a less consumer-driven economy base. However, failure to achieve these more traditional goals is for many individuals inevitable, as by falling short they are offered the opportunity to couch their failings as 'individuality', 'maintenance of independence' and other language more suited to the 'liquid life' identified by Bauman (2005). We can perhaps borrow from the psychological approach to explaining sociopathy (see for example, Millon, 2004) and describe socialisation as parasitic, with an emphasis on individualisation, benefiting at the expense of others and characterised by low levels of motivation and deferment of gratification. The birth of the infantile narcissist that has been permitted through the intervention of consumer capitalism within the individual's maturation process allows the individual to view his or her version of adulthood, be it, childless, single or married, as the right way of being adult, a version of rationality that can be viewed as being almost entirely driven by the consumer economy.

References

Arnett, J.J. 2000. Emerging adulthood: A theory of development from the late teens through the twenties. *American Psychologist*, 55(5): 469–480. doi:10.1037/0003-066X.55.5.469

Arnett, J.J. 2001. Conceptions of the transition to adulthood: Perspectives from adolescence to midlife. *Journal of Adult Development*, 8(2): 133–143. doi:10.1023/A:1026450103225

Barber, B.R. 2007. *Consumption: How markets corrupt children, infantilize adults, and swallow citizens whole*. New York: Norton.

Baudrillard, J. 1983. *Simulations*. New York City: Semiotext(e) Inc.

Bauman, Z. 1998. *Work, consumerism and the new poor*. Buckingham: Open University Press.

Bauman, Z. 2005. *Liquid life*. Cambridge: Polity.

Blatterer, H. 2007. Contemporary adulthood: Reconceptualizing an uncontested category. *Current Sociology*, 55(6): 771–792. doi:10.1177/0011392107081985

Bone, J. and O'Reilly, K. 2010. No place called home: The causes and social consequences of the UK housing 'bubble'. *British Journal of Sociology*, 61(2): 231–255.

Bourdieu, P. 1984. *Distinction: A social critique of the judgement of taste*. London: Routledge and Kegan Paul.

Chatterton, P. and Hollands, R. 2003. *Urban nightscapes: Youth cultures, pleasure spaces and corporate power*. London: Routledge.

Cheal, D. 1991. *Family and the state of theory*. Toronto: University of Toronto.

Coles, B. 1995. *Youth and social policy: Youth citizenship and young careers*. London: UCL Press.

Currie, E. 2005. *The road to whatever: Middle class culture and the crisis of adolescence*. New York: Henry Holt.

Dorling, D. 2010. *Injustice: Why social inequality persists*. Bristol: Policy Press.

Engineer, R., Phillips, A., Thompson, J. and Nicholls, J. 2003. *Drunk and disorderly: A qualitative study of binge drinking among 18- to 24-year olds*. London: Home Office.

Fisher, M. 2009. *Capitalist realism: Is there no alternative?* Ropley: John Hunt Publishing.

Hadfield, P. M. 2006. *Bar wars: Contesting the night in contemporary British cities*. Oxford: Oxford University Press.

Hall, S., Winlow, S. and Ancrum, C. 2008. *Criminal identities and consumer culture: Crime, exclusion and the new culture of narcissism*. Cullompton: Willan.

Hastings, G., Anderson, S., Cooke, E. and Gordon, R. 2005. Alcohol marketing and young people's drinking: A review of the research. *Journal of Public Health Policy*, 26(3): 296–311. doi:10.1057/palgrave.jphp.3200039

Hayward, K. and Hobbs, D. 2007. Beyond the binge in 'booze Britain': Market-led liminalization and the spectacle of binge drinking. *The British Journal of Sociology*, 58(3): 437–456. doi:10.1111/j.1468-4446.2007.00159.x

Health and Social Care Information Centre. 2012. *Statistics on alcohol: England, 2012*. Leeds: HSCIC.

Hollands, R. 2002. Divisions in the dark: Youth cultures, transitions and segmented consumption spaces in the night-time economy. *Journal of Youth Studies*, 5(2):153–171.

Lloyd, A. 2013. *Labour markets and identity on the post-industrial assembly line*. Farnham: Ashgate.

Lovatt, A. and O'Connor, J. 1995. Cities and the night-time economy. *Planning Practice and Research*, 10: 127–35.

Maggs, J. and Schulenberg, J. 2004. Trajectories of alcohol use during the transition to adulthood. *Alcohol Research and Health*, 28(4): 195–201.

Malbon, B. 1999. *Clubbing: Dancing, ecstasy and vitality*. London: Routledge.

Matza, D. 1964. *Delinquency and drift*. New Brunswick, N. J.: Transaction Publishers.

Millon, T. 2004. *Personality disorders in modern life*. 2nd ed. Hoboken, N. J.: Wiley.

Moore, L., Smith, C. and Catford, J. 1994. Binge drinking: Prevalence, patterns and policy. *Health Education Research*, 9(4): 497.

O'Connor, J. and Wynne, D. 1996. Introduction. In J. O'Connor and D. Wynne (Eds.), *From the margins to the centre: Cultural production and consumption in the post-industrial city*. Aldershot: Arena.

Office for National Statistics. 2013. General Lifestyle Survey, 2011. [Online]. http://www.ons.gov.uk/ons/rel/ghs/general-lifestyle-survey/2011/index.html (accessed 2 May).

Parsons, T. 1954. The incest taboo in relation to social structure and the socialization of the child. *British Journal of Sociology*, 101–117.

Parsons, T. 1955. *Family, socialization and interaction process*. Glencoe, Ill.: Free Press.

Plant, M. A. and Plant, M. 2006. *Binge Britain: Alcohol and the national response*. Oxford: Oxford University Press.

Power, C. 1992. Drinking careers: Lifestyles and life circumstances. In *Alcohol and young people: Learning to cope*. Proceedings of Addictions Forum, Alcohol Research Group Conference, October 1992. London: The Portman Group.

Seaman, P. and Ikegwuonu, T. 2010. *Drinking to belong: Understanding young adults' alcohol use within social networks*. York: Joseph Rowntree Foundation.

Skelton, T. and Valentine, G. 1998. *Cool places: Geographies of youth cultures*. London: Routledge.

Southwood, I. 2011. *Non-stop inertia*. London: Zero Books.

Smith, L. and Foxcroft, D. 2009. *Drinking in the UK: An exploration of trends*. York: Joseph Rowntree Foundation.

Smith, O. 2014. *Contemporary adulthood and the night-time economy*. London: Palgrave.

Virilio, P. 2005. *The information bomb*. London: Verso Books.

Virno, P. 1996. Virtuosity and revolution: The political theory of exodus. In P. Virno and M. Hardt (Eds.), *Radical thought in Italy: AA Potential Politics* (pp. 189–209). Minneapolis: University of Minnesota Press.

Wilkinson, R. and Pickett, K. 2010. *The spirit level: Why equality is better for everyone*. London: Penguin UK.

Willis, P. E. 1977. *Learning to labour*. Fansborough: Saxon House.

Winlow, S. 2001. *Badfellas: Crime, tradition and new masculinities*. Oxford: Berg.

Winlow, S. and Hall, S. 2006. *Violent night: Urban leisure and contemporary culture*. Oxford: Berg.
Wright, L. 1999. *Young people and alcohol: What 11 to 24 year olds know, think and do*. London: Health Education Authority.
Young, J. 1999. *The exclusive society: Social exclusion, crime and difference in late modernity*. London: Sage.
Žižek, S. 1999. *The ticklish subject*. London: Verso.
Žižek, S. 2009. *First as tragedy, then as farce*. London: Verso.
Žižek, S. 2010. *Living in the end times*. London: Verso.

Chapter 12

'There are limits on what you can do'

Biographical reconstruction by those bereaved by alcohol-related deaths

Christine Valentine, Lorna Templeton and Richard Velleman

> *There are limits on what you can do. Do what you can by all means but it may be you can't solve this problem . . . It may be that with all your best efforts the problem will still be there and . . . get worse and in the end it may result in death. (Bereaved father talking about son)*

Introduction

Drawing on interview narratives from family members bereaved following a death associated with serious alcohol problems[1], this chapter examines the experiences of a group largely hidden and neglected in research, policy and practice. These experiences provide a different and important perspective on alcohol use in contemporary Britain, yet those grieving a substance-related death have been largely ignored both in debates about alcohol or drug use, and in policy decisions around alcohol or drugs control. In analysing data from ongoing research[2] which has interviewed 106 adults, including six couples, bereaved following a drug- and/or alcohol-related death, we have found that these deaths can be particularly difficult to grieve, because of: 1) the pressures of coping with the person's substance use while they were alive; 2) the circumstances surrounding the person's death; 3) a culture that may stigmatise such deaths and pathologise the families, devaluing their grief and depriving them of social support; and 4) remembering and memorialising a life and death defined by alcohol and/or drugs and that the bereaved and/or others, may consider unfulfilled.

Focusing on a sub-sample of 14 interviews about problem alcohol-related deaths, which illustrates the difficulties involved in grieving this type of death, this chapter analyses how participants negotiated these four factors in reconstructing their own and the deceased's identity. It identifies dilemmas they encountered in attempting to make sense of and live with both the life and the death and how these reflected a social context lacking in support and understanding.

Background

Those bereaved following a substance-related death have been largely neglected in the academic literature, as well as in national and policy debates (Valentine, Bauld & Walter, 2016 forthcoming). Thus, few studies of this type of bereavement have been conducted in either substance use or bereavement fields (though see Guy, 2004; Noto & Formigoni, 2007; Feigelman, Jordan, McIntosh & Feigelman, 2012). Substance use studies have drawn attention to the experiences of families living with a relative's substance use, plus estimates of the numbers affected (Orford et al., 2005; Arcidiacono, Velleman, Procentese, Albanesi & Sommantico, 2009; Copello, Templeton & Powell, 2009). Yet, the impact on those families when the relative dies as a result of his or her substance use has received little academic attention, even though statistical recording of such deaths reveals their prevalence. There were 8,367 alcohol-attributable deaths registered in England in 2012 (Office for National Statistics, 2014) and 1,080 registered in Scotland in 2012 (General Register Office for Scotland, 2013)[3], with deaths more likely in males and in older age groups. While popular media often report such deaths, especially when of young people or celebrities[4], such reporting has been found to distance readers rather than invite empathy for grieving family members, who tend to be considered part of the problem (Riches & Dawson, 1998; Guy, 2004).

Bereavement studies have recognised that certain deaths are considered 'bad', in that they challenge perceptions of normalcy and naturalness (Seale & van der Geest, 2004), including sudden, violent and unanticipated deaths, such as those resulting from accidents, murder, suicide and substance use. Some bad deaths attract social stigma, particularly those considered to be self-inflicted and therefore preventable, such stigma extending to those left behind as being in some way complicit or having failed to prevent the death (Riches & Dawson, 1998). Reporting on suicide, Wertheimer (2001) has noted the challenges of making sense of something that 'outrages our basic assumptions', such as belief in the sanctity of life and the need to preserve it at all costs. With substance-related deaths, such outrage is also linked to deviant or morally reprehensible lifestyles (Guy, 2004; Feigelman et al., 2012). Thus, bad deaths are more difficult to grieve in that it is harder to make sense of an experience that defies the bounds of acceptability. With so-called self-inflicted deaths this situation is compounded by stigma and associated lack of sympathy and support from the wider society, though little research has explored bereavement following such deaths, particularly those resulting from substance use. There are personal testimonies published by the bereaved themselves, in some cases to challenge social stigma and dispel popular misconceptions (see, for example, Burton-Phillips, 2008; Skinner, 2012). Support agencies too have produced guidance leaflets, booklets and online information, and there have been some practice initiatives (see, for example, DrugFAM, 2013; Scottish Families Affected by Alcohol and Drugs, accessed 1 October 2014). Yet systematic research and evidence-based guidance for providers of either drug and alcohol treatment services or bereavement support are lacking.

Interviewing on substance-use bereavement

To address the situation just described, we interviewed (between March and December 2013, in South-West England and Scotland) a sample of 106 adults, including six couples, who recalled at length their experiences of bereavement following a substance-related death. Participants were targeted via local and national services, including drug and alcohol treatment services, generic bereavement services and the very few services offering specific support for this type of bereavement. This approach benefitted from having a bereaved family member on the research team, who, having set up a local charity to provide support for this type of loss, has forged strong links with relevant services. Because bereaved family members are a vulnerable and hidden group, we needed to rely on participant self-selection and convenience sampling. However, once interviewing was under way, we were able to use snowball and, later on, purposive sampling to increase diversity, for example, recruiting bereaved individuals who were themselves in treatment for or recovery from substance use.

This strategy produced a diverse sample in age, relationship to the deceased, time since death[5] and whether the participant was in treatment or recovery for an alcohol or drug problem. Of the 106 adults who took part, alcohol was implicated in 47 cases. The following analysis focuses on 14 of these (Table 12.1), representing a group where the relative who died had a serious alcohol problem (as opposed to acute alcohol intoxication or an alcohol-related road-traffic accident) and illustrating the difficulties of grieving this type of death. As will become evident from our analysis and Table 12.1, official causes of death, length of time bereaved and participants' experiences varied. Interviewers adopted an open-ended, conversational approach, which encouraged participants to tell their stories, while focusing on key areas such as the relationship with the deceased person before they died, the nature of their substance use, the circumstances and impact of the death, finding support and memory-making.

Interviewing took account of the emotional distress of recalling painful experiences that may be caused to participants both during and after the interview. Interviewers were also sensitive to concerns that members of this group may have about being stigmatised, potentially making them reluctant to share personal material. An open-ended approach to interviewing allowed participants to disclose only as much as they could manage and, as it turned out, almost all of them said they appreciated being able to share their stories. Indeed, it is well documented that talking about bereavement, though upsetting, may provide relief and reinforcement and that the lack of opportunity to do so only exacerbates the sense of isolation and exclusion (Walter, 1996; Riches & Dawson, 1996, Riches, 1998; Valentine, 2007).

Table 12.1 Profile of a sub-sample of interviews (conducted between March and September 2013)

Participant No.	Participant age at interview	Deceased age at death	Deceased year of death	Relationship of participant to deceased	Alcohol use	Final cause of death
1	F 35	F 64	2008 (5 years ago)	Daughter	Long-term, serious alcohol problem	Alcohol ketosis of the liver
2	F 37	F 54	1997 (16 years ago)	Daughter	Long-term, serious alcohol problem	Liver cirrhosis
3	F 33	M 51	1995 (18 years ago)	Daughter (in recovery for alcohol use)	Long-term, serious alcohol problem	Accidental death by fire, alcohol involved
4	F 42	F 53	1992 (21 years ago)	Daughter	Long-term, serious alcohol problem	Organ failure due to liver damage
5	F 24	M 45	1998 (15 years ago)	Daughter	Serious alcohol problem over two-year period	Chronic alcoholism – blood clot
6	F 30	F 40	2008 (5 years ago)	Daughter	Long-term, serious alcohol problem	Drug overdose with alcohol
7	F 37	F 63	2011 (2 years ago)	Daughter	Long-term, serious alcohol problem	Alcoholic hepatitis
8	M 24	M 49	2008 (5 years ago)	Son	Long-term, serious alcohol problem	Multiple organ failure
9	F 65	M 39	2012 (1 year ago)	Mother	Long-term, serious alcohol problem	Pneumonia and liver failure
10	F 50	M 22	2007 (6 years ago)	Mother	Long-term, serious alcohol and drug problem	Cardiac arrest brought on by illicit drugs and alcohol
11	M 74	M 30	1996 (17 years ago)	Father	Long-term, serious alcohol problem	Liver cirrhosis – organ failure resulting from alcoholism
12	F 53	M 32	1989 (24 years ago)	Wife	Long-term, serious alcohol problem	Aspiration of gastric contents
13	F 54	M 54	2007 (6 years ago)	Ex-wife	Long-term, serious alcohol problem	Death by ligature
14	F 24	M 45	2008	Niece	Long-term, serious alcohol problem	Heart attack

F = Female; M = Male

Mourning an alcohol-related death

The following thematic analysis of data drawn from the 14 interviews is structured by the four factors concerning the life, the death, the stigma and the memory, each raising painful dilemmas for those concerned. As a sensitive topic involving a vulnerable and little heard group, the analysis emphasises participants' version of events. As is illustrated, how participants negotiated these dilemmas in light of commonly held assumptions about this type of loss reflected the diversity of the sample and the responses of others, including family, friends, professionals and the wider society. Their biographical reconstructions, while diverse in how participants made sense of their loss, were similar in conveying the socially isolating impact of their experiences.

Coping with the person's alcohol problem

Bereavement more generally has been conceptualised as a major psycho-social transition (Parkes, 1988), the pain of which reflects the loss of meaning and identity arising from a severe disruption of one's 'assumptive world'. As such, bereavement involves adapting to a host of changes brought about by the death, including relationships, social status and economic circumstances. A resource that may assist this process is 'storying' grief (Walter, 1996; Neimeyer, 2002) in attempting to repair biographical continuity in the face of such disruption. However, with substance-related bereavement, one's assumptive world may already have suffered severe disruption prior to the death (Oreo & Ozgul, 2007), storying grief becoming both more urgent and more difficult.

Participants' narratives powerfully conveyed the considerable mental, emotional and social pressures and demands of living with another's excessive alcohol use, often for many years (Velleman, Copello & Maslin 2007). Their recollections are explored with reference to the impact on the family, feeling isolated from one's community and losing the person prior to their death.

The family

A father *[Participant 11]*[6] recalled feeling torn between the demands of his son's alcohol use (from the age of 17) and the needs of other family members:

> ... and gradually I felt driven to almost a choice, the drinking is causing great upset in the whole family. . . . Who do I look after? Do I expend loads and loads of time and effort trying to rescue him from this situation or do I think about the other members of the family . . . ?

Further still, he conveyed his sense of lost time following the final five years when his son's addiction seemed to gather momentum, until he died in hospital at age 30:

> I only gradually realised that he needed alcohol the way we need air . . . If you imagine the downward slope that got steeper over the last 5 years, and when it was all over . . . I felt that I'd lost 5 years of my life.

An ex-wife [P13] whose former husband's drinking eventually precipitated his suicide, felt torn between wanting to protect her two sons from their father's drinking and feeling obliged to keep the family together. Viewing his drinking as an illness, she believed he would eventually recover. Only when she had it on good authority that her husband was choosing to continue drinking and that her eldest son's mental health was at risk was she able to walk away from the situation:

> So the solicitor saying: "your husband obviously chose to drink again" was one clincher and the psychiatrist saying ". . . you have to leave your husband", was the other thing that made me leave, because I'd always thought, you know your marriage vows and you stay together through thick and thin . . . and I know that alcoholism is an illness so I sort of thought, oh he's trying . . . I just thought keeping the family together was important.

These examples convey how mourners may struggle with ongoing guilt and regret in that their efforts to limit the damage to family well-being and cohesion had ultimately failed to prevent the death. This struggle reflects wider social and political assumptions of family, which tend to emphasise cohesion, support and responsibility (Edwards, Ribbens-McCarthy & Gilles, 2012) against which families coping with a member's alcohol use may be viewed as troubled or dysfunctional (Guy, 2004).

Feeling isolated from one's community[7]

For those, particularly children of a parent with serious alcohol problems, for whom excluding the person from the home or walking away may not be an option, circumstances at home could isolate them from those outside the family. A daughter [P1] recalled the burden of responsibility she felt for defusing her mother's angry outbursts brought on by excessive drinking, while her neighbours, though aware of the situation, chose to ignore it:

> When the alcoholism got quite bad she would just basically scream at my dad for hours . . . I used to try and defuse things . . . anything to stop it all . . . I felt it was something I had to try and sort out . . . But yes it just got progressively worse . . . and it was just that thing that nobody [i.e., the neighbours] really talked about it, everyone knew what my mum was like but nobody really did anything about it.

For another daughter [P4], also affected by her mother's drinking, the lack of acknowledgement of her situation beyond the family left her feeling helpless and isolated. The extent of her predicament became apparent to her when sympathy was shown to a classmate whose mother was dying of cancer:

> I'd been up a lot of the night because Mum had been drunk and . . . I was very tired and I got to school the next day and I can remember thinking oh gosh

> I just can't hold this all in and a teacher coming in and saying well so and so is going to be off school for a while because her Mum's got cancer and me thinking oh god I really wish my Mum had cancer because then I could talk about it . . . say to people I can't cope, I haven't slept, . . . I had to cook all the meals at the weekend . . . and I couldn't because I was completely embarrassed.

In bereavement theory, *disenfranchised grief* (Doka, 2001) refers to grief that is not acknowledged by society, either because of the nature of the death or the status of the mourner, in either case leaving the bereaved person feeling unentitled to grieve and receive support. For this participant, it was her grief and need for support *while her mother was still alive* that was disenfranchised. Thus, when interviewed 21 years later, she acknowledged her ongoing struggle to make sense of her mother's life and death and their lasting impact on her own life:

> I still struggle with 'why didn't you take care of me . . . why did you let me down, why have you essentially left me with a lot of hang ups and a lot of things to deal with', you know? But also knowing that it was a disease and she couldn't help herself . . . so I constantly think 'could I have done more'?

The dilemma of needing to share one's predicament with a sympathetic other outside the family, while at the same time needing to protect one's own and the family's reputation, was conveyed by a woman [P12] whose husband was alcohol dependent. She acknowledged that her own guilt and shame contributed to her social isolation and lack of support:

> I would say there probably wasn't a lot of support around but I do think that I and an awful lot of people in the situation that I was in isolate ourselves. There is a lot of shame in it and guilt . . . and that feeling of 'it's all my fault' . . . So . . . I don't actually know how much help I could have accessed even if it had been there at the time.

Though she and her husband eventually sought help from a support group, her guilt was reinforced by the group's assumption that she, as his wife, was jointly responsible for her husband's alcoholism:

> The attitude was that this was a joint problem . . . my problem as much as . . . his. And I think I had already bought into that . . . so I would have done anything to have stopped him drinking. But I think the message that somehow I had some responsibility in it too came from . . . them.

In a context in which family members are supposed to be responsible for one another, individuals needing support in coping with a family member's alcohol use may find themselves feeling isolated, their predicament ignored and/or judged by those outside the family.

Losing the person before their death

Some participants described how living with another's alcohol use had damaged their relationship in that they felt they had already lost (to alcohol) the person they once knew and loved. A daughter [P3] who, at the time of being interviewed, was in recovery for her own alcohol use, recalled feeling rejected by her father who, as his drinking increased and his health and appearance deteriorated, became unavailable to her:

> And he didn't want me to see him like that. I understand that now but when I was younger . . . I felt rejected and very angry.

A mother [P9] described her experience of living with the possibility that her son's drinking might prove fatal. Having lived with his problem drinking from the age of 17 until he died at 39, each time she heard a car pull up outside the house she would expect it to be the police coming to inform her of his death:

> When [my son] didn't get back to me I knew the police would be coming to the door. So what I imagined in my mind a thousand times, it's exactly the way it happened, the only difference was I knew they were coming.

Thus, when the death occurs mourners may experience a further bereavement in that, prior to the death, they had been grieving for having already lost the person or in anticipation that they would eventually die (Oreo & Ozgul, 2007).

Circumstances of the death

The trauma of this type of death (Feigelman et al., 2012) reflects both the toll already taken by living with another's alcohol use and the often distressing circumstances surrounding the death. These circumstances included the stark contrast between the harsh realities of alcohol-related dying and commonly held norms about dying well, and the various statutory procedures involved in dealing with a death.

Dying norms

Participants' experiences of the death itself were influenced by socially accepted norms of where, how and in whose presence one should die. Studies have found these to include dying peacefully, at home, in character[8], with close others, being able to say goodbye and without too much pain (Kellehear & Lewin, 1988–1989).

However, for these family members, the reality could be far removed from the ideal, including their relative dying alone and/or away from home, without privacy or dignity, and far from peacefully. One daughter [P1] regretted that her mother had died alone in her flat, despite how difficult she was to live with:

> The neighbours alerted that nobody had seen her for a few days, because she lived at the front of a set of flats, and so police broke in and found her . . . I still feel really bad that she just died on her own, and she wouldn't have understood, she would have thought everyone had abandoned her because she never got that she actually drove everyone away.

Another daughter [P7] regretted the lack of privacy and dignity in her mother's dying on a hospital ward, these being qualities that were important to and characteristic of her mother:

> . . . and she was on a ward, full of people, confused, didn't want to be there . . . she had a catheter in and . . . and everybody just stared at us, it was horrendous and I kept saying this is just not dignified . . . my mum . . . was very private, liked her dignity and I just thought . . . she would be mortified by this. . . .

A mother [P10] whose son's drinking was linked to mental health problems, found it shocking to witness the far from peaceful way he died in intensive care after suffering a cardiac arrest from a drink and drug overdose:

> So we agreed to having the machine turned off. And he died I think it was a day later . . . But it was awful, because when they switch the machine off, if you can picture a fish out of water, that's what we were looking at. We had to watch him gasping and writhing for a day . . . he didn't slip away peacefully.

Even in more comfortable circumstances where saying goodbye was possible, doing so could be hampered by negative feelings about how the person's drinking affected those around them. One participant [P6], though intending to say goodbye to her dying mother, reported that to do so involved wrestling with considerable feelings of anger that her mother still aroused in her:

> The more I kept looking at her the more angry I was getting . . . I thought: what's the point? . . . she is going to die, there is no point in being angry and shouting. But when I looked at her . . . a lot of [bad] memories were coming back . . . but no, I just took her hand and I didn't want that, I had said the goodbye I had wanted to give her.

For some participants, the death could bring relief, both for themselves and the deceased, as experienced by a niece [P14] when her uncle died:

> Sometimes I do think to myself, maybe it was better for him to pass away because of the pain he was just going through. You know every day was a battle with him. His addiction was just too powerful . . . And I just sometimes think maybe now he's at peace. . . .

Yet, as one daughter [*P1*] explained about her mother's death, the sense of relief could be accompanied by guilt and questioning one's right to grieve:

> So for me when she first died it was a relief that that was over and . . . it is difficult because you feel guilty for feeling like that . . . and therefore you feel that perhaps you don't have the right to grieve and be so upset . . . it took me a while to realise that I had the right to be upset.

Thus, whether or not the death brought a sense of relief, participants still struggled with norms about dying and entitlement to grieve (Doka, 2001).

Encounters with officials

Participants' experiences were also affected by how the death was handled and how in the immediate aftermath they were treated by officials, including hospital staff, the police, the coroner and the undertaker, as well as professionals who would have known about the death, such as general practitioners, employers and teachers. While some reported being treated with kindness, others met with responses that reinforced the sense that their loss was considered less important than that associated with other types of death. Poor treatment affected both their experiences of being informed of the death as well as managing the processes involved.

For officials involved in the immediate aftermath, a particularly difficult and sensitive part of their job involves informing next of kin that their relative has died. Unless the death has occurred in hospital with family members present, this task usually falls to the police or, in some cases, the coroner. For the police, bearing bad news may not sit easily with the normal routine business of policing. Indeed, shifting from business as usual to a softer, more sympathetic approach may not be easy whatever the cause of death. However, when substances are implicated, negative assumptions about such deaths may reinforce a business-like approach (Walter et al., 2015) as conveyed by a mother [*P9*] whose son was found dead in his flat:

> You know it was just routine to them . . . you are going in to tell a mother that her son just died, it doesn't matter what kind of person she is or what kind of person he was, you try and show a bit of compassion. You don't just go in as if it was an ordinary run of the mill thing.

Such insensitivity could include disregarding the bereaved person's privacy. The ex-wife [*P13*] whose former husband took his own life was appalled to discover that, against the advice of her husband's doctor, the police had initially visited her workplace, where colleagues and customers would have been in earshot, to inform her of her husband's death:

> . . . his doctor . . . had said to the police, 'can I come with you to tell her?' And they said, 'No you can't, you know we're going to do this'. And they went

to [place of work] and asked to speak to me – he [the doctor] mentioned how I would have reacted if I'd been at work and two policemen walked in . . . [crying] . . . And I knew the minute I saw them and I think if they'd have done that to me at work, that would have been unforgiveable.

Then, after the initial impact of the death, participants often felt, as one daughter [P5] put it, 'simply left to get on with it'. She recalled the situation she found herself in after losing the father she had experienced as a quiet, intelligent man who loved helping others; his drinking began after an accident left him disabled and unemployed, and he died as a result two years later:

> Looking back it's worrying how little support from school was there. We had nothing from any other services, kind of external services. The things that are kind of pinnacle in society . . . such as police and school and social services they were non-existent, which I find surprising.

With substance use deaths being perceived as self-inflicted, such experiences only served to reinforce the sense that the deceased's death was less worthy of dignified treatment and, as the following section illustrates, mourners of sympathy and support.

Social stigma

Sharing one's grief with sympathetic others has been found to assist finding meaning and coherence in the loss (Walter, 1996; Neimeyer, 1998). However, social stigma, both actual and perceived, and the consequent sense of shame and unworthiness to grieve, can make it hard to find or trust others sufficiently to be able to confide in them. In addition, cultural stereotypes of an 'alcoholic lifestyle', exacerbated by media reporting, may encourage distancing rather than sympathy for the family (Riches and Dawson, 1996; Guy, 2004). Such distancing and lack of sympathy could be experienced from another family member, as reported by a mother [P9] after her son's death from alcohol:

> My sister never said anything about him, you know, a lot of people think: well he caused his own death, so I don't think you get the sympathy that you would get normally.

Sharing one's grief within the family may also be inhibited by fears of causing tension or conflict. Thus the ex-wife [P13] whose former husband took his own life came up against other family members refusing to acknowledge the role of alcohol in her husband's death:

> At the funeral I wanted any proceeds to go to Nacoa [National Association for the Children of Alcoholics] but . . . my brother-in-law didn't want the funeral to have any mention of alcohol. So I thought this is what killed him but we're not to mention it.

Beyond the family, one mother [*P10*] whose son's drinking was linked to a mental health condition felt distanced by professionals both before and after the death. The mental health issue combined with his drinking produced extreme mood swings and violent behaviour, but her repeated attempts to find support for him were largely met with what she experienced as 'professional indifference'. Her hopes were raised when the GP referred her son to the mental health services, only to be dashed when the psychiatrist concluded that the evidence pointed not to a mental health difficulty, but to a dysfunctional family:

> ... he was referred to the mental health services and I was full of hope, and we had an appointment with the psychiatrist. And ... they immediately went down the route of what's going on in the family? ... this is a family that aren't functioning well together. Rather than thinking, well, we wouldn't be functioning well if somebody is smashing up your home, they were looking at kind of the other way around – that [our son] was in difficulty because of something to do with us.

When her son died, she continued to feel abandoned by the professionals she felt should have shown more care and concern, in that none of them took the trouble to contact her:

> From the day we got home, we just thought, well, what do we do now? I mean, I find it extraordinary that, given that ... our GP ... and ... that health centre, knew so much about us in our family, that nobody ... thought to pick up the phone and ring us.

However, stereotypical assumptions, which misrepresented the identities and relationship of both the bereaved and deceased, could be challenged, as conveyed by a son [*P8*] talking about his father and a daughter her mother [*P2*]:

> I was really conscious of the fact that I didn't want anyone to think just because he was an alcoholic and just because he died young doesn't make him a bad dad, he was a fantastic father ... and I wanted people [at the funeral] to know how special he was to us [*P8*]
>
> I won't have anyone speak ill of my mum ... she is not here ... I am very protective of my mother despite what she has done .... [*P2*]

Stigma could be challenged through studying alcohol dependence and using the knowledge to try and dispel popular assumptions. Thus the daughter [*P5*] who, following her father's death, felt unsupported by her teachers, and now a teacher herself, felt in a position to use her own learning to benefit others:

> So making people more aware for me is important and not demonising the alcoholic ... I am hoping ... to start building educational materials for PSHE

[Personal, Social and Health Education] so that teachers can kind of pull it off of the database . . . A good set of resources with backup material, so they can feel more confident in teaching about alcoholism.

Thus, perceptions of stigma could inhibit sharing one's grief, even within families. Stigma felt prior to the death could shape the bereaved person's experiences after death, leaving them vulnerable to an ongoing sense of isolation. However, stereotypical assumptions could be challenged through protecting and asserting the deceased person's memory and integrity, as the following section elaborates.

Remembering a life and death defined by alcohol

Finding comfort in sharing and preserving memories of the deceased person's life has been found to be crucial to making sense of loss and repairing identities of both bereaved and deceased, as well as the relationship between them (Rosenblatt, 1993). However, as the previous section illustrated, feeling stigmatised, as well as painful memories of the person's life and death, may inhibit remembering, sharing and finding meaning in those memories.

For one daughter [*P5*], remembering her mother evoked lost hope, while for another daughter [*P1*], childhood memories produced considerable bitterness:

> I always had this hope . . . [but] when she died I lost my hope and that was the saddest thing for me that there was no hope of it ever getting better. [*P5*]
>
> I am still bitter about my mother, very, very bitter. And still to this day blame her. And even . . . if she was alive today in this room honestly I wouldn't even be sitting in the same room as her, mother or not. [*P4*]

Such deaths are also considered premature and untimely, in the case of a child, outside the natural order of things (Seale & Van der Geest, 2004). For one father [*P11*], his son's death evoked a sense of wasted life:

> And having to get to grips with the death was overlaid with having to get to grips with the fact that this sense of waste . . . this total waste of a life.

Yet, as two daughters [*P4* and *P6*] reflected, bad memories could be tempered by choosing to hold on to positive images of the person prior to their drinking:

> Yes, I do believe that she's like in heaven having a lovely time . . . Do I imagine her with a drink or without a drink? Or would I rather have her back with all her problems? . . . you wish them to all go away – but then you just think well I'd like to have her back with that just as much as without. [*P4*]
>
> God bless her she was a good woman. Apart from her drink problem, she loved her kids and she was a good mum . . . I do try to think a lot of the good time. [*P6*]

Another daughter [P7] conveyed how memories of bad experiences could be made good through trying to understand what drove the person to drink, to develop empathy for their predicament, and to discover more about the family dynamic and its influence on one's own identity:

> But for me I wanted to understand why she drank . . . I don't have the answer . . . but I think I've tried to understand a bit more about my family dynamic . . . going by how it's affected me in positive as well as negative ways . . . would I change it? I would like some of the pain to have gone away but I do think the relationship I have with my mum has made me who I am and from that I have a lot of empathy and . . . determination and it has enabled me to achieve things in my life that I may not have done otherwise.

Despite painful memories of the life, some participants found ways of reconnecting with and including the deceased in their ongoing lives. Thus one mother [P10] recovered her relationship with her son through writing to him and creating a memory box of the letters, while a niece [P14] continued her relationship with her uncle through talking to him at his graveside:

> Well, it started with our first Christmas without [him]. I decided I would write him a Christmas card . . . and I dated and sealed it and put it in a tin. And then just after Christmas with what would have been his 24th birthday, I sent him a birthday card and put it in the tin. And then when it got to . . . the first anniversary, I wrote him a letter and told him about things that had happened since he died. So this tin is now absolutely full of letters . . . and I'm still writing to him. [P10]
>
> I just go on my own and have a chat to him . . . because he understood me so well that I can almost imagine the kind of reply he would give me . . . So it's definitely really important to just keep that going, like I will always visit his grave. If it's looking tatty, I would always clean it. I will always take him a little something and . . . write him a poem or a letter, because he's still there. [P14]

In reporting how they actively continued their relationship with the deceased person, both participants represented this process as mutually reinforcing and restorative. Thus, in a social context which may severely undermine the integrity of both bereaved and deceased, the relationship between them (Valentine, 2008) and, of the family, some participants found ways of remembering and including the deceased in their ongoing lives that enabled recovery of identities and their relationship.

Conclusion

As illustrated, the group represented by these interviews face some complex and distressing issues, which have been linked in our analysis to four key factors, and which make this type of death and loss particularly difficult. Furthermore, as discussed, grieving may not necessarily diminish over time. Thus, prior to the death, the demands and impact of the person's drinking could threaten both individual and family well-being and integrity, as well as social identity and feeling connected to and supported by the local community. It could mean living with a sense of having lost the person to their alcohol problem and the knowledge that this might eventually kill them. The death itself could present those left behind with the painful gap between the ideal of dying well and dying alone, in painful and distressing circumstances. Encounters with officials could reinforce the sense of social exclusion already experienced during the person's life. A context of social stigma was implicit in participants' accounts of coping with both the life and the death, as well as explicit in accounts of others' distancing themselves, both within and outside the family. Yet some participants found ways of negotiating negative stereotypes and protecting the deceased's memory, though taking comfort from fond memories could be threatened by painful memories of wasted years, lost hope and bitterness. Comfort could be found in holding onto positive memories of the person, trying to understand their alcohol problem and finding ways to include them in one's ongoing life.

By focusing on the predicament of those who have lived with both the life and the death of someone with serious alcohol problems, these findings may not necessarily reflect the range of alcohol-related deaths, though there are likely to be similarities. There are also similarities to bereavement following other types of bad deaths, particularly suicide (Feigelman et al., 2012). Yet, as illustrated, there are a combination of factors that make the task of recovering integrity – their own, their family's and the deceased's, as well as relationships – particularly difficult and precarious, which may be unique to this type of bereavement (including substance use generally). With policy and practice initiatives related to excessive drinking focused on prevention, control and treatment, those grieving someone whose drinking could not be treated or their death prevented, are inevitably excluded. Indeed, as conveyed by the bereaved father, they serve as reminders that such efforts may fail, suggesting that dependency on drink and/or other substances may be a far more complex and nuanced issue than is apparent. It also suggests that there is much to be learned from those who have been most closely affected by another's alcohol use.

While these findings, as indicated, address a significant gap in the bereavement and addiction literature, they also resonate with other social science, particularly social geographical, perspectives, such as the way alcohol use is constructed within the family space and its role in negotiating family ties (see, for example, Jayne, Valentine & Holloway, 2001) and on alcohol use as a means of coping with the stigma of being unable to locate oneself in an accepted social space (Staddon, 2005). For example, for the bereaved father and the ex-wife, the sense of threat posed by a member's alcohol use to both family space and relationships between family members were constructed within normative expectations of family well-being and integrity. For the mother whose son suffered from mental health problems, her attempts to legitimise and find support for both her son's condition and the impact his behaviour was having on the family only served to exacerbate the sense of feeling stigmatised and isolated. However, these experiences also provide a further dimension to considerations of space, location, gender, status/identity and relationships between people in mediating attitudes to alcohol use, that being the impact of death and loss on such attitudes. While our findings provide further examples of the way alcohol use is constructed within a range of spaces and relationships, our participants' recollections also draw attention to spaces and relationships not yet considered by the literature. These include the various spaces of dying, death, memorialisation, disposal and commemoration, such as the hospital, the morgue, the inquest and the funeral, and a range of relationships and activities within which both their own and the 'spoiled' identity of the deceased person were negotiated.

Notes

1 We exclude those who died in other ways related to substance use, such as acute alcohol intoxication, alcohol-related road-traffic accident or a range of deaths associated with drug (rather than alcohol) use.
2 A study funded by the Economic and Social Research Council (Understanding and responding to those bereaved through their family members' substance misuse, 2012–2015) of the experiences and needs of families and individuals bereaved by a substance use–related death.
3 The collection of these statistics focuses on 'alcohol-attributable' deaths, those which are most closely and directly associated with alcohol. This covers a range of conditions and diseases, including liver cirrhosis, but the estimates are likely to be under-estimates because they exclude alcohol-related deaths such as road traffic and other accidents.
4 Hearsum (2012), on the death of the singer, Amy Winehouse, notes that media reporting typically emphasises such deaths as punishment for reckless behaviours and fails to consider the underlying reasons for the person's substance use.
5 Stage theories of grief have been discredited in the bereavement literature (see, for example, Valentine, 2008) and, as our sample confirms, it has been found that the intensity of grief, particularly for difficult deaths, does not necessarily decrease with time, but rather may fluctuate and recur many years later.
6 See Table 12.1.
7 Also see section 3 on social stigma.
8 For instance, as the person they were when they were alive (and not, for example, showing an altered personality through, for example, dementia).

References

Arcidiacono, C., Velleman, R., Procentese, F., Albanesi, C. and Sommantico, M. 2009. Impact and coping in Italian families of drug and alcohol users. *Qualitative Research in Psychology*, 6(4): 260–280.

Burton-Phillips, E. 2008. *Mum can you lend me twenty quid? What drugs did to my family*. London: Piatkus Books.

Copello, A., Templeton, L. and Powell, J. 2009. *Adult family members and carers of dependent drug users: Prevalence, social cost, resource savings and treatment responses. Final report to the UK Drug Policy Commission*. London: UK DPC.

DrugFAM, 2013. *Bereaved by addiction. A booklet for anyone bereaved through drug or alcohol use*. Available at: www.drugfam.co.uk

Doka, K. (Ed.), 2001. *Disenfranchised grief: New directions, challenges, and strategies for practice* (pp. 95–117). Champaign, Ill.: Research Press.

Edwards, R., Ribbens-McCarthy, J. and Gilles, V. 2012. The politics of concepts: Family and its (putative) replacements. *The British Journal of Sociology*, 63(4): 730–746.

Feigelman, W., Jordan, J.R., McIntosh, J.L. and Feigelman, B. 2012. *Devastating losses: How parents cope with the death of a child to suicide or drugs*. New York: Springer Publishing Co.

General Register Office for Scotland, 2013. *Alcohol-related deaths*, General Register Office for Scotland, Edinburgh, Available online at: http://www.groscotland.gov.uk/statistics/theme/vital-events/deaths/alcohol-related/

Guy, P. 2004. Bereavement through drug use: Messages from research. *Practice* 16(1): 43–54.

Hearsum, P. 2012. A musical matter of life and death: The morality of mortality and the coverage of Amy Winehouse's death in the UK press. *Mortality*, 17(2): 182–199

Jayne, M., Valentine, G. and Holloway, S.L. 2011. *Alcohol, drinking and drunkenness: (Dis)orderly spaces*. Burlington: Ashgate.

Kellehear, A. and Lewin, T. 1988–1989. Farewells by the dying: A sociological study. *Omega*, 19: 275–292.

Neimeyer, R. 1998. *Death, loss and personal reconstruction*. London: Sage.

Noto, A. and Formigoni, M. 2007. Death by drug overdose: Impact on families. *Journal of Psychoactive Drugs*, 39(3): 301–6.

Office for National Statistics, 2014. *Alcohol-related deaths in the United Kingdom, registered in 2012*, Office for National Statistics: Newport.

Oreo, A. and Ozgul, S. 2007. Grief experiences of parents coping with an adult child with problem substance use. *Addiction Research and Theory*, 15(1): 71–83.

Orford, J., Natera, G., Copello, A., Atkinson, C., Tiburcio, M., Velleman, R. . . . and Walley, G. 2005. *Coping with alcohol and drug problems: The experiences of family members in three contrasting cultures*. London: Taylor and Francis.

Parkes, C. 1988. Bereavement as a psycho-social transition: Processes of adaption to change. *Journal of Social Issues*, 44(3): 53–65.

Riches, G. 1998. Families bereaved by murder. *Mortality*, 3(2): 143–160.

Riches, G. and Dawson, P. 1996. Making stories and taking stories. *British Journal of Guidance and Counselling*, 24(3): 357–365.

Rosenblatt, P. 1993. Grief: The social context of private feelings. In M. Stroebe, W. Stroebe and R. Hansson (Eds.), *Handbook of bereavement research: Theory, research and intervention* (Ch. 7, pp. 102–111). Cambridge: Cambridge University Press.

Scottish Families Affected by Alcohol and Drugs. *Drug related deaths*. Available at: http://www.sfad.org.uk/supporting_yourself/drug_related_deaths (accessed 1 October 2014).

Seale, C. and Van der Geest, S. 2004. Good and bad death: Introduction. *Social Science and Medicine*, 58: 883–885.

Skinner, P. 2012. *See you soon: A mother's story of drugs, grief and hope*. UK: Presence Books in partnership with Spoonbill Publications. Available at: www.seeyousoon.me.uk (accessed 1 October 2014).

Staddon, P. 2005. Labelling out: The personal account of an ex-alcoholic lesbian feminist. *Journal of Lesbian Studies*, 9(3): 69–78, doi: 10.1300/J155v09n03_07

Valentine, C. 2007. Methodological reflections: The role of the researcher in the construction of bereavement narratives. *Qualitative Social Work*, 6(2): 1–22.

Valentine, C. 2008. *Bereavement narratives: Continuing bonds in the twenty first century*. London, New York: Routledge.

Valentine, C.A., Bauld, L. and Walter, T. (2016, forthcoming) Bereavement following substance misuse: a disenfranchised grief. *Omega Journal of Death Studies*, 72.

Velleman, R., Copello, A. and Maslin, J. 2007. *Living with drink: Women who live with problem drinkers*. Reissued Edition, 2007. London: Pearson Education.

Walter, T. 1996. A new model of grief: Bereavement and biography. *Mortality*, 1(1): 7–25.

Walter, T., Ford, A., Templeton, L., Valentine, CA. and Velleman, R. 2015. Compassion or Stigma? How adults bereaved by alcohol or drugs experience services, *Health & Social Care in the Community*. Available at: *http://onlinelibrary.wiley.com/enhanced/doi/10.1111/hsc.12273/*

Wertheimer, A. 2001. *A special scar: The experiences of people bereaved by suicide*. London: Brunner-Routledge.

Chapter 13

Drinking dilemmas
Making a difference?

Mark Jayne and Gill Valentine

Introduction

The chapters in this book have contributed to a long tradition of applying sociological and cultural analysis to understanding alcohol, drinking and drunkenness. From the Mass Observation (1987) movement of the 1930s, and in response to the challenges laid down in the seminal book *Constructive Drinking* edited by Mary Douglas (1987), published almost 30 years ago, writers have sought to influence dominant representations and theorisations of drinking. The chapters have all, in various ways, added to our understandings of how alcohol, drinking and drunkenness are social and cultural practices that are shaped by, and therefore help us to further our understandings of, place, sociability and selfhood.

Taking the three broad themes of the collection in turn, the contributions made by the chapters becomes clear. Identity has been a prominent theme throughout the volume. Specifically, chapters have detailed the prominence of alcohol beverages and branding in constructions of personal, national and local identity (Ross-Houle, Atkinson and Sumnall; Thurnell-Read), constructions of youth identity (Wilkinson), the precarious and for some incomplete transition to adulthood (Smith) and in the negotiations of the stigmatised identities of those 'after drink has killed' (Valentine, Vellman and Templeton). Social class (Hollands; Nicholls) and, in particular, gender (Ross-Houle, Atkinson and Sumnall; Thurnell-Read; Riches; Gaussot, Le Minor and Palierne) have been of particular prominence. In relation to culture, while each chapter is in itself a demonstration of the plurality and diversity of drinking cultures, specific chapters have shown how drinking practices are intertwined with parental styles and normative cultural expectations (Gaussot, Le Minor and Palierne) and that particular drinks (Thurnell-Read), drinking venues (Nicholls; Smith) and drinking spaces (Charman; Bonte; Riches; Wilkinson) are very much embedded in the wider web of cultural history and belonging. Finally, chapters have explored the contested development of urban leisure spaces (Hollands; Charman; Bonte), the salience of space and place in discourses of 'good' and 'bad' drinking (Nicholls) and the spatial drinking practices of young people in suburban (Wilkinson) and subcultural (Riches) spaces.

In this concluding chapter we offer insights into the strengths and weaknesses of this academic work. In doing so, we reflect on the ability of social and cultural researchers to challenge orthodoxies that dominate popular, political, policy and academic understanding of alcohol, drinking and drunkenness[1].

Drinking dilemmas?

Elsewhere we have argued that 'alcohol studies' across the social and medical sciences is defined by an 'impasse where alcohol consumption is conceived as a medical issue, pathologised as a health, social, legislative, crime or policy problem *or* as being embedded in social and cultural relations – with limited dialogue between these approaches' (Jayne, Valentine & Holloway, 2008a, p. 247). With this backdrop of distanced traditions it is nonetheless scientific research, lab-based experimentation, statistical measurement, modelling and numerical proxies which define alcohol-related harm. Indeed, scientific and quantitative findings capture newspaper headlines, dominate popular imaginations and representations and influence political decision-making and policy formation. Moreover, pathologisation of alcohol and its effects as health, social, legislative and criminal problems is entrenched because social and cultural researchers, despite offering rich and detailed evidence with reference to diverse alcohol-related topics and case studies around the world, have overwhelmingly failed to critique dominant ontologies and epistemologies.

Such comments notwithstanding, there is a voluminous amount of academic research that has offered vital theoretical and empirical insights into the discursive and differential construction of 'problem' and 'constructive' drinking with reference to diverse spaces, cultures and identities around the world. *Mass Observations: The Pub and the People* (1937–1943) was undertaken because of a contemporary dissatisfaction with the way in which drinking was reported by official statistics, and also a concern that political, policy and policing measures to curb drunkenness failed to grasp the experience and context of drinking. Mass Observation was part of a wider documentary movement in the UK, Europe and the United States that aimed to rejuvenate a public sphere corrupted by unrepresentative government, a biased press and advertising. In January 1936, Mass Observation recruited amateur observers to complete diary entries, collect newspapers cuttings, overhear conversations, and professional observers carried out covert and overt participation (see Kneale, 2001). Mass Observation studies of pub life were undertaken in Bolton, Blackpool, Plymouth, Liverpool and Fulham, and, prior to this research, drunkenness had generally been considered as a social problem that required reform and legislation.

In seeking alternative meanings of alcohol consumption, observers noted that alcohol was not the sole reason for public drunkenness, and that pub sociality encouraged a relaxing of sober self-control even for those who were not drinking (Kneale, 2001). The Mass Observation importantly also described the symbolic importance of drinking, and that rooms within pubs were strictly gendered; the vault and taproom were masculine spaces, while the lounge or parlour were dominated by couples or mixed groups. Observers noted practices such as drinking rates, where groups all drank at the same rate and took similar sized sips in order to ensure social bond and equivalence between drinkers. This highlighted the ways in which drinking was a way of creating and transforming social relationships with associations of drink as being bound up with trust, reciprocity and a relaxing of formal social relations.

The working-class drinking practice of 'rounds' and 'treating' one another reproduced social ties and obligations, and hence drinking can be seen to have played an important role in making connections between people. Drink was equated with social worth, trust, reciprocity and fraternity. Drunkenness was bound up with group intoxication as a social phenomenon of self-liberation from the weekly routine and the time-clock of the factory whistle. It was also argued that sobriety and drunkenness were controlled through social hierarchies and particularly through the guidance of older drinkers. In these terms, then, although drunkenness created particular bonds of sociality between drinkers and temporary suspension of particular social divisions that brought people together, there were still social norms to adhere too. In these terms, drinkers did not consider that they were involved in a transgressive practice, but rather that drinking was simultaneously about being part of the community and also about being a good customer.

One of the most important features of the Mass Observation research related to drinking and public space. The formation of crowds of people, drunk and not so drunk, engaging with one another and with other users of public space was seen as a key feature of drunken behaviour. In particular, the promenading of people after closing time, in large but temporary groups, was shown to be a key component of urban drinking. Such depictions critiqued historical political and popular representations of drinking and public space that are still pertinent today. Indeed, the township shebeen (Charman, this volume), the parks and bedrooms of suburban Manchester (Wilkinson, this volume) and the bars and cafés of Beirut's Mar Mikhael neighbourhood (Bonte, this volume) are all spaces where the gaze of politics and policy can be tempered by these insights into the social value of drinking in forging connections and belonging.

More recently, the landmark publication of the book *Constructive Drinking*, edited by Mary Douglas (1987), was influential in challenging researchers to move beyond a research agenda dominated by the limiting theorization of the pathologising of alcohol consumption. Douglas advocated the need to address the everyday social relations and cultural practices bound up with drinking. Moreover, other important publication prior to, and following *Constructive Drinking*, such as McAndrew and Edgerton's *Drunken Comportment* (1969) and Burnett's *Liquid Pleasures: A Social History of Drink in Modern Britain* (1999) touched on similar terrain. Responding to challenges laid down by these theorists, work across the social sciences has investigated the relationship between alcohol consumption, space/place, and identity, lifestyle and forms of sociability in different locations around the world (see, for example, de Garine & de Garine, 2001; Share, 2003; Wilson, 2005).

Other studies have considered drinking and gender in India (Chatterjee, 2003); gender and sexuality in San Francisco (Bloomfield, 1993); drinking and young people in Vietnam (Thomas, 2002); young people in rural areas of Australia and Wales (Jones, 2002; Kraack & Kenway, 2002; Kelly & Kowalyszyn, 2003); masculinity and identity in Newcastle upon Tyne (Nayak, 2003); alcohol-related service provision for Indian, Chinese and Pakistani young people in Glasgow (Heim, Hunter, Ross, Bakshi, Davis, Flatley & Meer, 2004); Sikh, Hindu, Muslim and white male drinking in the West Midlands (Cochrane & Bal, 1990); and research that asked respondents whether they thought that it is acceptable that Australian supermodel Elle McPherson drinks beer (Pettigrew, 2002). Such writing has engaged with everyday social and cultural practices bound up with alcohol consumption as well as considering how, when, why and for whom drinking is constructed as demanding of legislation, policy and policing strategies (Kneale, 1999; Hubbard, 2005; Wilson, 2005; Holt, 2006; Leyshon, 2008; Beckingham, 2008; Waitt, Jessop & Gorman-Murray, 2011; Jayne, Holloway & Valentine, 2006; Jayne, Valentine & Holloway, 2008b; Valentine, Holloway, Knell & Jayne, 2007; Shaw, 2014).

These selected examples of social and cultural approaches to understanding alcohol, drinking and drunkenness just scratch the surface of the voluminous amount of theoretical and empirical work across the social sciences that has investigated the discursive and differential construction of 'problem' and 'constructive' drinking. At its best, research has highlighted, firstly, how the study of drinking can make important contributions to academic disciplines – giving space to the study of alcohol, drinking and drunkenness in the research agendas of sociology, and more recently geography, but also anthropology, criminology, economics, English, history, politics, psychology and urban studies. Secondly, writing has also highlighted how disciplinary perspectives offer particular contributions to 'alcohol studies'. Thirdly, writing with a critical edge has made significant progress in showing how the study of alcohol, drinking and drunkenness can contribute to broader foundational social science research agendas relating to a diverse range of key academic debates, relating to, for example, capitalism, gender, class, ethnicity, sexuality, imperialism, globalisation, post-colonialism, post-modernism, post-industrialisation and so on. Finally, there can be little doubt that academic research which applies social and cultural approaches to understanding alcohol, drinking and drunkenness has been utilised by a diverse range of key actors, organisations and institutions in explicit and implicit ways to inform policy formation and practice.

The rich and detailed theoretical, empirical, policy and practice insights offered by sociological approaches have nonetheless done little to challenge a stubborn impasse where alcohol, drinking and drunkenness is considered either as a medical issue involving the pathologising of alcohol as a health, social, legislative, crime or policy problem, or as a practice embedded in social and cultural relations – with limited dialogue between these distinct approaches (Jayne, Valentine & Holloway, 2008c). With such a long tradition of important writing being produced by social and cultural researchers across the social sciences it is clearly disappointing that scientific research – namely, lab-based experimentation, statistical measurement, modelling and numerical proxies – continue to define alcohol-related harm and dominate popular imaginations and representations and influence political decision-making and policy formation. As such, while bearing in mind the strengths of research that has advanced social and cultural understanding of alcohol, drinking and drunkenness, there is clearly much more that needs to be done to critique dominant ontologies and epistemologies and to influence popular, political and policy debate. It is towards such a challenge that the remainder of this chapter turns.

Making a difference?

Our selves, and our geography colleagues, are relative latecomers to the theoretical and empirical terrain that constitutes 'alcohol studies'. Despite this inexperience, geographers have looked at alcohol, drinking and drunkenness in terms of a range of different topics, with varying focus and depth of interest. These include, for example, studies of the entertainment/night-time economy (Malbon, 1999; Thomas & Bromley, 2000; Chatterton & Hollands, 2002, 2003; Latham, 2003; Latham & McCormack, 2004; Hubbard, 2005); pub life and identity (Hall, 1992; Kneale, 1999, 2004; Leyshon, 2005; Maye, Ilbery & Kneafsy, 2005; Edensor, 2006; Valentine, Holloway, Knell & Jayne, 2007); temperance (Kneale, 2001); family life (Lowe, Foxcroft & Sibley, 1993); the relationship between drinking and health (Twigg & Jones, 2000; Philo, Parr & Burnes, 2002); historical geographies of wine production and consumption (Unwin, 1991); the distribution of working men's clubs (Purvis, 1998); the policing of urban public space (Bromley, Thomas & Millie, 2000; Bromley & Nelson, 2002; Bromley, Tallon & Thomas, 2003; Jayne et al., 2006); assemblages of human and non-human actors bound up with alcohol consumption, and emotions, embodiment and affect relating to alcohol, drinking and drunkenness (Jayne, Valentine & Holloway, 2010; Waitt et al., 2011; Shaw, 2014).

Geographers can be criticised for undertaking research that is often focused on case studies of specific people and places, replicating weaknesses of alcohol studies research. However, where research has sought to make connections among different people, places, practices and processes, addressing similarities, differences and mobilities at different spatial scales, human geographers *are* nonetheless developing important new insights (see Jayne et al., 2008a). This represents a conceptual *and* empirical approach that offers opportunities to draw together topics related to production, regulation and legislation, consumption, identity, lifestyle and forms of sociability, representation and emotional and embodied issues, and so on (see Jayne et al., 2008a; Jayne, Valentine & Holloway, 2011b). The most important contribution of geographers to 'alcohol studies' has been to highlight that space and place are not passive backdrops, but active constituents of alcohol drinking and drunkenness, deserving of sustained attention. As the interdisciplinary contributions to the volume attest, the uptake of space and spatiality in sociological approaches to alcohol studies indicates recent and ongoing cross-fertilisations between the two disciplines that continue to prove fruitful.

However, it is fair to say that our own writing, to a large degree, mirrors the strengths and weaknesses of 'alcohol studies' literature previously outlined. We have focused on making a case for the importance of engagement with alcohol, drinking and drunkenness within the discipline of geography, and highlighted how geographical perspectives contribute to both 'alcohol studies' and broader foundational social studies debates (Jayne et al., 2008c; Jayne et al., 2011b; Jayne, Valentine & Holloway, in press, 2016a, 2016b). For example, our research has focused on urban and rural public spaces (Jayne et al., 2008b, 2016b); drinking at home (Holloway, Jayne & Valentine, 2008); masculinity and femininity (Holloway, Valentine & Jayne, 2009); ethnicity (Valentine, Jayne & Holloway, 2009); young people (Valentine et al., 2007); intergenerational transmission of drinking cultures (Valentine, Jayne, Gould & Keenan, 2010a; Valentine, Jayne & Holloway, 2010b); mobilities (Jayne, Gibson, Waitt & Valentine, 2012a); and children, childhood and family (Jayne, Valentine & Gould, 2012b; Valentine, Jayne & Gould, 2013; Jayne & Valentine 2015, 2016a, 2016b).

There are, nonetheless, also a number of ways in which our work has sought to challenge orthodoxies that dominate 'alcohol studies'. Firstly, we have developed theoretical perspectives that seek to overcome the artificial separation of biological, physiological and psychological impacts of alcohol consumption and drinking as a social and cultural practice, arguing that there has been an under-theorisation of the relationships between emotions, embodiment, affect and everyday uses of alcohol (Jayne et al., 2010). Both Wilkinson and Riches, in their contributions to this volume, demonstrate the importance of embodiment and affect in their respective case studies. We developed theoretical insights into the ways in which interdisciplinary work can combine medical with social science methodologies in a manner that offers possibilities to advance understanding of geographies of alcohol, drinking and drunkenness. Similarly, we have unpacked the multiple spatialities bound up with the consumption of 'units' as the dominant means of diagnosing 'health-related' alcohol problems and measuring 'drunkenness' in international alcohol policy and research. In order to question the power afforded to units we investigated the intersection of theoretical debates concerning biopower and governmentality; emotional, embodied and affective geographies and actor-network theory. We highlighted the need for dialogue between social, health and medical scientists in order to develop more pertinent ways of understanding and representing the risks and benefits of alcohol consumption (Jayne, Valentine & Holloway, 2011a). Finally, we have challenged ontologies and epistemologies of alcohol-related violence and disorder and uncovered problematic 'imaginaries' that underpin academic, political, popular debate and policy. We critiqued widely held views that violent behaviour and disorder are ubiquitous and offered theoretical and policy relevant understandings of better ways to theorise, research and tackle alcohol-related violence and disorder (Jayne & Valentine, 2015). While the arguments made in these few papers barely scratch the surface of long-traditions of 'alcohol' research, they nonetheless, at the very least, offer fruitful avenues for dialogue between distanced traditions of social and medical/ health sciences approaches.

Secondly, and just like many other social and cultural theorists whose research focuses on alcohol, drinking and drunkenness, our research was developed in partnership with policy makers and practitioners. Working in the UK with the Joseph Rowntree Foundation, in collaboration with a diverse range of partners, including Alcohol Concern and the Drinkaware Trust (see Valentine, Holloway, Jayne & Knell, 2008;Valentine et al., 2010a); and along with other geographers we contributed to the Royal Geographical Society's (with the Institute of British Geographers) report *Consumption Controversies: Alcohol Policies in the UK* (2010), highlighting the productive ways that geographers contribute to policy debate. Indeed, our personal research goals have been driven by a desire to generate theoretically informed empirical research that is relevant to policy makers and practitioners (see Valentine et al., 2010a, Valentine et al., 2008).

However, while there are undoubtedly a significant number of theorists and researchers, in sociology, geography and beyond, who have published their academic work in accessible policy/practice friendly documents, webpages, newsletters and so on, more needs to be done to ensure that theoretical and empirical work is easily accessible and useful to diverse audiences that might benefit from research findings, analysis and discussion. In these terms we challenge alcohol researchers from across the social sciences to ensure that their work is better communicated to diverse political/policy/practice audiences. There is also clearly a need for social scientists to facilitate sustained engagement with medical and health scientists with regards to alcohol, drinking and drunkenness and, on their part, for health research and policy professionals to ensure that they are receptive to such social and cultural insights.

Finally, at the intersection of the foregoing two issues is the recent opportunities to assess the *impact* of policy-relevant theoretically and empirically robust academic work. For those working beyond the UK, the 'impact agenda' emerged from prior attempts to map what previously had been known in various guises as 'academic enterprise' or 'policy and knowledge transfer'. Under the periodic review of academic research in the UK, the Research Excellence Framework 2014 (in earlier years known as Research Assessment Exercise) now requires collation of *evidence* of *impact* defined as:

> . . . an effect on, change or benefit to the economy, society, culture, public policy or services, health, the environment or quality of life, beyond academia . . . [edit] Impact **includes**, but is not limited to, an effect on, change or benefit to: the activity, attitude, awareness, behaviour, capacity, opportunity, performance, policy, practice, process or understanding of an audience, beneficiary, community, constituency, organisation or individuals; vin any geographic location whether locally, regionally, nationally or internationally . . . [edit] Impact **includes** the reduction or prevention of harm, risk, cost or other negative effects.
> (Higher Education Funding Council for England, 2012, p. 48)

In responding to the new imperative to gather robust *evidence* of how our work was being used by policy makers and practitioners, we of course drew heavily on our already existing partnerships (as previously outlined). In doing so we found that our research into alcohol, drinking and drunkenness had been utilised by research organisations (Joseph Rowntree Foundation, Royal Geographical Society), campaigning groups (Alcohol Concern, Quaker Action on Alcohol, Drugs, Family and Alcohol Alliance) and trade-led bodies (Drinkaware Trust, Portman Group). Our research had also fed into national policies and ongoing programmes, including the UK Government 'Youth Alcohol Action Plan' (2008), and the House of Commons Health Committee inquiry (and report) on the Government's 'Alcohol strategy' (2012). Our numerous keynote lectures at policy conferences and workshops, attended by large numbers of key actors, organisations and institutions involved in policy and practice, were now considered as 'pathways to impact'.

We were also able to gather evidence via testimony from our partners that our research findings had affected the following policies, practices, initiatives and campaigns, inspiring the Joseph Rowntree Foundation's (JRF) 'Alcohol Programme' to foregrounding geographical approaches to understanding alcohol consumption. Moreover, drawing on our research, JRF worked closely with the alcohol strategy/ policy teams in Westminster, Scotland and Northern Ireland. We also gathered statistical-based evidence to show how our research on childhood and family life (Valentine et al, 2010a) had directly influenced the content of the Drinkaware Trust's campaign 'Your Kids and Alcohol', especially the production of an online video which was viewed more than 800,000 times, as well as the content of an advice leaflet which was requested by, and delivered to 100,000 families. The Drinkaware trust also significantly drew on the research into alcohol, families and childhood to develop *In:tuition*, a course of 10 primary lessons and 11 secondary lessons aimed at building young people's confidence, decision-making and communication skills. To date, 751 schools and 909 other organisations (primary care trusts, Youth Services, local authorities, etc.) have utilised this resource. *In:tuition* was then rolled out to 650 schools in the UK from 2013 to 2014. In addition, we gathered evidence showing that our research also generated strong traditional and social media interest and debate.

It is fair to say that we were genuinely surprised by these selected examples and other detailed *evidence* of the *impact* of our research. We are sure that there are many other individuals and research groups that have similarly uncovered impressive evidence of the ways in which their social and cultural approaches to understanding alcohol, drinking and drunkenness has influenced policy and practice. Indeed, we argue that the process and outcome of gathering evidence of impact from partnership working is worthwhile whether or not the findings are used for Research Excellence Framework or not. However, what is vital is that there is a process of collation, summary and widespread distribution of the evidence of the impact that social and cultural theorists and researchers have collected which highlights influence on policy and practice. Bodies such as the British Sociological Association's Alcohol Study group are just one example of disciplinary organisations that could contribute to this project so that this new resource of impact data is purposively utilised as an evidence base in order to highlight the important work that is being done. Such work is fundamentally important if the voluminous, rich and diverse work utilising social and cultural approaches to understand alcohol, drinking and drunkenness is to offer a more significant alternative to medical discourses and engage in critical dialogue with orthodoxies that dominate alcohol studies.

Conclusion

The chapters in this book offer a valuable contribution to the long tradition of applying social and cultural theory and methods to understanding alcohol, drinking and drunkenness. The drinking 'dilemmas' of the volume's title have, through all the chapters, been brought to the fore in accounts of the contested, at times controversial, and certainly complex nature of alcohol and drunkenness as it relates to individual identities and diverse social space.

Such comments notwithstanding, we have argued in this chapter that despite offering rich and detailed evidence with reference to diverse alcohol-related topics and case studies around the world, social and cultural approaches to alcohol, drinking and drunkenness have failed to develop significant and sustained critique of dominant ontologies and epistemologies. To a large degree, there has been little progress in overcoming the impasses that inspired the work of Mass Observation and publications such as *Constructive Drinking* (Douglas, 1987). It still is overwhelmingly scientific research which captures newspaper headlines, dominates popular imaginations and representations and influences political decision-making and policy formation. Despite such a pessimistic statement, we are nonetheless convinced that the *impact* agendas in higher education in the UK are an important opportunity for the collation and application of an 'evidence base' of social and cultural approaches to alcohol, drinking and drunkenness that must be grasped if the long-standing dominance of medical and health sciences influence on political, policy and practice is to be meaningfully challenged.

Note

1 This chapter draws on, updates and advances previous arguments made in Jayne, M., Valentine, G. and Holloway, S.L. (2011b) *Alcohol, drinking, drunkenness: (Dis)orderly spaces*. Aldershot: Ashgate; Jayne, M., Valentine, G. and Holloway, S.L. (2011a) What use are units? Critical geographies of alcohol policy. *Antipode*, 44(3): 828–846; Jayne, M., Holloway, S.L. and Valentine, G. (2006) Drunk and disorderly: Alcohol, urban life and public space. *Progress in Human Geography*, 30(4): 451–468; and Jayne, M. and Valentine, G. (2015) Alcohol-related violence and disorder: New critical perspectives. *Progress in Human Geography*, (OnlineFirst).

References

Allaman, A., Voller, F., Kubicka, L. and Bloomfield, K. 2000. Drinking and the position of women in nine European countries. *Substance Abuse*, 21(4): 231–247.

Beckingham, D. 2008. Geographies of drink culture in Liverpool: Lessons from the drink capital of nineteenth-century England. *Drugs: Education, Prevention and Policy*, 15(3): 305–313.

Benson, D. and Archer, J. 2002. An ethnographic study of sources of conflict between young men in the context of a night out. *Psychology, Evolution and Gender*, 4(1): 3–30.

Bloomfield, K. 1993. A comparison of alcohol consumption between lesbians and heterosexual women in an urban population. *Drug and Alcohol Dependence*, 33: 257–269.

Bobak, M., Mckee, M., Rose, R. and Marmot, M. 1999. Alcohol consumption in a sample of the Russian population. *Addiction*, 94(4): 857–866.

Bromley, R. D. F. and Nelson, A. L. 2002. Alcohol-related crime and disorder across urban space and time: Evidence from a British city. *Geoforum*, 33(2): 239–254.

Bromley, R. D. F., Tallon, A. R. and Thomas, C. J. 2003. Disaggregating the space-time layers of city centre activities and their users. *Environment and Planning A*, 35: 1831–1851.

Bromley, R. D. F., Thomas, C. J. and Millie, A. 2000). Exploring safety concerns in the night-time city. *Town Planning Review*, 71: 71–96.

Burnett, J. 1999. *Liquid pleasures: A social history of drinks in modern Britain*. London: Routledge.

Chatterjee, P. 2003. An empire of drink: Gender, labor and the historical economies of alcohol. *Journal of Historical Sociology*, 16(2): 183–208.

Chatterton, P. and Hollands, R. 2002. Theorising urban playscapes: Producing, regulating and consuming youthful nightlife city spaces. *Urban Studies*, 39(1): 95–116.

Chatterton, P. and Hollands, R. 2003. *Urban nightscapes: Youth culture, pleasure spaces and corporate power*. London: Routledge.

Cochrane, R. and Bal, S. 1990. The drinking habits of Sikh, Hindu and Muslim men in the West Midlands: A community survey. *British Journal of Addiction*, 85: 759–769.

De Garine, I. and De Garine, V. C. 2001. *Drinking: Anthropological approaches*. Oxford: Berg.

Douglas, M. 1987. *Constructive drinking*. Cambridge: Cambridge University Press.

Edensor, T. 2006. Caudan: Domesticating the global waterfront. In D. Bell and M. Jayne (Eds.), *Small cities: Urban experience beyond the metropolis*. London: Routledge.

Gefou-Madianou, D. 1992. *Alcohol, gender and culture*. London: Routledge.

Hall, T. 1992. 'The postmodern pub, hegemonic narrative, nostalgia and collective identity in the construction of postmodern landscapes: A problem for research'. Discussion paper, Department of Geography, University of Birmingham.

Heim, D., Hunter, S. C., Ross, A. J., Bakshi, N., Davis, J. B., Flatley, K. J. and Meer, N. 2004. Alcohol consumption, perceptions of community responses and attitudes to service provisions: Results from a survey of Indian, Chinese and Pakistani people in Greater Glasgow, Scotland, UK. *Alcohol and Alcoholism*, 39(3): 220–226.

Higher Education Funding Council for England. 2012. *Research excellence framework: Assessment framework and guide on submission*. HEFCE: Bristol.

Holloway, S. L., Jayne, M. and Valentine, G. 2008. 'Sainsbury's is my local': English alcohol policy, domestic drinking practices and the meaning of home. *Transactions of the Institute of British Geographers*, 33: 532–547.

Holloway, S. L., Valentine, G. and Jayne, M. 2009. Masculinities, femininities and the geographies of public and private drinking landscapes. *Geoforum*, 40(5): 821–831.

Holt, M. P. 2006. *Alcohol: A social and cultural history*. London: Berg.

Hubbard, P. 2005. The geographies of 'going out': Emotion and embodiement in the evening economy. In J. Davidson, L. Bondi and M. Smith (Eds.), *Emotional geographies* (pp. 117–134). Aldershot: Ashgate.

Hunt, G. and Satterlee, S. 1980. Cohesion and division: Drinking in an English village. *Rural Studies*, 21: 521–537.

Jayne, M. and Valentine, G. 2015. Alcohol-related violence and disorder: New critical prerspectives. *Progress in Human Geography*, (OnlineFirst).

Jayne, M. and Valentine, G. 2015a. *Childhood: Families and alcohol*, Aldershot: Ashgate (in press).

Jayne, M. and Valentine, G. 2016a. 'It makes you go crazy': Children's knowledge and experience of alcohol consumption. *Journal of Consumer Culture* (in press).

Jayne, M. and Valentine, G. 2016b. Alcohol consumption and geographies of childhood and family life. In T. Skelton, J. Horton and B. Evans (Eds.), *Geographies of children and young people: Play recreation, health and well-being*. Springer: London (in press).

Jayne, M., Gibson, C., Waitt, G. and Valentine, G. 2012a. Drunken mobilities: Alcohol, backpackers and 'doing' place'. *Tourist Studies*, 12(3): 1–21.

Jayne, M., Holloway, S. L. and Valentine, G. 2006. Drunk and disorderly: Alcohol, urban life and public space. *Progress in Human Geography*, 30(4): 451–468.

Jayne, M., Valentine, G. and Gould, M. 2012b. Family life and alcohol consumption: The transmission of 'public' and 'private' drinking cultures. *Drugs: Education, Prevention*, 19(3): 192–200.

Jayne, M., Valentine, G. and Holloway S. L. 2008a. Geographies of alcohol, drinking and drunkenness: A review of progress. *Progress in Human Geography*, 32(2): 247–263.

Jayne, M., Valentine, G. and Holloway, S. L. 2008b. Fluid boundaries. 'British' binge drinking and 'European' civility: Alcohol and the production and consumption of public space. *Space and Polity*, 12(1): 81–100.

Jayne, M., Valentine, G. and Holloway S. L. 2008c. The place of drink: geographical contributions to alcohol studies. *Drugs: Education, Prevention and Policy*, 1–14.

Jayne, M., Valentine, G. and Holloway, S. L. 2010. Emotional, embodied and affective geographies of alcohol, drinking and drunkenness. *Transactions of the Institute of British Geographers* 35(4): 540–554.

Jayne, M., Valentine, G. and Holloway, S. L. 2011a. What use are units? Critical geographies of alcohol policy. *Antipode*, 44(3): 828–846.

Jayne, M., Valentine, G. and Holloway, S. L. 2011b. *Alcohol, drinking, drunkenness: (Dis) orderly Spaces*. Aldershot: Ashgate.

Jayne, M., Valentine, G., and Holloway, S. L. 2016a. Consumption and context. In T. Kolind, B. Thom and G. Hunt (Eds.), *Handbook of drug and alcohol studies: Social science perspectives*. London: Sage (in press).

Jayne, M., Valentine, G. and Holloway, S. L. 2016b. Geographical perspectives on drug and alcohol studies. In T. Kolind, B. Thom and G. Hunt (Eds.), *Handbook of drug and alcohol studies: Social science perspectives*. London: Sage (in press).

Jones, J. 2002. The cultural symbolisation of disordered and deviant behaviour: Young people's experiences in a Welsh rural market town. *Journal of Rural Studies*, 18: 213–217.

Kelly, A. B. and Kowalyszyn, M. 2003. The association of alcohol and family problems in a remote indigenous Australian community. *Addictive Behaviour*, 28: 761–767.

Kneale, J. 1999. A problem of supervision: Moral geographies of the nineteenth-century British public house. *Journal of Historical Geography*, 25(3): 333–348.

Kneale, J. 2001. The place of drink: Temperance and the public, 1956–1914. *Social and Cultural Geography*, 2(1): 43–59.

Kneale, J. 2004. 'Drunken geographies: Mass observation's studies of 'a social environment . . . plus alcohol, 1937–48'. Unpublished paper (available from author).

Kraack, A. and Kenway, J. 2002. Place, time and stigmatised youth identities: Bad boys in paradise. *Journal of Rural Affairs*, 18: 145–155.

Latham, A. 2003. Urbanity, lifestyle and making sense of the new urban cultural economy: Notes from Auckland, New Zealand. *Urban Studies*, 40(9): 1699–1724.

Latham, A. and McCormack, D. P. 2004. Moving cities: Rethinking the materialities of urban geographies. *Progress in Human Geography*, 28(6): 701–724.

Leyshon, M. 2005. No place for a girl: Rural youth pubs and the performance of masculinity. In J. Little and C. Morris (Eds.), *Critical studies in rural gender issues* (pp. 104–122). Aldershot: Ashgate.

Leyshon, M. 2008. 'We're stuck in the corner': Young women, embodiment and drinking in the countryside. *Drugs: Education, Prevention and Policy*, 15(3): 267–289.

Lowe, G., Foxcroft, D. R. and Sibley, D. 1993. *Adolescent drinking and family life*. London: Harwood Academic Publishers.

Malbon, B. 1999. *Clubbing: Dancing, ecstasy and vitality*. London: Routledge.

Mass Observation. 1987. *The pub and the people*. London: The Cresset Library.

Maye, D., Ilbery, B. and Kneafsy, M. 2005. Changing places: Investigating the cultural terrain of village pubs in south Northhamptonshire. *Social and Cultural Geography*, 6(6): 831–847.

McAndrew, C. and Edgerton, R. B. 1969. *Drunken comportment: A social explanation*. London: Nelson.

Nayak, A. 2003. Last of the 'real Geordies'? White masculinities and the subcultural response to deindustrialization. *Environment and Planning D: Society and Space*, 21: 7–25.

Pettigrew, S. 2002. Consuming alcohol: Consuming symbolic meaning. In S. Miles, A. Anderson and K. Meethan (Eds.), *The changing consumer: Markets and meanings* (pp. 104–116). London: Routledge.

Philo, C., Parr, H. and Burns, N. 2002. *Alcohol and mental health* (draft). Published by the Department of Geography and Topographical Science, University of Glasgow. Available at: http://www.geog.gla.ac.uk/olpapers/cphilo015.pdf

Purvis, M. 1998. Popular institutions. In J. Langton and R. J. Morris (Eds.), *Atlas of industrial Britain 1780–1914*. London: Methuen.

Share, P. 2003. A genuine 'third place'? Towards an understanding of the pub in contemporary Irish society. Paper presented at the 30th SAI Annual Conference, Cavan, 26 April.

Shaw, R. 2014. Beyond night-time economy: Affective atmospheres of the urban night. *Geoforum*, 51: 87–95

Thomas, C. J. and Bromley, R. D. F. 2000. City-centre revitalization: Problems of fragmentation and fear in the evening and night-time city. *Urban Studies*, 37(8): 1403–1429.

Thomas, M. 2002. Out of control: Emergent cultural landscapes and political change in urban Vietnam. *Urban Studies*, 39(9): 1611–1624.

Twigg, L. and Jones, K. 2000. Predicting small-area health related behaviour: A comparison of smoking and drinking indicators. *Social Science and Medicine*, 80(11): 9–20.

Unwin, T. 1991. *Wine and the vine: An historical geography of viticulture and the wine trade*. London: Routledge.

Valentine, G., Holloway, S. L., Jayne, M. and Knell, C. 2008. *Drinking places: Where people drink and why*. York: Joseph Rowntree Foundation.

Valentine, G., Holloway, S. L., Knell, C. and Jayne, M. 2007. Drinking places: Young people and cultures of alcohol consumption in rural environments. *Journal of Rural Studies*, 24: 28–40.

Valentine, G., Jayne, M. and Gould, M. 2013. The proximity effect: The role of the affective space of family life in shaping children's knowledge about alcohol and its social and health implications. *Childhood: A Journal of Global Child Research*, 21(1): 103–118.

Valentine, G., Jayne, M., Gould, M. and Keenan, J. 2010a. *Family life and alcohol consumption: The transmission of drinking cultures*. York: Joseph Rowntree Foundation.

Valentine, G., Jayne, M. and Holloway, S. L. 2009. Contemporary cultures of abstinence and the night–time economy: Muslim attitudes towards alcohol and the implications for social cohesion. *Environment and Planning A*, 42(1): 8–22.

Valentine, G., Jayne, M. and Holloway, S. L. 2010b. Generational patterns of alcohol consumption: Continuity and change. *Health and Place*, 16: 916–925.

Waitt, G., Jessop, L. and Gorman-Murray, A. W. 2011. 'The guys in there just expect to be laid': Embodied and gendered socio-spatial practices of a 'night out' in Wollongong, Australia. *Gender, Place and Culture*, 18(2): 255–275.

Wilson, T. M. 2005. *Drinking cultures*. Oxford: Berg.

Index

addiction 151, 191, 195, 201
affect 82, 99, 101–3, 105, 106, 109, 110, 111, 133, 140–2, 144–5, 210
alcohol industry 6, 9, 20–1, 35, 36, 56–7
alcohol in Islamic countries 84
ale 6, 21, 46, 48–55, 57, 58, 105, 106

Bauman, Zygmunt 173, 176, 183
beer 21, 33, 34, 45–7, 50, 52, 54, 55, 56, 65, 67, 84, 90–1, 100, 139, 174
Bigg Market, the (Newcastle) 16, 114, 124–8
Billig, Michael 47, 51
binge drinking 1, 4, 13, 45, 124
bouncers 2, 19, 67, 143
Bourdieu, Pierre 29–30, 38, 47
branding 18–21, 23, 28, 33–6, 39, 45, 46–8, 51–3, 55, 57, 91, 174, 205

Campaign for Real Ale (CAMRA) 9, 48–50, 53, 56, 57, 60
celebrities 20, 31, 33, 38, 188
champagne 21, 34, 87
'chavs' 20, 34, 37, 132
cost considerations of alcohol 89, 91–2, 126, 133, 137–8, 145
crime 65, 75, 125, 133, 206, 208
Criminal Justice Act 22
cultural capital 30, 34, 88

dancing 22, 72, 75, 91, 107, 120, 175
deregulation 63
Douglas, Mary 1, 13, 45–6, 51, 58, 205, 207
drinking venues 17, 21, 64, 66–9, 75–7, 82, 87–91, 100, 109, 118, 125, 126, 128, 132, 137, 138, 175, 205
drink spiking 31

drunkenness 1–4, 9, 13, 66, 75, 83, 88, 91, 92, 95, 101, 104, 106, 108–9, 111, 114, 117, 120–3, 125, 128, 139, 144, 164, 206–7

economic change 17
elites 9
embodiment 29, 46, 55, 88, 99–102, 104, 106, 109–11, 114, 116, 118, 120, 124, 132, 141, 143, 165, 209
exclusivity 31, 34

Facebook 35–7, 57, 83, 118, 134, 142
femininity 31, 32, 39, 56–7, 102, 106, 114–18, 124, 127, 165, 210
France 8, 45, 150, 166
friendship 1, 7, 17, 22, 38, 50, 72, 85, 87, 92, 110, 119–20, 135, 140, 177, 180–3, 191

gender 3, 6, 7, 9, 14, 28–35, 37–8, 47, 54–5, 99–100, 104, 110, 115, 117, 123, 150, 154, 156–8, 162, 166, 206
gentrification 6, 18, 20, 21, 63, 88
geographical approaches to alcohol 1, 4–5, 64, 82, 85, 96, 135, 201, 208–10, 212
Giddens, Anthony 49, 52
globalisation 3, 208

Happy Hour 91
health 4–5, 13, 36, 39–40, 64–5, 165, 194, 202, 209, 210, 211
heritage 46–7, 51–5, 57–8
Hollands, Robert 2, 8, 9, 15–17, 18–19, 132
homogenisation 6, 18, 20, 48, 95, 175

Index

identity 1, 3, 17, 22–3, 28–30, 32, 37–40, 45–8, 49–54, 55, 58, 101, 106, 118–20, 145, 165, 172–3, 177, 180, 183, 187, 200–1, 205
illegal drinking venues 22, 62–3, 77, 89
informal drinking spaces 62–4, 92–3, 136

Klein, Naomi 22

leisure 2, 18, 30, 32, 52, 63, 69, 81–2, 91, 94, 172, 178, 180, 181
LGBT drinkers 19, 93–4
licensing 17, 64, 84, 89, 132, 136, 140

masculinity 32–3, 46, 54–5, 100, 106, 115, 163, 208, 210
Mass Observation 45, 205–7, 213
Measham, Fiona 2, 122
media representations 2, 9, 13, 16–17, 29–33, 35, 55, 114, 118, 125, 126, 188, 197
middle-class 9, 30, 32–4, 63–4, 114, 117–18, 124–8, 139, 145
Mill, C. Wright 15
music 111, 133, 138–40, 142, 145, 175

national identity 45–7
nightclubs 28, 31, 81, 86, 87, 88, 109, 137
non-commercial drinking 132, 136, 144
non-drinkers 9, 120, 160, 163
non-representation theory 102, 104, 106, 109–11

outdoor drinking 133, 135, 137–8, 143–4

physical appearance 31, 38, 165
police 19, 69–71, 73, 125, 139, 142, 194–7
post-industrial cities 6, 14, 23, 118
pre-loading 28, 38, 133
prohibition 64–4, 84–5
public houses (pubs) 14, 15, 16, 20, 21, 30, 33, 45, 47, 51, 54, 86, 90, 100, 103, 136, 172, 182, 206
pub closure 172

religion 82, 84
research methodologies: interviews 16, 17, 37, 48, 67, 83, 103, 114, 135, 152, 187; participant; observation 16, 19, 48, 83; surveys 84, 152
respectability 7, 82, 114–17, 123–5, 127–8
risk 1, 30–1, 66–7, 75–6, 99–100, 109, 114, 118, 120, 124, 125, 139, 151, 156, 161, 165

safety 30, 73, 75–5, 109, 125
segregation 64
sex 17, 23, 122, 128, 164
sexism 55–7, 103
sexuality 5, 31, 115–16, 121, 127–8, 156, 162, 163, 208
shots 174, 175
Skeggs, Beverly 30–1, 115, 128
sociability 7, 13, 15, 24, 62, 64, 75, 77, 83, 105, 159, 164, 166, 205, 207
social change 17, 58
social class 4–5, 9, 29, 32–4, 82, 115, 150, 152
social media 4, 6, 36, 212
sobriety 88, 107–10, 122, 206
spirits 45, 87, 91, 17
street drinking 91, 132, 137
subcultures 15, 99–100, 103, 110, 132

Twitter 35, 36, 134

underage drinking 15, 36, 136
units of alcohol 120, 210

violence 2, 4, 13, 17, 23, 65, 70, 76, 77, 96, 114, 125, 127–8, 210
VIP 9, 73–5
vomit 121, 123, 137
Youth Culture 6, 19, 22, 33, 36, 132–3, 135, 140, 144

wine 33–4, 45–6, 54, 72, 84, 87, 140, 162, 177, 183, 209
working-class 2, 9, 19, 30–3, 39, 45, 62, 64, 76, 114, 117–19, 124–7, 134, 139, 145, 150, 180, 207

Žižek, Slavoj 173, 177